NEW YORK
JETS

THE COMPLETE ILLUSTRATED HISTORY

Mark Cannizzaro
Foreword by Joe Namath
Afterword by Woody Johnson

MVP
BOOKS

First published in 2011 by MVP Books, an imprint of MBI Publishing Company and the Quayside Publishing Group, 400 First Avenue North, Suite 300, Minneapolis, MN 55401 USA

Text copyright © 2011 by Mark Cannizzaro
Photo copyrights as indicated.

MVP Books titles are also available at discounts in bulk quantity for industrial or sales-promotional use. For details write to Special Sales Manager at MBI Publishing Company, 400 First Avenue North, Suite 300, Minneapolis, MN 55401 USA.

To find out more about our books, visit us online at www.mvpbooks.com.

Library of Congress Cataloging-in-Publication Data

Cannizzaro, Mark.
 New York Jets : the complete illustrated history / Mark Cannizzaro.
     p. cm.
Includes index.
 ISBN 978-0-7603-4063-9 (hardback w/jkt)
 1. New York Jets (Football team)—History. I. Title.
GV956.N37C357 2011
796.332'64097471—dc22

2011006119

On the front cover (inset): Joe Namath, 1972 (Tony Tomsic/Getty Images).

On the back cover (upper left to lower right): Darrelle Revis, 2011 (Heinz Kluetmeier/Sports Illustrated/Getty Images); Super Bowl III, 1969 (Kidwiler Collection/Diamond Images/Getty Images); Mark Sanchez, 2009 (John Iacono/Sports Illustrated/Getty Images); Laveranues Coles, 2001 (Keith Torrie/NY Daily News Archive/Getty Images); Jets fans, 2010 (Per-Anders Pettersson/Getty Images); Don Maynard, circa 1970 (Focus on Sport/Getty Images); Mark Gastineau and Marty Lyons, 1988 (Rick Stewart/Getty Images); Wayne Chrebet, 1998 (Mike Albans/NY Daily News Archive/Getty Images); Curtis Martin, 1998 (Al Tielemans/Sports Illustrated/Getty Images).

On the frontispiece: Jets at the line of scrimmage, 2010 (Scott Boehm/Getty Images).

On the title page: Mark Sanchez in action, 2010. (Joe Robbins/Getty Images).

On this page: Mark Gastineau, 1983 (Focus on Sport/Getty Images).

On the facing page: Joe Namath in action, Super Bowl III, 1969 (Herb Scharfman/Sports Illustrated/Getty Images).

Edited by Josh Leventhal
Design manager: Kou Lor
Book designer: John Barnett
Layout by Greg Nettles

Printed in China

CONTENTS

FOREWORD
by Joe Namath

WHEN I THINK about the history of the Jets, I think about the loyalty of the fans.

Jets fans are unlike any other sports fans, and I really didn't understand that until I became a Jet. I can remember going to New York for the first time and learning about fans of pro sports teams, and it was those Jets fans who helped me become a fan. The Jets fans became family, just like the fans at home in Beaver Falls always were.

Growing up I was a fan of baseball, basketball, and football. That's all I knew, and that's all we had at home with our local teams. So I knew Beaver Falls fans. I knew the neighborhood people that were pulling for us. They were like family or friends.

I have friends who were Jets fans back in the 1960s and I still maintain those friendships. They used to come watch our practices on Long Island and come to Shea Stadium for the games, and we developed real-life friendships. When I met those people I started to recognize how many similarities I had with the fans.

Ever since I was a kid in Beaver Falls, Pennsylvania, I was always a ballplayer first and a fan second. I spent more time practicing and playing than watching.

But when I did watch, my guys were Roberto Clemente, Otto Graham, Vito "Babe" Parilli, Johnny Unitas, Stan "The Man" Musial, Bill Mazeroski, Jerry West—I could go on.

Because I was always a ballplayer, I judge things differently than a pure fan does. I look for the reason for the failure. I try to analyze and rationalize why my team lost and how we can get better. Over the years, I've learned what it's like to go through the emotional peaks and valleys of being a fan.

I've learned that on Sundays after the game and when you get up on Mondays we're happy when the Jets win—when *we* win. I have a different physiological feel when the Jets win as opposed to how I feel after a Jets loss.

MVP Books Collection

Kidwiler Collection/Diamond Images/Getty Images

As players, we need to keep the fans happy. And as a fan, you only want to be happy. Together, we're pulling for people we care about with people we care about.

Sharing it, man, that's the joy. Sharing the history of the franchise we love is what convinced me to write this foreword. Having seen and lived through the transformation of the team and how far it's come—from practicing in an empty lot alongside the Grand Central Parkway and Rikers Island Prison to our current home at the state-of-the-art Atlantic Health Training Center in New Jersey—makes me proud to be a Jet and a Jets fan.

I was honored to have been on the Jets with three of the original Titans players: Don Maynard, Larry Grantham, and Bill Mathis. They were the nucleus of our championship team in 1968 and helped lead us to victory in Super Bowl III.

We players were lucky to have the support and guidance of our ownership as well as the expert leadership of our general manager and head coach, Hall of Famer Weeb Ewbank.

To me, winning that championship doesn't feel like a long time ago. I can still remember the tense atmosphere in the locker room on game days as if it were yesterday. I remember dreading Shea's swirling winds. They, along with the bone-chilling rain and snow, won't easily be forgotten. But despite the elements, I can still feel the ground vibrating in Shea from the fans going crazy, as they always would. And it helped us win!

Wesley Hitt/Getty Images

As players, we feel the energy coming from the fans, and it inspires us physically and mentally to give the extra effort it takes to be successful. There really is a lot to be said about home-field advantage, and that's because of the fans.

Fans provide that extra shot of adrenaline that players crave and thrive off of. Fans are the catalyst for the sense of urgency we players need. Hearing the roar of 82,000 fans chanting "J-E-T-S, JETS! JETS! JETS!" is undeniably motivating.

Today I no longer find myself on the field, but I'm often in the stands with the fans pulling for the team that we all love.

I've often heard people complaining about time flying. It's been 42 years since the Jets won the Super Bowl—which is hard to believe, but the time has flown by for me.

When I hear people complaining about time flying, I ask, if it's not flying then what's happening? It's dragging. Time drags when you're sick, when business is lousy, when your love life's askew, when your team's on a losing streak, things like that. For me, these last 42 years have been flying for the most part, and I'm thankful for it.

I would love to see the Jets win another Super Bowl.

It would mean that people I know personally and Jets fans in general would once again have something to cherish for a good while.

I know as a player what it's like to win a Super Bowl, but I want our fans—some who have waited so long for another one and some who have never had one to cherish—to experience the elation.

The passion that we have as fans we share with our friends and family. It's about sharing. To see the Jets win another championship would allow us to share these feelings and celebrate the emotional high that only champions feel.

Woody Johnson and Rex Ryan have our Jets in position to accomplish their goal of winning another Super Bowl. Having been to the AFC Championship Game in 2009 and 2010, our hopes are high, and we expect to bring home the Lombardi trophy soon! Go Jets!

PREFACE

I HAD NO IDEA what I was getting into.

I grew up in southern Connecticut, where I was a New England Patriots fan living in the heart of New York Giants country. While in high school in the late 1970s, I trekked up Interstate 95 on weekends to Foxborough, Massachusetts, as a season-ticket holder and had little idea what the plight of the Jets fan was—nor did I care.

I started to understand in the mid-1980s, when I took a job covering both the Jets and the Giants for the *Bridgewater Courier-News*. It was then that I began to see not only the stark differences between the two competing New York franchises, but also the different mindsets and expectations of the fans of the two teams.

I was never a true Jets fan, but after covering the team for more than a quarter of a century I've come to empathize and respect them. I even root for them, because few fans of any professional sports team in America deserve a winner more than Jets fans do. Few have been tortured and teased the way the Jets fan has been over the years. It's not easy being green.

Sure, the Jets won the Super Bowl in 1969. But is that it? One sniff of glory? One trip to Nirvana? Is that all? Who can eat just one potato chip?

The Giants have been to three Super Bowls and won two since the Jets played in their one and only championship game.

As I look back on the years I've covered the Jets, I differentiate the eras by the head coaches, and there have been many.

When I first came on the scene in 1986, the Jets were coached by Joe Walton. It was perhaps fitting that the first season I covered the team for the *Courier-News*—1986—turned into one of the worst teases in franchise history.

The Jets jumped off to a 10–1 start and appeared to be headed for a magical ending. They lost the last five regular-season games and limped into the playoffs as a wild-card entrant.

A 35–15 wild-card playoff win over the Chiefs was followed by a devastating double-overtime loss to the Browns in the AFC divisional round. That game, of course, was marred by Mark Gastineau's infamous roughing-the-passer penalty.

The Jets were never the same after that, sinking to 6–9 the following year and limping to 8–7–1 in 1988. Then came the '89 season, my lasting memory of which is being on the field at the end of a 37–0 home loss to the Buffalo Bills in the finale of a 4–12 season.

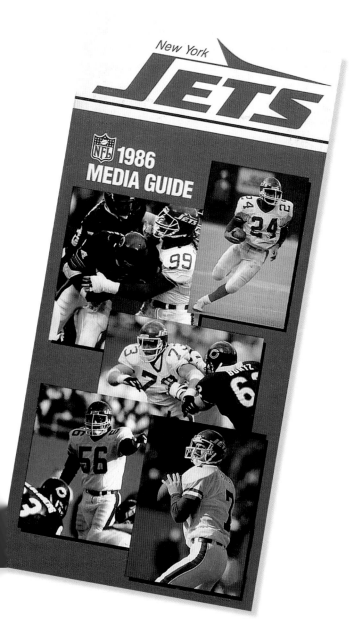

As Walton trotted off the Giants Stadium field and into the end zone tunnel for the final time (he would soon be fired), fans threw beer on him and screamed, "Joe Must Go!"

It was a humiliating moment, and though I was never really close to Walton, I felt terrible for him.

As it turned out, Walton's demise was the first of many endings to head coaching eras that I would cover.

Rex Ryan, the current head coach, is the ninth Jets head coach since 1986 and the 17th since the franchise's founding in 1960.

Most of the tenures didn't end well, for varying reasons.

The Walton era, of course, ended ugly. That was followed by Bruce Coslet, who was hired by Dick Steinberg, the general manager that team owner Leon Hess hired to right his struggling franchise before the 1990 season.

Steinberg was a quiet, classy, dignified man with a solid football background. His personality and the humble way in which he carried himself belied that of Coslet, who despite being a first-time head coach acted like he invented the game. That arrogance ended up being Coslet's downfall, getting fired after four largely unproductive seasons.

Coslet's Jets twice posted 8–8 records, and they even got into the playoffs once with their 8–8 mark, in 1991.

So while the Giants were winning their second Super Bowl in five years, the Jets benchmark for success was not losing as many games as they won. A mere .500 record was considered an accomplishment.

Coslet was replaced by Pete Carroll, his defensive coordinator. The much more affable Carroll brought a unique coaching style. Gone was Coslet's constant paranoia. Carroll brought a fresh, new-world approach to the game, trying to promote fun in work.

Unfortunately the fun didn't translate into wins, and after a 6–10 season in 1993, Carroll was out. To this day, I think Carroll got a raw deal. No head coach should be given only one year to implement a program. Carroll landed on his feet, of course, winning multiple collegiate national championships at USC.

The Jets? Not so much.

Rich Kotite's calamitous two years are well chronicled in this book. Suffice it to say, Kotite was a nice guy who simply wasn't a very good head coach.

Bill Parcells brought immediate credibility to the Jets, but he coached only three years and, in my opinion, never finished the job. I'd have liked to have seen Parcells coach another couple of years, because he had gotten the team so close in 1998.

Al Groh was a good man who realized quickly (after one year) that NFL head coaching wasn't his thing. So he fled to college and his alma mater Virginia.

Enter Herman Edwards, one of my personal favorites, and a coach whom I believe never got his due from Jets fans. People preferred to nitpick the failures rather than focus on the fact that Edwards took the team to the playoffs in three of his first four seasons—more than any coach in franchise history, the great Parcells included.

History will show that Edwards was one of the best coaches the Jets ever had.

Eric Mangini was a pretty good coach, too, but he was another first-timer learning on the fly. Although he made his mistakes, Mangini, like Edwards, had his worst seasons when his starting quarterback, Chad Pennington, suffered season-ending injuries.

Ryan, who was hired at the start of the 2009 season, is unlike any of them, a 24-7 newsmaker. Through his first two seasons, he led the Jets to two AFC Championship Games. But Ryan, like everyone else since Weeb Ewbank coached those 1968–1969 Jets to the Super Bowl, was always trying to reach that promised land of the Super Bowl.

As much as I'll always remember the coaches I've covered, the fellow beat writers, particularly those I encountered early on, will always have a fond place in my heart.

Gerald Eskenazi of the *New York Times* was the dean of the beat and a man with the perfect temperament to handle the wild and wacky world of the New York Jets. Eskenazi, late in his time covering the team, wrote a terrific book on the franchise called *Gang Green*.

Don Williams of the *Newark (NJ) Star-Ledger* was another longtime beat writer. His crusty exterior could easily intimidate a younger reporter like myself, but Williams possessed one of the best, most sarcastic senses of humor around. In order to cover the Jets, a sense of humor was an absolute requirement.

Paul Needell of the *New York Daily News* was my chief competition when I took over covering the Jets for the *New York Post*. We were the two tabloid writers in New York City constantly trying to outdo each other with a scoop or any kind of nugget.

Despite being serious competitors, though, Paul was always a classy friend who cared about you personally more than he cared about kicking your butt in the newspaper wars.

There are many other colleagues whom I've covered the team alongside, too many to mention, who have made this a fun ride.

As the Jets again got so close to reaching the Super Bowl in the 2010 season, I was asked by many people if I was rooting for that to happen. Selfishly, I told people I thought it would be cool to see the team I've covered for so long finally play in a Super Bowl.

My overriding thought, though, was for the Jets fans who've waited so long. For those deserving fans—and I'm friends with many of them—I want to see the Jets get back to the Super Bowl and win it so they can finally enjoy the fruits of so much labor over too many years.

One day in my lifetime, I'd like to see a second Lombardi Trophy on display at the Jets team facility.

1 FROM TITANS TO JETS TO CHAMPIONS

1960–1969

THE LONE SYMBOL of what all NFL teams chase sits in an enclosed case like a priceless museum artifact inside the lobby of the New York Jets' state-of-the-art training facility in Florham Park, New Jersey.

It's inside that airy lobby, sitting proudly to the left of the reception desk, where the Vince Lombardi Trophy sits, a symbol of the Jets' most glorious, unforgettable moment—their Super Bowl III triumph in January 1969.

That trophy and that game, however, did not even exist when the Jets were born. In fact, the Jets weren't even born the Jets. They came into existence as the New York Titans in 1960 as members of the fledgling American Football League, which was trying to rival the established National Football League. These rivals would soon merge to form an even more potent and competitive professional football league.

TERRIBLE TITANS

From the start, the NFL owners considered the American Football League an inferior stepchild, and the AFL owners even referred to themselves as the "Foolish Club" for going up against the powerful NFL. But the new league competed right away for the same players that the NFL went after, and in fact, half of the first-round choices in the 1960 NFL draft went on to sign with the AFL. Among the high-profile converts was Billy Cannon, the LSU All-American and 1959 Heisman Trophy winner, who was selected first overall by the Los Angeles Rams in the NFL draft but signed instead with the AFL's Dallas Texans.

The Titans' roster in 1960 was made up of a combination of first-year players, such as Bill Mathis of Clemson and Mississippi's Larry Grantham, and former NFLers who were either outcasts or opted to jump to the new league, including veteran quarterback Al Dorow, second-year end Art

Powell, and defensive lineman Sid Youngelman, an NFL pro since 1955.

The Titans' representative in the "Foolish Club" was Harry Wismer, a former football broadcaster and one of only two AFL owners who had prior experience in sports-team ownership. Wisner had previously been a part owner of the Detroit Lions and the Washington Redskins (Buffalo's Ralph Wilson also had been a part owner of the Lions).

A flamboyant, swashbuckling fast-talker and self-described hustler, Wismer was also known as a heavy drinker. His lifestyle and volatile personality would occasionally lead to clashes not only with fellow owners but with the league commissioner, Joe Foss, as well as the media. Because Wismer's money was completely tied up in the Titans, he also lacked the kind of funds enjoyed by other owners, whose wealth came from sources outside of sports. That financial insecurity ultimately led to Wismer's downfall as an owner.

The eight franchises of the newly formed American Football League were determined to challenge the more established rival league head on, and that chip-on-the-shoulder competitiveness was the reason behind the New York team being named the Titans.

"Titans are bigger and stronger than Giants," Wismer told everyone, referring to the well-established New York Giants of the NFL.

In another bold move intended to draw attention to his franchise, Wismer hired former Washington Redskins quarterback Sammy Baugh to be the Titans' first head coach. Baugh, known as "Slingin' Sammy" from his playing days, was one of the biggest names in football, and Wismer figured his hiring would bring immediate cachet to his team.

The Titans wore blue-and-gold uniforms from 1960 to 1962, with an AFL innovation: They put the names of the players on the backs of the jerseys in an effort to create a new identity separate from the old school.

There were other outward signs of how the Titans set out to take New York. They played their home games at the Polo Grounds, which was located across the river from Yankee Stadium, where the Giants played. The Polo Grounds also had been the home of the New York Giants baseball team before it left for San Francisco.

Even the Titans' first big-name player, receiver Don Maynard, was a former Giant. The Texas-born Maynard

Titans owner Harry Wismer shares a light moment with coach Sammy Baugh prior to a game against the Denver Broncos at the Polo Grounds in 1961. Baugh, a Hall of Famer as a quarterback, lasted only two seasons as coach after back-to-back 7–7 finishes. *Harry Harris/ AP Images*

Coach Baugh (center, with cap) checks out the potential recruits, who are getting a real workout at Titans training camp in July 1960 in Durham, North Carolina. *AP Images*

DON MAYNARD

RECEIVER

1960–1972

DON MAYNARD holds the unique distinction of being the only player to play for the New York Titans, Jets, and Giants.

Maynard was a deep-threat receiver from deep in the heart of Texas who played his way into the Pro Football Hall of Fame. He is also one of three Jets to have his number retired (along with Joe Namath and Weeb Ewbank). Maynard finished his career leading the Jets in all-time receptions (627), receiving yards (11,732), and touchdowns (88).

When Maynard retired in 1973 with 633 career catches, 11,834 receiving yards, and 88 touchdowns (including his stats from his brief turns with the Giants and Cardinals), those were all NFL career records. Through 2010, his reception average of 18.7 yards per catch was the highest in NFL history for anyone with more than 600 catches.

Maynard caught 68 passes for 1,218 yards and 14 touchdowns in 1965, Joe Namath's rookie year. He was a big factor in leading the Jets to the Super Bowl in 1969, making six receptions for 118 yards and two touchdowns in the AFL title game win over the Oakland Raiders.

By far, Maynard's finest personal triumph was the Super Bowl III victory, even though he was hobbled with a hamstring injury. He had been cut by the Giants nearly a decade earlier, and he wanted revenge against the league that didn't want him.

"I'd been waiting ten years to get even with the NFL," Maynard said after the Super Bowl win. "Was it extra special? Absolutely."

Seen here making a leaping catch in a game circa 1970, Don Maynard was with the Titans in the team's inaugural season and stayed with them for 13 years. Today he stands as the franchise leader in catches, receiving yards, and touchdowns. *Focus on Sport/ Getty Images*

had been drafted by the Giants in the ninth round in 1957 and appeared in 12 games in 1958, primarily as a kick and punt returner. But Giants coach Allie Sherman didn't like his go-for-broke running style, so Maynard was cut, and he became the first player to sign with the Titans.

Maynard not only would go on to become the franchise's first real star, but he also would be enshrined in the Pro Football Hall of Fame in Canton, Ohio, after setting numerous Jets franchise records, some of which remained intact a half century later.

Before the Titans' inaugural season, Baugh and the coaches held tryouts at the Polo Grounds and then ran a training camp in Durham, New Hampshire. To get ready for the 14-game season, the team went on a six-exhibition-game road trip.

The Titans won the first regular-season game of their existence, a 27–3 victory over the Buffalo Bills on September 11, 1960, with just over 10,000 in attendance at the Polo Grounds. After spotting the Bills an early 3–0 lead, New York scored 27 unanswered points. Quarterback Dorow scored two rushing touchdowns in the inaugural game, and Maynard led the way with 116 receiving yards and was awarded the game ball for his efforts.

One of Dorow's finest performances that year came during a 31–28 win over the Oakland Raiders in Week 13. He threw for 375 yards and three touchdowns while running

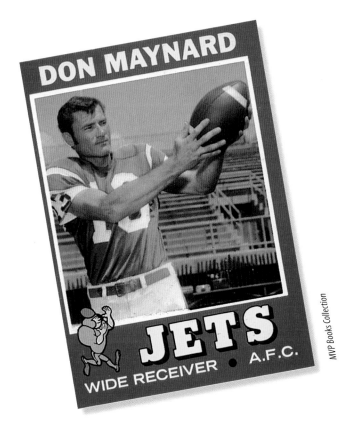

Halfback Dewey Bohling (36) throws a block on a Bills defenseman as quarterback Al Dorow (12) heads upfield during the Titans' franchise debut on September 11, 1960. Dorow ran for two scores in New York's 27–3 victory. *Frank Hurley/NY Daily News Archive/Getty Images*

AL DOROW

QUARTERBACK
1960–1961

THE FIRST QUARTERBACK of the New York Titans was Al Dorow. The Michigan native who played college ball at Michigan State spent four years in the NFL with the Redskins and Eagles in the mid-1950s before going to play for the B.C. Lions of the Canadian Football League. He ended up leaving the Lions following a disagreement with his coach about who would call the plays.

Dorow, who knew Sammy Baugh from their time together in Washington, contacted Harry Wismer and asked him about the new league. Next thing he knew, he was the starting quarterback for Wismer and Baugh's Titans.

Dorow led the team to a 7–7 record in that inaugural season, good enough for a second-place finish in the four-team Eastern Conference. He led all AFL passers with 26 touchdown passes and was voted the team's Most Valuable Player. He completed 201 of 396 passes for 2,748 yards, throwing mainly to Don Maynard and Art Powell. Dorow, a scrambling quarterback, also led the Titans—and all AFL quarterbacks—in rushing with 453 yards on 90 carries.

The Titans had another 7–7 finish in 1961 while Dorow, despite a bad shoulder, led the AFL in passes attempted (438) and passes completed (197). His 19 touchdown passes were good enough for second best in the league, but his 30 interceptions were also more than any other quarterback.

Dorow was traded to Buffalo during training camp in 1962 following a dispute with Wismer over delinquent payments of Dorow's salary.

for another 43 yards and a touchdown. He was responsible for 418 of New York's 471 yards on offense.

In his first season with the Titans, Maynard established himself as one of the game's first true deep-threat receivers, catching 72 passes for 1,265 yards in the 14-game season. A 1,200-yard receiving season today, in a 16-game season, is considered Pro Bowl-caliber production.

Other than Maynard, the primary recipient of Dorow's prolific passing was Art Powell. The 23-year-old Texas native, who played one season as a reserve for the Philadelphia Eagles before coming to the AFL, made 69 catches for 1,167 yards in his debut season with New York. One of the league's first stars, Powell led the AFL in receiving touchdowns (14) in 1960 and in receiving yards in 1962 (1,130); after going to the Raiders in 1963, he led the league in both categories.

The performance of Powell and Maynard in 1960 made them the first receiver tandem ever to each gain more than 1,000 receiving yards in the same season. They repeated the feat two years later.

On the defensive side of the ball, the young Titans had a budding star in Larry Grantham. From his left outside linebacker position, Grantham was one of the team's leading tacklers over the next decade. He was named to the AFL all-star team five times and earned five straight All-Pro selections from 1960 to 1964. Grantham was one of only 20 players who played in the AFL for its entire 10-year existence, and one of only seven who played their entire careers

in one city. He stuck around long enough to enjoy the fruits of the New York Jets' Super Bowl glory in January 1969.

Despite the talented players on the Titans' 1960 roster, with the well-established Giants playing at Yankee Stadium, the fans didn't exactly flock to Titans games at the Polo Grounds. In that first year, newspapers estimated an average crowd of about 10,000, but that was documented to be a rather generous estimate.

Still, amidst the chaos of being a first-year franchise and Wismer's antics, Baugh led the Titans to a 7–7 record. Little did anyone know at the time, but that mediocre .500 record

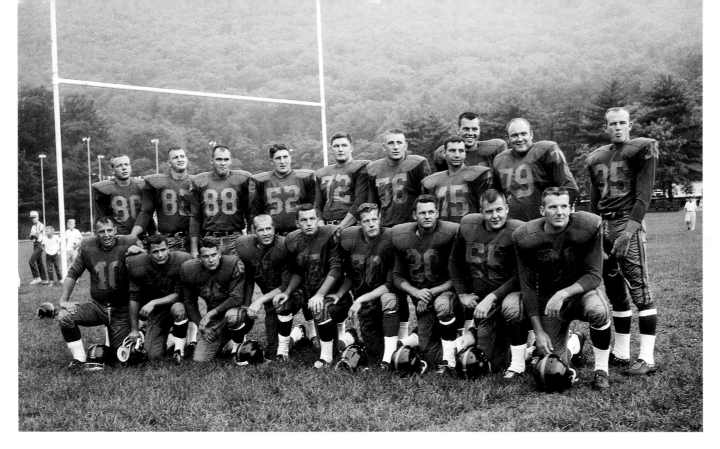

The New York Titans pose at their training facility at Bear Mountain, New York, in July 1961. Front row: Joe Pagliei, Fred Julian, Dewey Bohling, Dick Felt, Dick Jamieson, Larry Grantham, Curley Johnson, Bob Marques, Bill Mathis. Back row: Dave Ross, Ed Cooke, Thurlow Cooper, Mike Hudock, Dick Guesman, Roger Ellis, Nick Mumlay, Dick Christy, Bob Reifsnyder, Roger Donnahoo. *Joe Petrella/NY Daily News Archive/Getty Images*

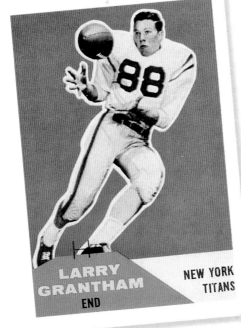

Although he's identified as an end on his rookie card from 1960, Larry Grantham was a cornerstone of the Titans/Jets defense as linebacker for more than a decade. A five-time first-team All-Pro, Grantham had 24 interceptions during his career, ranking him among the top five on the franchise list. *MVP Books Collection*

would be fitting and symbolic, given the organization's profound mediocrity in the years to follow.

The Titans went 7–7 in their second season as well, and they were still not generating any excitement on the New York sports scene—particularly with the Giants, led by quarterback Y. A. Tittle and coached by Allie Sherman, on their way to a third NFL Championship Game in four years.

In 1961, the Titans won their season opener for the second time in as many years—eking out a 21–20 win over the Patriots in Boston—and were victorious in three of their first four games. But even with Al Dorow completing a league-high 197 passes and All-Pro fullback Bill Mathis piling up 846 rushing yards on 202 carries, the team failed to establish much consistency during the season. Even their formidable receiving duo had a down year, with Powell hauling in 71 receptions for 881 yards and five touchdowns and Maynard, slowed by injuries, catching 43 passes for 629 yards and eight touchdowns.

Baugh's reign as the Titans' first head coach ended after two years because Wismer didn't want to pay him his $28,000 salary. Wismer, in fact, had stopped paying Baugh during the 1961 season because of financial problems. The

Bill Mathis lunges for extra yards during a 25–10 loss to the Chargers at home on October 15, 1961. Mathis amassed a league-high 202 carries that season en route to an All-Pro selection while posting career bests in rushing yards (846) and touchdowns (7). *Charles Payne/NY Daily News Archive/Getty Images*

owner, hoping the problems would simply go away, suddenly hired Clyde "Bulldog" Turner, the Hall of Fame center who played for the great Chicago Bears teams of the 1940s, to replace Baugh in 1962.

For his book *Gang Green*, *New York Times* sportswriter Gerald Eskenazi interviewed Baugh, then 83 years old, about the calamity that ensued when Wismer hired Turner.

"Harry never called me, never wrote me a letter [telling me] that I was fired," Baugh said. "He still owed me money, but he hired 'Bulldog' Turner. What Harry wanted me to do was just not come out there, but I knew damn well I wouldn't get the rest of my money because he'd say I didn't report."

Baugh, who knew Turner, called his replacement and was welcomed back to the team long enough to get his money from Wismer.

Baugh recalled in *Gang Green* how crazy the financial situation was under the ownership of Wismer. He told Eskenazi, "It got so bad, when they started passing out the checks, guys ran to the banks as fast as they could."

Incredibly, but somewhat fitting for the organization, Baugh's 14–14 record over two seasons stood as the best record of any coach in franchise history until Bill Parcells, who took over in 1997 and in his three seasons became the first Jets coach with a winning record.

Baugh wasn't the only victim of Wismer's financial troubles. Dorow was traded away prior to the 1962 season after

Titans tackle/kicker Dick Guesman practices his placekicking in the rain during a workout at the Polo Grounds in 1961, while backup quarterback Dick Jamieson holds. Despite a 32 percent career success rate at field goals, Guesman ranked in the AFL's top 10 for accuracy in both of his seasons as the Titans' primary placekicker (1961 and 1963). He hit nearly 97 percent of his extra points. *Ossie LeViness/NY Daily News Archive/Getty Images*

Halfback Dick Christy (45) was an all-star in 1962, leading the Titans with 535 rushing yards while also pulling in 62 pass receptions. He ran for one touchdown during New York's 17–6 win over the Buffalo Bills on September 22.
Robert L. Smith/Getty Images

he contacted the league office about the lack of payment. Years later, Dorow explained his departure from the team in an interview. "Harry Wismer borrowed money to keep up with the expenses of the team," explained Dorow. "At the end of the second year, he owed me money. I didn't get paid for the last three or four games. I was bucking Wismer for my money, and we argued about it. Wismer let Sammy Baugh go, and he brought in Bulldog Turner. Bulldog was a great guy, but not a great head coach.

"In training camp in 1962 I was still owed from the previous season, and Wismer couldn't get the money. I went to the AFL commissioner, Joe Foss, and he said, 'Harry says he's going to get the money.' When Harry found out that I saw Joe, he traded me to Buffalo."

With Johnny Green, Lee Grosscup, and Butch Songin taking turns at quarterback, the Titans went 5–9 under Turner in 1962. It was one-and-done for Turner, who never coached again at the pro level after his brief stint in New York. In their last home games in 1962, the Titans drew 4,011 fans

for the Buffalo Bills (a 30–3 loss) and 3,828 for the Houston Oilers (a 44–10 loss).

Eventually Wismer could no longer afford to meet payroll. On November 8, 1962, the AFL took over operations of the team. The franchise ended up in bankruptcy court, and on March 28, 1963, the Titans were purchased by a five-person ownership group headed by David A. "Sonny" Werblin, a legendary businessman and a bit of a showman. Also among the investors was Leon Hess, the chairman of the Amerada Hess Corporation. Hess would later become the primary owner of the team from 1977 until his death in 1999.

A month after taking control of the team, the new owners changed the name to the New York Jets.

Werblin saw the depressed state of the team, which was generating zero buzz on the New York sports scene, and he knew it needed some star power to generate excitement and interest. The star would soon be found in Alabama in a quarterback named Joe Namath.

SONNY WERBLIN: PRESCIENT SHOWMAN

AP Images

A BRILLIANT VISIONARY, Sonny Werblin was, in many ways, one of the most important figures in New York sports history. Not only did he help purchase the Jets and build a championship-caliber team, but he was the first chairman of the agency that built the Meadowlands Complex where Giants Stadium was built. He also served as chief executive officer of Madison Square Garden. Moreover, Werblin's signing of Joe Namath in January 1965 helped start a bidding war for players that led to the merging of the NFL and AFL.

In a career that spanned more than 50 years, Werblin became an agent with the Music Corporation of America in the 1930s and later built its television division into such a power that it represented such high-profile clients as Elizabeth Taylor, Johnny Carson, and Ronald Reagan and put together such television hits as the Ed Sullivan and Jackie Gleason shows.

Once Werblin got into sports, his successes were no less remarkable.

At one time or another, Werblin owned a share of the Monmouth Park racetrack, ran Madison Square Garden, and rejuvenated downtrodden New York Knicks and Rangers teams. He also helped create the $340 million Meadowlands Sports Complex in New Jersey, which instantly became one of the nation's premier sports venues and was copied by many others around the country.

Werblin landing Namath, though, perhaps defined him more than anything.

"He knew the value of the fan and the star system," Namath said of the former Jets owner. "Over the years, he adopted me. He made sure I was getting along well. He told me to get to know New York, that it was the greatest city."

As Werblin, who with his partners bought the Titans for $1 million, explained when he gave Namath the then-outlandish contract of $427,000: "A million-dollar set is worthless if you put a $2,000 actor in the main role."

Some 18 months later, the NFL agreed to a merger with the AFL, and the Super Bowl was created as an annual championship game.

Upon Werblin's death, broadcasting legend Howard Cosell said, "He single-handedly changed the face of sports in America."

One of the greatest shames in New York sports history was that Werblin was not able to enjoy the Jets' Super Bowl victory as a team owner. His partners had become uncomfortable with all the attention being paid to Werblin, and they bought him out before the start of the 1968 season. They paid $1.2 million for a share that had cost Werblin $250,000 less than six years earlier.

Werblin, after all he did to put the franchise on the map, was out.

For the next 20 years, he pursued his other sports ventures and, with his wife, ran the David and Leah Ray Werblin Foundation in support of charitable and philanthropic causes. He died in 1991 at age 81.

"When I found out he had died, it was an empty feeling, a hollow feeling," Namath said at Werblin's funeral. "Then, right away, I thought of how up and busy and full of life he was. He was here a good while with a wonderful wife and family. I got to thinking he had a wonderful life, and that made it easier."

Paul Tagliabue, the NFL commissioner at the time, called Werblin "the consummate showman" who "had a profound impact on the entire entertainment industry, including pro football."

Although he described their relationship as being "rivals almost to the point of being enemies," New York Giants co-owner Wellington Mara praised Werblin for creating the Meadowlands complex, which still houses both teams. "This is the outstanding sports complex in this country," Mara said, "and without [Werblin], the thing never could have been dreamed up, financed, or built."

Werblin, summing up his own brilliant and full life, once famously said, "My life has been selling tickets."

Few, if any, did it better.

Before the 1963 season, Weeb Ewbank was named the third head coach in the history of New York's AFL franchise. He remained with the team for 11 seasons, longer than any other Jets head coach. Most importantly, he led the Jets to their greatest success. *Wire photo/MVP Books Collection*

THE WEEB YEARS

Two years before Werblin brought Namath to the Big Apple, he made another significant move as team owner: hiring Weeb Ewbank as head coach.

Ewbank, just three years removed from leading the Baltimore Colts to a second consecutive NFL championship, was fired by Baltimore following the 1962 season. (The Colts let Ewbank go so they could hire Don Shula, who would go on to great things as head coach of the Colts and the Miami Dolphins.) The Jets pounced, naming Ewbank head coach and general manager on the same day they changed the team's name from the Titans to the Jets. Finally, they had head coaching credibility.

Ewbank brought in a strong assistant coaching staff that included Walt Michaels, Chuck Knox, and Clive Rush, all of whom would later become head coaches, including Michaels with the Jets. Upon being hired by the Jets, Ewbank said, "I had a five-year plan in Baltimore and I don't see why we can't build a winner here in five years."

That comment proved to be most prescient. Although Ewbank's first three seasons produced a trio of 5–8–1 records, the Jets jumped to 8–5–1 in his fifth season (1967). In his sixth year on the job they claimed the one and (through the 2010 season) only Super Bowl victory in franchise history.

In 1963, the Jets won their first three home games with Ewbank as head coach while jumping out to another 3–1 start, but a 1–6 road record for the year, and an offense that scored fewer than 18 points per game (worst in the league), left the team in last place in the AFL East. Bake Turner, a transplant from the Colts, replaced Art Powell at wide receiver and was named an all-star with his career-best 71 catches and 1,009 receiving yards.

After Ewbank's first season, the Jets moved out of the Polo Grounds and into the newly constructed Shea Stadium

in Flushing, Queens, which would be their home for the next 20 years. The only problem with the Jets' new stadium was that it was also the Mets' home, and the baseball club took precedence. Consequently, the Jets were not allowed to practice in the stadium while baseball season was in progress because they would chew up the field.

The Jets ended up finding some practice fields on the Rikers Island prison grounds. The prison officials allowed the Jets to practice there as long as they let the prisoners watch, which they did.

Most importantly, however, pieces were gradually being put in place that would build the winner that Ewbank had promised would come within five years.

In 1964, the Jets outbid the Giants for Matt Snell, a top running back out of Ohio State. This was a landmark moment, as Snell became the first player to spurn the Giants for the upstart Jets. As a rookie, Snell carried the ball 215 times for 948 yards while also tallying 56 receptions for 393 yards, all of which were career highs for the three-time Pro Bowler.

On the defensive side of the ball, linebacker Larry Grantham earned his fifth consecutive All-Pro selection, and

Shea Stadium, seen here under construction in October 1962, would become the Jets' new home in 1964. *AP Images*

safety Dainard Paulson led the league with 12 interceptions—a Jets franchise record that still stood through 2010.

Suddenly, that star power that Werblin craved was beginning to show results—at the ticket booth if not yet in the win column. The Jets drew their largest crowd to date in the 1964 season opener when 44,497 came to Shea to see them beat the Denver Broncos 30–6. Later that season, on November 8, the Jets experienced another watershed moment. The team drew 61,929 at Shea Stadium, virtually the same number the Giants drew that same day at Yankee Stadium.

The team's performance away from Shea that season was uninspiring, however, as the Jets went 0–7 on the road, with double-digit losses in five of those contests.

ENTER BROADWAY JOE

Although stealing Snell away from the Giants and competing with their cross-town rival for New Yorkers' attention were all significant small victories for the Jets, things got real interesting in Queens in 1965, when Joe Namath joined the team.

Namath, fresh off a brilliant collegiate career at Alabama under legendary coach Bear Bryant, was signed by the Jets one day after the 1965 Orange Bowl. Werblin wasn't fooling around. The Jets were ready to pounce on Namath as soon as his college career was finished. New York signed Namath

to a three-year, $427,000 contract, which seems like pocket change compared to today's mega-contracts but at that time was big money.

The young quarterback hit it off with his coach almost instantly. In fact, Namath revealed years later that Ewbank was a big reason he opted to sign with the Jets instead of the St. Louis Cardinals, who had selected him with the 12th overall pick in the NFL draft. Namath was impressed by the work that Ewbank had done with the great Baltimore quarterback, Johnny Unitas.

"What made him special for us was his knowledge of the game and what we needed to do to get the job done," Namath said of Ewbank. "I took a liking to him early when he insisted on excellent pass protection."

According to Namath, Ewbank understood what went through a quarterback's mind, but at the same time the coach was never afraid.

"I used to marvel at him when he wanted to run a play that seemed a little hairy," Namath recalled. "He showed respect for other teams, but never showed an ounce of fear for other teams. . . . He always pumped us up and always had us thinking we were going to win."

Namath called Ewbank "one of the best coaches that ever lived, ever coached the game of football."

"With every new coach I played for," Namath said, "Weeb got better and better. He had something very special, and one

The signing of Alabama quarterback Joe Namath (right) in January 1965 was a watershed moment for the Jets and the entire American Football League, proving that the upstart AFL could attract the big-name college stars. Coach Weeb Ewbank (left) and team owner Sonny Werblin (center) show their pleasure about the signing. *AP Images*

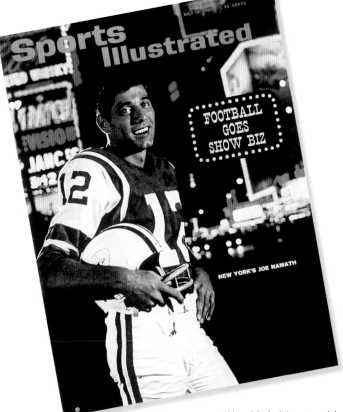

Although he hadn't yet earned the "Broadway Joe" nickname, Namath's arrival in New York was the big sports story of 1965. *James Drake/Sports Illustrated/Getty Images*

thing he shared with all of us was winning championships. He did it in New York and did it in Baltimore, and people will never forget that."

People wouldn't soon forget Namath, either. From the big contract signing as a 21-year-old, the Namath legend grew and grew to the point where now, decades after he began playing, he remains not only the most iconic figure in Jets franchise history but one of the most influential players in pro football history.

On the field, Namath could be prolific. Three times he led the league in passing yards, and in 1967 he became the first quarterback to throw for 4,000 yards in a 14-game season. Off the field, he was all Broadway. He wore long hair and a Fu Manchu mustache, starred in commercials for panty hose, wore mink coats, and went to all the New York City clubs. Wherever Joe went was the cool place to be.

What makes Namath's legacy so confounding, though, is that his career statistics were mediocre at best, and he didn't produce a lot of winning seasons.

Namath played in 140 games in the AFL and NFL, and as a starter he won 62, lost 63, and tied 4. In those 140 career games, he threw 173 touchdown passes and 220 interceptions, and he had more TDs than interceptions in only two

In 1967, Namath helped the Jets to their first winning season while leading the league in pass completions and passing yards. Although Broadway Joe couldn't help New York defeat Kansas City in Week 8 (seen here), the 5–1–1 start got the Jets off on the right foot. *Focus On Sport/Getty Images*

seasons. He had a pedestrian 50.1 percent completion rate for his career and threw for 27,663 yards, which ranked him 49th all time (through 2010). Even in the Super Bowl season of 1968, Namath completed just 49.2 percent of his passes and threw 15 touchdowns against 17 interceptions. In his 13 seasons, Namath played for three division champions (the 1968 and 1969 AFL East champion Jets and the 1977 NFC West champion Rams) and won one league championship and one Super Bowl.

Still, the future Hall of Famer made an impact practically right out of the gate as a rookie in 1965. Although he won only three starts that season, Namath threw 18 touchdown passes against just 15 interceptions and had the third-highest passer rating in the league. In his first pro start, he attempted 40 passes in a 33–21 loss to Buffalo. In his fifth

start, he tossed four touchdown passes in a 41–14 romp of the Houston Oilers. Two of those scores were to fellow Pro Bowler Maynard, who led the AFL with 14 receiving touchdowns that year.

A third straight 5–8–1 finish was followed in 1966 by a slightly improved 6–6–2 record. Things started off very strong, as the team didn't lose its first game until Week 6, but a four-game losing streak that followed ensured another season without a playoff appearance.

Namath continued his development, leading the AFL in pass attempts (471), completions (232), and yards (3,379) in 1966. He improved on those numbers in 1967, posting career bests in all three categories (491, 258, 4,007), while the team improved to 8–5–1, the first winning season in franchise history. The Jets won five of their first seven

JOE NAMATH

QUARTERBACK

1965–1976

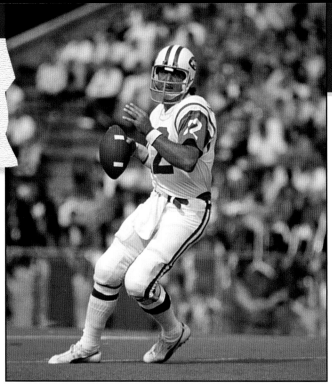

JOE NAMATH was raised in tiny, rural Beaver Falls, Pennsylvania, and nobody could have predicted the larger-than-life sports figure he would become. Namath, much like Michael Jordan in basketball and Tiger Woods in golf, would transcend sports. He was a brand as much as he was an athlete.

And Namath was quite an athlete.

When he graduated high school, Namath received offers from six Major League Baseball teams—the Yankees, Mets, Indians, Reds, Pirates, and Phillies—but football was his true love.

Namath has told interviewers that he wanted to sign with the Pirates and play baseball like his idol, Roberto Clemente, but he elected to play football because his mother wanted him to get a college education. Ironically, Namath, who went to the University of Alabama, would not earn his degree until 2006 when he returned to college in an online program.

During his time at Alabama, Namath led the Crimson Tide football team to a 29–4 record over three seasons. Alabama coach Bear Bryant once called Namath "the greatest athlete I ever coached."

Many speculated that Namath's relationship with his college coach was a rocky one because he was so free-spirited and

From the moment he entered the league, Joe Namath was often the center of attention. Here he jokes around with the Playboy Bunny touch football team, of which he was the honorary coach, in October 1967. Quipped the former Alabama star, "Bear Bryant never told me I'd run into anything like this." *James Garrett/NY Daily News Archive/Getty Images*

Bryant so rigid. But that's something Namath vehemently disputes. Namath called Bryant "the smartest coach I ever knew and the man who taught me the meaning of integrity."

Despite suffering a serious knee injury in his senior year, Namath was drafted by teams in both the National Football League and the American Football League. The two competing leagues held their respective drafts on the same day, November 28, 1964.

The NFL's St. Louis Cardinals selected Namath 12th overall in their draft, while the Jets selected him with the AFL's first overall pick. He opted to sign with the Jets.

Some contend that part of the reason Namath opted to play for the Jets was that he had developed a dislike for the NFL when the Giants used the first overall pick that year to draft Tucker Frederickson, who played at Auburn, Alabama's biggest rival. Hailing from tiny Beaver Falls, Namath also embraced the underdog status of the fledgling AFL

As Namath became a football star in New York, his stardom soon went beyond the playing field. He became a sought-after advertising pitchman, selling everything from shaving cream to panty hose. Namath's nickname "Broadway Joe" was given to him by tackle Sherman Plunkett, a Jets teammate.

Namath wore a full-length fur coat on the sidelines, something not allowed by the NFL, as that league required all team personnel (players, coaches, athletic trainers) to wear official team apparel issued by the league's athletic supplier on the sidelines. He also stood out from the rest of his Jets teammates by wearing white shoes on the field, rather than the traditional black.

"Whatever individuality I had was condoned by coach Bryant, and also Weeb Ewbank with the Jets," Namath said. "I was team captain at Alabama and in New York and always got along with fellow players. In practice, and on game days, nobody accused me of screwing off.

Broadway Joe was often seen in the company of high-profile actresses and other celebrities. Here he accompanies Raquel Welch to the Academy Awards in 1972. *Fotos International/ Getty Images*

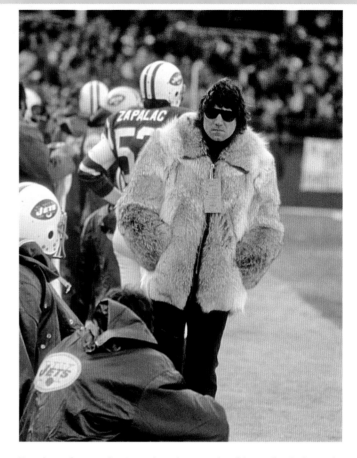

Namath, out of action with an injury, dons a fur coat on the sidelines at Shea Stadium in the early 1970s. *Focus on Sport/Getty Images*

"Flamboyant? It was probably my white football shoes, when all other players wore black. I stood out, but that was the idea. Sonny Werblin, the Jets owner, had a lot to do with molding my style. He was a show-business exec and became the first owner of a pro sports team to promote a star system. Maybe he and I were both a little ahead of our time."

However big Namath got, he never changed.

"He treated everybody nice; he was my favorite," longtime Jets equipment manager Bill Hampton said. "He'd buy you dinner. He was a class guy then and he still is. He hung around with the trainer and with me. He was a regular guy."

Hampton recalled always carrying an extra jersey for Namath and no one else to road games, saying, "One time in Kansas City, someone broke into the locker room the night before the game . . . and stole Namath's number twelve."

Namath's popularity was widespread, even reaching his peers. Dallas Cowboys quarterback Roger Staubach once said: "I enjoy sex as much as Joe Namath. Only I do it with one girl."

One of Broadway Joe's off-field endeavors was Bachelors III, a bar on Manhattan's Upper East Side. NFL Commissioner Pete Rozelle had demanded that Namath sell his interest in the bar because it reflected badly on the league's image. Namath refused, and he briefly retired before the 1969 season, until he and Rozelle reached a compromise. *Vincent Riehl/NY Daily News Archive/Getty Images*

Emerson Boozer (left) and Matt Snell (right) provided a ground-game complement to Joe Namath's aerial attack in the late 1960s and early 1970s. As of 2010, both Snell, a three-time Pro Bowler with New York from 1964 to 1972, and Boozer, a two-time Pro Bowler from 1966 to 1975, rank among the franchise's top five in career rushing yards. *Pictorial Parade/Getty Images*

games with one tie, but three losses in the final four weeks left them one game out of the division lead.

Namath didn't do it alone, of course. End George Sauer, who like Namath was a rookie in 1965, combined with Maynard to form a dangerous receiving corps. Both caught more than 70 passes and collected more than 1,000 receiving yards in 1967. More than 40 years later, Maynard's 1,434 yards remained a franchise record, and Sauer's 1,189 rank sixth on the Jets' single-season list. Although halfback Emerson Boozer and fullback Matt Snell, both Pro Bowlers in 1966, missed a combined 13 games to injuries, the pair helped give the Jets a legitimate running game.

The pieces were starting to fit together to form a winning team.

THE ROAD TO A MIRACLE

The 1968 Jets team was largely unchanged from the squad that won eight games the previous year. Other than the addition of three-time All-Pro guard Bob Talamini, acquired from Houston, and rookie tackle Sam Walton, all the offensive starters from 1967 were back. On the defensive side, John Elliott moved into the starting role at defensive tackle and responded with his first of three straight Pro Bowl seasons.

The Jets opened the '68 season with three road games and came away with two victories. A tight 20–19 win over Kansas City in the opener was followed by a 47–31 shoot-out victory at Boston in which cornerback Randy Beverly ran back an interception 68 yards for a first-quarter touchdown and Mark Smolinski scored on a blocked punt. After

Don Maynard beats Chiefs defensive back Goldie Sellers on a 56-yard touchdown pass during New York's 20–19 win at Kansas City in the 1968 season opener. Maynard had 203 receiving yards in the game and led the league with 99.8 yards per game for the year, with a total of 1,297 receiving yards. *William P. Smith/AP Images*

coming up short against Buffalo in a 37–35 loss—despite 124 yards rushing by Snell and four touchdown passes by Namath—the Jets came from behind in the fourth quarter to defeat San Diego in the home opener, with the go-ahead touchdown provided by Boozer on a one-yard run.

A 21–13 loss to Denver put the Jets at 3–2, but eight wins in their final nine games catapulted New York to an 11–3 record, a full four games ahead of the second-place Oilers in the East Division. The Jets' explosive offense put up 510 yards in a 37–15 thrashing of the Chargers in Week 11. Maynard, who had 166 receiving yards in that game, averaged nearly 100 yards per game on the year, best in the league. In all, the Jets outscored their opponents 419–280 in the 14 games.

Interestingly, Namath remembers those disappointing losses to Buffalo and Denver during the historic championship season as vividly as he does the great wins.

"The things that stand out, other than winning, were losing to the two last-place teams in the league with that same team," Namath said. "I threw five interceptions in each of those two losses—ten interceptions for those two games. But for the year we had seventeen, so the other games were good."

About the Buffalo game, Namath said, "If a loss could be put on one guy's shoulders, that one certainly was put on me, because I did everything to foul up our plan that day, not intentionally certainly. Our defensive coordinator, Walt Michaels, left me a note after the game, maybe to

THE "HEIDI GAME"

THE 1968 JETS didn't make history solely with their Super Bowl III triumph. Earlier that season, they were unwittingly a part of television history during a game against the Oakland Raiders.

The game that came to be known as the "Heidi Game" took place on November 17, 1968, at the Oakland Coliseum, when the two playoff-bound teams with identical 7–2 records were embroiled in a nip-and-tuck contest. The Jets took a 32–29 lead on Jim Turner's 26-yard field goal with 1:05 remaining in the game.

That's when officials from NBC-TV decided to end the game broadcast and air the children's movie *Heidi*, to be shown at its scheduled time.

The TV viewers who were locked into the tense football game missed Oakland scoring two touchdowns in the span of 42 seconds that led to a shocking 43–32 Raiders victory.

One of those viewers was Weeb Ewbank's wife, Lucy. Shortly after NBC switched to *Heidi*, Lucy Ewbank called the Coliseum to congratulate her husband on the Jets victory she thought she saw. When the switchboard operator put the call through to the locker room, Ewbank said, "Congratulations? What do you mean congratulations? We lost! We blew it!"

Oakland's improbable comeback began when Raiders quarterback Daryle Lamonica connected with running back Charlie Smith on a 43-yard scoring pass to put Oakland ahead 36–32. Then, with 42 seconds remaining, Jets returner Earl Christy fumbled the kickoff at the 10-yard line, and Oakland's Preston Ridlehuber recovered it and ran it in for a touchdown and a 43–32 Raiders lead. In a span of nine seconds, while the opening credits were probably running for *Heidi*, the Raiders scored 14 points.

"We thought it was in the bag," running back Emerson Boozer recalled. "Anything that can go wrong did. There were a bunch of freak incidents. The Raiders didn't beat us. We beat ourselves."

Due to NBC's decision to cut away from the game, viewers also lost out. The network's gaffe caused angry fans to flood the switchboard with complaints. The next day, NBC Program Director Julian Goodman issued a public apology.

"People still remember it now," Curt Gowdy, the veteran announcer, said. "It was a real happening in pro football. It was the best 'mistake' they ever made. It got more publicity than it would have if NBC had stayed with the game. But it wasn't planned; NBC just blew it."

give more thought on how to approach the thing and looking at the other side of the ball, and we started playing that way afterwards."

Even if Namath remains hard on himself for those defeats, his performance during the year was good enough to earn him league Most Valuable Player honors and the lone All-Pro selection of his career.

The only AFL team that put up more points than the Jets in 1968 was the West Division champion Oakland Raiders, their opponent in the AFL title game. Although the 12–2 Raiders lacked any single star with the draw of Namath, the defending AFL champs had a high-powered offense led by quarterback Daryle Lamonica and a stingy defense that allowed the second-fewest points in the league in 1968.

The AFL Championship Game was a rematch of the classic "Heidi Game" of six weeks earlier, when the Raiders defeated the Jets 43–32 with a stunning comeback in the final minute.

To prepare for the title game, Namath said he went to a bar, "grabbed a girl and a bottle of Johnnie Walker Red and went to the Summit Hotel and stayed in bed the whole night with the girl and the bottle." Broadway Joe played through his hangover and threw three touchdowns passes against the Raiders. The final one was a 6-yarder to Maynard with 7:47 remaining to give the Jets a 27–23 lead.

Led by Lamonica, who threw for 401 yards in the game, the Raiders then marched down the field to the Jets' 12-yard line with just over two minutes remaining. From there, he threw a quick screen to Charlie Smith, but the ball floated over Smith's head and was picked up by Jets linebacker Ralph Baker. Because the pass was ruled a lateral, New York got possession, sealing the game and a trip to the Super Bowl.

THE GUARANTEE

As much as the Jets' upset victory in Super Bowl III forever altered the pro football landscape, it was a simple sentence uttered by Joe Namath days before the game that lives on in most people's minds.

"The Jets will win Sunday. I guarantee it," Namath said upon being heckled by a Colts fan during a gathering at the Miami Touchdown Club three days before the game. There were few reporters present, and Namath's guarantee didn't really make headlines at the time. Now, of course, the guarantee is legend.

Joe Namath fires a pass over the head of Raiders defender Ben Davidson (83) to Jets end George Sauer (83) in the second quarter of the AFL Championship Game on December 29, 1968. Namath and Sauer—both named first-team All-Pros that year—led New York to a 27–23 win to clinch a trip to Super Bowl III. *Gene Kappock/NY Daily News Archive/Getty Images*

Namath's boast actually sabotaged the pre-game strategy Weeb Ewbank had been cooking up to get the Colts to take his Jets team lightly.

"I could have killed him," Ewbank said years later. "We were seventeen-point underdogs and I said, 'I like this.' But, talking to the squad, I said, 'I don't want you guys doing anything that will bring the Colts alive and get them mad at us.' I said, 'Now don't pay any attention to what I say [to reporters] because if I can make us twenty-one-point underdogs I will.'"

Ewbank recalled speaking at a press conference the day after Namath's guarantee, not knowing what his star quarterback had said.

"I went out there to meet all the writers, three hundred or so from all over the country, and they said, 'What do you think about what Joe said last night?'" Ewbank recalled. "I said, 'What'd he say?' They said he'd guaranteed it. I said,

'Well, sorry he said it, but I hope he's right.' What could you say? It was done."

Namath recalled Ewbank being "upset . . . very upset" about his bold guarantee of victory.

"And he was right," Namath added, "because he wanted the Colts overconfident and I had messed things up, it appeared. Coach Ewbank said they would put that up there [on the bulletin board] and it would give them extra incentive, and I laughed. I said, 'If they need clippings for the bulletin board, they are in trouble.'

"He told me to behave myself from there on. He knew I could dig a big hole for myself, so he said, 'Don't say anything from here on in.' He made me become a little wary of what I would say. I honest to God felt bad he was upset about it."

Ewbank wasn't the only person upset with Namath's burst of bravado. Jets tackle Dave Herman, who was going to be tasked with trying to block massive defensive end

A relaxed Joe Namath chats with members of the media and fans at the Jets' Fort Lauderdale hotel a couple of days before the Super Bowl. *Walter Iooss Jr./Sports Illustrated/Getty Images*

Bubba Smith, was hardly pleased. "He wanted to choke me," Namath recalled.

"Joe went out and said quite innocently, 'I guarantee we're going to win,' and I went up and said, 'I've got a guy six-eight, three hundred and twenty pounds. We don't need to excite him any more than he's going to be,'" Herman said.

"The guy is crazy," Jets linebacker Ralph Baker recalled thinking of Namath's guarantee.

"Namath talks too much," Colts defensive tackle Billy Ray Smith said at the time. "He should keep his mouth shut. He'll keep his teeth a lot longer."

The concerns of Ewbank and Herman turned out to be unfounded, because despite Namath's guarantee, the Colts didn't take the Jets seriously.

"All we did was laugh," Colts Hall of Fame tight end John Mackey said. "We thought it was a joke. And that was the problem. We had the wrong attitude."

The Colts, after all, entered the game with a 15–1 record and had outscored their opponents 460–158. They had just trounced the Cleveland Browns 34–0 in the NFL title game.

"I think the biggest mistake was that we believed we were a nineteen-point favorite," Mackey said. "We just believed all we had to do was show up. We had announced the victory party the Wednesday before and cut up the winners' share at the pre-game meal. Now, can you believe that?"

Mackey added that he believed the Colts' cavalier attitude was bred by the team's owner, Carroll Rosenbloom, who had arranged for the players' families to make the trip to Miami and who treated Super Bowl week like a vacation.

"Distractions hurt us," Mackey said. "Our owner, Carroll Rosenbloom, took everybody on the trip but family pets. We had wives, kids, everyone. In our hotel lobby, I remember my son asking me why all these people were around asking some guy to write his name on a piece of paper. It was Frank Sinatra."

Namath said his guarantee "was not planned, it wasn't premeditated; it was just anger and frustration, and I really believed we were going to win the game.

"You get angry when told you're going to lose, and lose big, day after day. And, you know, anger can be a good thing when you're playing sports."

Namath wasn't alone in his confidence that the Jets would win; he was just the only one to say it publicly.

"We were watching film of the Colts and we just knew we could beat them," Jets guard Randy Rasmussen recalled. "But Weeb kept reminding us, 'Don't say anything to the press. Just keep quiet.' Then Joe Namath spoke out and took the pressure off us and put it on himself."

Namath wasn't the only Jets player who was confident about the team's chances against the Colts in Super Bowl III—he was just the only one to say so publicly. Tight end Pete Lammons, seen here warming up with his quarterback two days before the game, expressed concern that the Jets might be *over*confident. *AP Images*

Jets coach Weeb Ewbank wasn't thrilled with his quarterback's pre-game boast, but he was on the sideline ready to lead his team to fulfill Namath's guarantee on January 12, 1969, at the Orange Bowl in Miami. *Walter Iooss Jr./Sports Illustrated/Getty Images*

Defensive back Johnny Sample, a former Colt, said, "People just believed the hype from the NFL machine because they had killed the AFL in the first two Super Bowls. But they didn't take the time to analyze the two teams. We had so much more talent than the Colts."

Jets tight end Pete Lammons recalled saying to teammates in the week leading up to the game, "If we watch any more of these Colts game films, we're going to get overconfident."

Ewbank provided some motivational gems of his own by prodding the players on his team who had played for the Colts, such as Sample, kicker Jim Turner, and even offensive lineman Winston Hill, who had been drafted by Baltimore but was cut before he had a chance to play.

"Some of you young men used to be with the Colts, but that team decided that you didn't have the skills to stay with them," Ewbank reportedly told the players. "Now you're opposing that team. You've proven to yourself that you're capable. Now you've got an opportunity to prove it to that team." (Of course, Ewbank himself had been told by the Colts that he wasn't wanted there as a coach, so he surely had similar motivation.)

According to Gerald Eskenazi's *Gang Green*, after the team prayer before the game, Ewbank left his players with this final thought: "One more thing. When we win, don't pick me up and ruin my other hip. I'll walk."

JANUARY 12, 1969: THE GAME

What was perhaps most remarkable about the Jets' 16–7 upset of the Colts in Super Bowl III on January 12, 1969, at the Orange Bowl in Miami is the fact that the Colts, favored by as many as 19 points by some oddsmakers, really had no chance. The underdogs dominated the game so convincingly, building a 16–0 lead in the fourth quarter, that Joe Namath didn't throw a single pass in the final period.

With his top big-play receiver, Don Maynard, suffering with a hamstring injury, Namath went with an uncharac-

teristically conservative game plan on offense. That, coupled with a Jets defense that befuddled the Baltimore offense, gave the Jets the greatest win in franchise history.

"Weeb Ewbank had coached the Colts before coming to the Jets and Weeb was a guy who watched about ten years' worth of film," Jets kicker Jim Turner recalled. "He knew the Colts' weaknesses, and they fit right into our strengths."

The Jets, seeing that the right side of the Baltimore defense was aging and vulnerable with Ordell Braase (36) playing defensive end, Don Shinnick (33) at linebacker, and Lenny Lyles (32) at cornerback, attacked the Colts there. Snell ran behind the blocks of tackle Winston Hill and fullback Emerson Boozer and battered the Baltimore defense with 30 carries for 121 yards.

Namath and the Jets came out firing in Super Bowl III at the Orange Bowl. By the time it was all over, the Vince Lombardi trophy would be heading to New York. *Lou Witt/Getty Images*

"We didn't understand why other teams hadn't taken advantage of what Baltimore was telegraphing on its plays," Namath said. "Every time, ahead of time, I knew what defense they were going to be in."

Many believed that Snell should have been named the game's Most Valuable Player. Afterward, he said he had no problem with Namath (17-for-28, 206 yards) being named MVP.

"When a guy makes a prediction like he did, then goes out there and wins the game, he's got to be the MVP," Snell said.

Namath threw a lot of short, quick passes to tight end Pete Lammons and receiver George Sauer, who caught eight passes for 133 yards.

As heralded as Namath was, the Jets defense brought a major contribution to the upset. The secondary picked off four Baltimore passes, two by cornerback Randy Beverly and one

SUPER BOWL III FACTS AND FIGURES

JANUARY 12, 1969
ORANGE BOWL, MIAMI, FLORIDA
NEW YORK JETS 16, BALTIMORE COLTS 7

Score by Quarter	1	2	3	4	Final
Jets	0	7	6	3	16
Colts	0	0	0	7	7

Attendance: 75,389

Point Spread: Colts by 18

MVP: Joe Namath, New York quarterback

Broadcast Network: NBC

Announcers: Curt Gowdy, Al DeRogatis, and Kyle Rote

Neilsen TV Rating: 36.0

Market Share: 71

Cost of a 30-Second Commercial: $55,000

National Anthem: Anita Bryant

Running back Matt Snell (41) saw plenty of openings in the Baltimore defense during Super Bowl III. With 121 yards rushing, Snell (along with Baltimore's Tom Matte) became the first back to gain more than 100 yards in a Super Bowl. *Kidwiler Collection/Diamond Images/ Getty Images*

each by cornerback Johnny Sample and safety Jim Hudson, all deep in Jets territory or in their own end zone.

"Our defense was underrated," Herman said. "Most of the guys weren't that big, but they were strong."

New York's opportunistic defense forced five turnovers in the game and caused the Colts to squander several scoring chances. Starting quarterback Earl Morrall led Baltimore on six first-half drives. Two ended with missed field goals, and three ended with interceptions inside the Jets' 15-yard line.

The play that most haunted the Colts came in the final minute of the half. With the Jets up by a touchdown and the ball on the Jets' 41, Baltimore receiver Jimmy Orr got open in the end zone on a flea-flicker, but Morrall never spotted him. Instead, Morrall was picked off by Hudson on a pass over the middle intended for Jerry Hill.

"Morrall was flustered," Jets defensive end Gerry Philbin said. "We gave them a different look they really weren't used to seeing."

According to Jets safety Jim Richards, defensive coordinator Walt Michaels told the team before the game, "I don't want to see you guys come into this locker at halftime and talk about how you can come back. I want you in here with a lead."

Indeed, the Jets closed out the first half leading 7–0 thanks to a four-yard touchdown run by Snell in the second quarter. Never before had an AFL team led in a Super Bowl.

Two Turner field goals put the Jets ahead 13–0 late in the third quarter, and Baltimore head coach Don Shula yanked Morrall in favor of the 35-year-old Johnny Unitas, who had been injured. Unitas' reputation as one of the all-time great quarterbacks fostered some nervousness on the Jets sideline when they saw the future Hall of Famer heading into the game.

"When he came on the field, my heart went to my feet," recalled Herman.

Jim Hudson runs back his interception of an Earl Morrall pass intended for Jerry Hill (45) as time expired in the second quarter. One of four interceptions by New York in the game, Hudson's pick was a key play heading into halftime. *Tony Tomsic/Getty Images*

Guarantee fulfilled. *Walter Iooss Jr./Sports Illustrated/Getty Images*

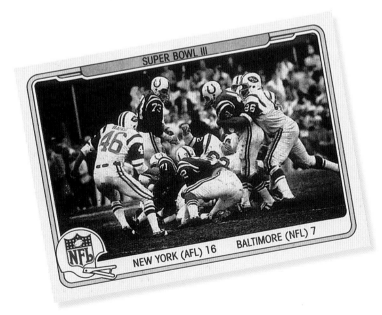

"I'm telling you, man, it sent chills," Snell said, "because if you grew up like myself watching him take teams from behind to victory, you knew this was a legend coming in."

"I thought we could win all along; I thought we were supposed to win," Namath said. "But until you do it, you can't be sure. I'll admit when Unitas came on the field, my heart almost stopped."

The Jets defense would hold on, not letting Unitas engineer one of those comebacks. Unitas did get the Colts into the end zone once, but he also threw a damaging interception.

"I want this moment to last, and last, and last, and last," Sample told reporters in the locker room after the game.

When it was over, as Namath triumphantly trotted off the field with his right index finger held high in the air, it signaled more than just a glorious moment for the New York Jets and their fans. The victory sent shockwaves throughout professional football, as the young upstarts from the American Football League had firmly asserted their place as equals alongside the long-established National Football League.

THE AFTERMATH

Although the NFL and AFL had announced in June 1966 their agreement to merge into a single league with two conferences beginning with the 1970 season, the Jets' improbable win in Super Bowl III brought added legitimacy to the junior league. After decisive victories by the NFL champion Green Bay Packers in the first two Super Bowls, the superiority of the older league was almost taken as a given by most observers and particularly by those within the NFL organization. But Broadway Joe and his guaranteed victory in Super Bowl III put the sports world on notice that the AFL was legit.

After the game Namath proclaimed, "Listen, the AFL is here to stay, and you'd better believe it. I guarantee."

That, of course, proved to be another guarantee Namath was spot on about. And he wasn't alone in that assessment. Curt Gowdy, the legendary sportscaster who did the play-by-play of Super Bowl III, called the Jets' victory the "most financially important game" in American sports history.

"That changed the whole thinking of the sportsman's mind," Gowdy said. "Most guys were, 'Ah, that AFL, who are they?' Like the AFL players came from upper Slobovia and the NFL players came from the colleges. You couldn't tell 'em the AFL was getting better every year until the Jets beat Baltimore. The next year, Kansas City beat Minnesota

Thousands gathered at New York's City Hall in January 1969 to celebrate the Jets' stunning Super Bowl win over the Colts. It marked the city's first sports championship since the Yankees in 1962.
Phil Stanziola/NY Daily News Archive/Getty Images

soundly [23–7 in Super Bowl IV]. Suddenly, everybody was, 'Hey, it's all over now. The AFL is as good as the NFL.'"

To this day, the significance of the win is not lost on the Jets players who were involved in the moment.

"Any time you're part of history to some degree, you feel great," Don Maynard said. "The AFL was great for football. Media people knocked the league, the players, and the coaches. I always said, 'Why don't you accept that it's a new job opportunity for thirty-three players, five to seven coaches, and the front-office staffs? And how about fans getting to watch pro football in towns that never had it—like Denver, Houston, Boston, Buffalo?'

"America is the land of opportunity, and the AFL was an opportunity for a lot of people."

Indeed, the championship stands out as a peak moment for many of the players from the 1968 Jets. Namath called it "a dream come true."

"When I came in as a rookie, the dream was to make the team, regardless of whether you were the No. 1 draft choice or whatever," he said. "You know you've got to make the team and convince your teammates. Your second goal is to win a championship, and we did that. Those are the only two goals—make the team and win a championship."

Namath said he had no idea how iconic a moment that Super Bowl victory would become.

"Because it was a championship, I knew it was big-time," he said. "But I knew it was even more meaningful for us because we were representing the league, the American

Emerson Boozer finds a hole and heads for the end zone in the fourth quarter of a 23–17 win over the Patriots on October 26, 1969. The Jets beat New England twice that season, and Boozer ran the ball 130 times for 604 yards in 14 games. *Dan Farrell/NY Daily News Archive/Getty Images*

Football League. We'd lost two in a row, and, as a player, you do hear players in the other league talking about you not in a very nice way, or talking about how the Raiders and Kansas City, they weren't good enough."

Namath and the other players understood that losing a third Super Bowl in a row could even bring doubts into the minds of the AFL players themselves. "But we weren't looking to lose," he said. "We were looking to win, and we did."

The winning continued during the 1969 regular season, but not much beyond that. With the New York Mets in residence at Shea Stadium and in the midst of a heated playoff race, the Jets opened the year with five straight away games. They lost two of the first three before rallying with a six-game winning streak that ended with a 34–16 loss to the Chiefs, the eventual Super Bowl champion. The following week, four Jim Turner field goals and two Namath-to-Sauer touchdown passes staked New York to a 26–0 lead before backup quarterback Babe Parilli led them the rest of the way to a 40–7 final.

The Raiders, who went 12–1–1 that season, handed the Jets their fourth loss of 1969, but then Namath's crew notched

back-to-back road victories at Houston and Miami to finish the year at 10–4 and capture another Eastern Division title. The postseason life was brief, however, as Kansas City's fourth-quarter, tie-breaking touchdown secured a 13–6 win in the opening round.

The Jets would go 12 years before having another winning season.

Many wondered how that Super Bowl team could have fallen off the face of the map so quickly. Cornerback Randy Beverly said money and age broke up the team.

"I got $12,500 for the 1968 season," Beverly told Gerald Eskenazi in the book *Gang Green*. "I had two interceptions in that [Super Bowl] game. I asked Weeb about a raise for the next season. I said, 'I'd like a $1,500 increase,' and he said, 'You're pricing yourself out of the league.'"

Beverly called himself and a number of the other lesser-known Jets on that championship team "the forgotten few."

"People don't remember us," he said. "They remember the win."

And Namath.

The Jets' 1969 season came to a disappointing end in the AFL Championship Game against the Chiefs, as Joe Namath completed only 14 of 40 passes and threw three interceptions in the 13–6 loss at Shea Stadium on December 20. *Herb Scharfman/Sports Imagery/Getty Images*

② DARK DAYS AND TEASES
The 1970s and 1980s

MVP Books Collection

SOME PEOPLE HAVE SUGGESTED that the New York Jets sold their soul to the devil to win Super Bowl III, grabbing the glory of that historic victory in exchange for years of failure to come.

Certainly, since that magical January day in Miami, iconified by Joe Namath running off the field with his index finger pointed toward the sky, the Jets and their fans have lived on that moment. In the decade following that Super Bowl victory, fans endured a series of mind-numbing, nondescript seasons.

The Jets, to put it bluntly, might as well have not shown up for the 1970s. Their cumulative record in the decade was 53–91. They posted not a single winning season and managed to finish at .500 four times.

During one stretch, the Jets had four different head coaches in two seasons and five in three seasons.

WEEB'S FINAL YEARS

After two straight playoff years featuring double-digit win totals, the Jets fell hard and fast in 1970, the first season of a fully merged league. A six-game losing streak began with the Bills' comeback victory in Buffalo on October 4 when the Jets let a 31–20 fourth-quarter lead slip away. The Jets rallied back from a 17–0 deficit against their one-time Super Bowl foe, the Baltimore Colts, in Week 5 before losing by a touchdown, a game in which Joe Namath's 397 passing yards were clouded, to say the least, by his six interceptions.

The streak ended with the Jets' first-ever regular-season win against an original NFL team, a 31–20 road victory over the Los Angeles Rams. Al Woodall, who had taken over for an injured Namath as the Jets' starting quarterback in Week 6, threw for 261 yards and three touchdowns against the

The Jets opened the 1970 season at Cleveland in the first game ever aired on ABC's *Monday Night Football*. Although Matt Snell (41) ran for 108 yards in the game, New York lost the historic contest 31–21 as the Browns intercepted Joe Namath three times and Cleveland's Homer Jones ran back a kickoff for a 94-yard touchdown. *Herman Seid Collection/Diamond Images/Getty Images*

Rams' vaunted defense. New York secured another impressive win two weeks later, defeating the defending NFL champion Vikings 20–10, but a one-point loss to the Raiders kicked off a three-game slide to close out the 4–10 season.

Woodall filled in admirably for Namath, throwing nine touchdown passes in nine starts. But the offensive line didn't make things easy for the 25-year-old Duke University product, allowing him to be sacked 29 times.

Namath and Woodall combined to start only seven games the following year, as Bob Davis took a majority of the snaps in 1971—and the Jets finished last in the NFL in passing. The running game was bolstered by the selection of Kansas' John Riggins with the sixth overall pick in the draft. The bruising fullback ran for 769 yards on 180 carries in his rookie season while also leading the team with 36 pass receptions. Notwithstanding a 14–13 road win over the eventual AFC champion Dolphins—secured by two fourth-quarter rushing touchdowns from George Nock—the 6–8 season offered few highlights. The 22–0 loss to Baltimore in the season opener, as the Jets amassed 118 yards of total offense, set the tone for what would be a feeble year for the New York offense.

Broadway Joe was back for 1972, and he had his best season of the new decade. Namath led the league with 2,816 passing yards and 19 touchdown tosses while completing 50 percent of his passes. Riggins improved in his second season (944 rushing yards), and Emerson Boozer chipped in with 14 total touchdowns. Third-year tight end Rich Caster benefited from Namath's resurgence, earning his first Pro Bowl berth by pulling in 39 catches for 833 yards and 10 touchdowns.

Rich Caster shakes hands with Bills running back O. J. Simpson following New York's 41–3 thrashing of Buffalo at Shea Stadium on November 12, 1972. Caster caught only one pass in the game, but his 39 receptions for 833 yards and 10 touchdowns on the season led all Jets in 1972. *Ross Lewis/Getty Images*

This potent offense put more than 40 points on the board four times during the season, starting with a 41–24 win over Buffalo and a 44–34 triumph over Baltimore in the season's first two games, both on the road. Against Baltimore, Namath piled up 496 yards and threw six touchdown passes, both career bests, on just 15 completions.

At the halfway point of the season, the Jets were 5–2, but they went 2–5 the rest of the way. The only win in the final five weeks was a narrow 18–17 victory over the Saints, who won only two games all year.

Another injury-plagued season for Namath in 1973 led to a major backslide for the Jets, who finished 4–10, with all four victories coming against the Colts and Patriots. And with that, the Weeb Ewbank era came to an end. Although his time with the Jets ended on a negative note, Ewbank's legacy will also be tied to the amazing championship season of 1968.

COACHING CAROUSEL

Charley Winner, Ewbank's son-in-law, took over the head coaching duties for 1974, although the former St. Louis Cardinals coach didn't quite live up to his name.

Winner's Jets got off to a horrendous 1–7 start in 1974, with the only victory coming against Chicago in Week 2—a game they won by a 23–21 margin after taking a 20–0 first-quarter lead. A 26–20 overtime road win against the Giants not only stopped the bleeding but kicked off an improbable six-game winning streak to close the season. They finished at 7–7.

The 1975 season started off only slightly better than 1974, as the Jets went 2–7, but this time Winner didn't get a chance to right the ship. Instead, Ken Shipp took the helm after Winner was fired following a 52–19 romp by Baltimore. The first-time NFL head coach, who had served as the team's receivers coach and offensive coordinator, didn't fare much

Running back John Riggins spent the first five years of his Hall of Fame career with the Jets (1971–1975). His best season in New York was his last, when he carried the ball 238 times for 1,005 yards and eight touchdowns. *Focus On Sport/Getty Images*

better. The Jets went 1–4 under Shipp to close the season. That was the extent of Shipp's reign in New York.

The 3–11 season, during which the Jets boasted the lowest-ranked defense in the league, was highlighted only by Riggins' 1,005 rushing yards, which made him the first running back in Jets history to break the 1,000-yard barrier. Riggins, who played in the only Pro Bowl of his career that year, bolted for the Washington Redskins the next season.

Lou Holtz, who had been working in the college ranks as an assistant and then head coach since 1960, was hired as the Jets' new head coach for 1976 after a failed bid by New York to lure Ara Parseghian, who had just left Notre Dame. Holtz's Jets promptly lost 10 of his 13 games, and he was replaced by Mike Holovak for the final game of that season.

Holtz, who would go on to legendary success as a college head coach, was overmatched from the start as an NFL

head coach. After a preseason loss, Holtz admitted to Gerald Eskenazi of the *New York Times*, "If I knew that coaching in the pros was going to be like this I would never have taken the job."

Those words, mind you, came *before* Holtz had coached a regular-season NFL game.

Of the three games the Jets won under Holtz, two came against the lowly Buffalo Bills, who won only two games themselves that season. The other win came against the expansion Tampa Bay Buccaneers, who didn't win a game all year. So Holtz's three wins as an NFL head coach came against teams with a combined record of 2–26.

Holtz tried to be a college coach in the pros and it, quite simply, didn't work. He wrote a fight song for the team, ran a veer offense in training camp, and never really figured out the pro game.

Lou Holtz had been coaching at the collegiate level for more than a decade but had never worked in the NFL when the Jets hired him to be their new head coach in February 1976. Holtz's tenure with New York lasted less than one year, as he bailed to take a job at Arkansas before the last game of the Jets' season. *MVP Books Collection*

At the time of his hiring, Holtz said, "McDonald's doesn't change the menu, and it's successful. Lou Holtz will not change."

Amidst the mess he created—the team was 3–10 and a laughingstock of the league—Holtz resigned with one game to play in the 1976 season. He returned to the college game, taking the head coaching job at the University of Arkansas, and Holovak assumed the Jets' head coach position on an interim basis.

Holovak had previous success coaching in New England in the 1960s and finished his NFL head coaching career with a respectable 53–48–9 record (including playoffs). His career with the Jets lasted only one game, however.

Despite Namath's creaky knees, Holovak opted to start the veteran quarterback in the 1976 finale, which would be Namath's last action as a Jet. As Holovak explained to reporters, "This may be the only time in my life I get a chance to start Joe Namath at quarterback."

The Jets lost 42–3 to the Bengals at Shea Stadium on December 12. Namath completed as many passes to his own receivers (four) as he threw interceptions. He finished the year with four touchdowns and 16 interceptions.

Namath's departure from New York was handled poorly by the Jets, who always seemed to be cursed with poor public relations skills. Namath was a free agent, and because of the injuries and age that had eroded his skills, New York had no interest in re-signing him. They had taken Richard Todd, another former Alabama quarterback, in the 1976 draft to replace Namath.

So the Jets, with no fanfare, quietly let Namath sign with the Los Angeles Rams. He spent one year in L.A., playing in four games and throwing three touchdowns and five interceptions, before hanging up his white cleats for good.

MICHAELS BRINGS STABILITY

After the Winner-Shipp-Holtz-Holovak era produced a combined record of 13–29, the hiring of Walt Michaels to replace Holovak on January 5, 1977, was probably the best thing to happen to the Jets in the 1970s. Though Michaels was hardly a resounding success—a 39–47–1 overall record in six seasons—he at least brought some amount of respectability to the team and even led them to the playoffs twice.

The first post-Namath season brought a repeat 3–11 record, as 24-year-old Richard Todd did the bulk of the quarterbacking in 1977. Rookie Wesley Walker, the team's second-round draft pick, hauled in 35 passes for 740 yards, but otherwise the Jets offense failed to generate much of a spark. In fact, it failed to score in three of 14 games.

New York was third in the NFL in points scored in 1978, but the 27th-ranked defense limited the Jets to an 8–8 finish in the first year of the 16-game schedule. They went 6–2 within the division, including a 33–20 season-opening win over the eventual East champion Dolphins; both losses were to the Patriots. Matt Robinson started 11 games at quarterback, and Walker was named a first-team All-Pro thanks to his league-leading 1,169 receiving yards. In just his second year on the job, Michaels was named UPI's AFC Coach of the Year.

Another .500 finish followed in 1979, and the team took a big step backward in 1980. New York fell to 4–12, making Michaels' job status tenuous. A particularly low point came in mid-December, when Todd completed just 10 of 27 passes and was intercepted twice in a 21–20 loss to the New Orleans Saints. It was the Saints' only win that season.

For their 10th win of the 1981 season, the Jets easily defeated the Packers 28–3 in the finale at Shea Stadium. Johnny "Lam" Jones (80) caught a 47-yard touchdown pass from Richard Todd, beating Green Bay defensive backs Mark Lee (22) and Estus Hood (38). *Vernon Biever/Getty Images*

RICHARD TODD

QUARTERBACK
1976–1983

RICHARD TODD was given the unenviable task of replacing Joe Namath on the New York Jets. He also played college ball at the University of Alabama under legendary coach Bear Bryant, as had Namath a decade earlier.

When Namath was released by the Jets after the 1976 season, Todd, age 23, was named the starter. However, Todd's accomplishments never approached those of Namath.

Throughout his time in New York, Todd was booed by fans and ripped by the media. In November 1981, he famously shoved *New York Post* reporter Steve Serby against a locker after reading a story by Serby that supported backup quarterback Matt Robinson.

Todd's finest on-field moment came in 1981, when he led the Jets to their first winning record (10–5–1) since 1969. In the wild-card playoff game, he brought them back from a 24–0 deficit but ultimately fell short. The next year, he led New York to the playoffs again and made it all the way to the AFC Championship Game, but he threw five interceptions in the Jets' 14–0 loss.

Todd's final year with New York was 1983, Joe Walton's first season as head coach. The Jets finished 7–9, and Todd was traded to the Saints, where he would play two more seasons.

Todd finished his Jets career with 1,433 completions, a 54.6 completion percentage, 18,241 yards, 110 touchdowns, and 138 interceptions. He also scored 14 rushing touchdowns. In 1980, Todd set a dubious NFL record by throwing at least one interception in 15 games in the same season.

Richard Todd quarterbacked the Jets offense for eight years, but he was never quite able to bring consistent leadership or success to New York. *NFL Photos/AP Images*

In 1981, Michaels' Jets turned it around dramatically, producing the team's first winning season since 1969. After losing their first three games and four of their first five, the Jets finished strong, going 9–1–1 in their last 11 games, to earn their first postseason appearance in 12 years.

The 10–5–1 record was particularly impressive considering the Jets didn't win their second game until the sixth week. With a talented offense featuring Todd at quarterback, Walker at wide receiver, and rookie running back Freeman McNeil, plus the formidable Sack Exchange pass rush on defense, New York finished second in the AFC East and clinched a wild-card spot in the playoffs.

Their stay in the postseason, however, was short, as the Jets lost 31–27 to the Buffalo Bills at Shea Stadium. Though the final score was close, the Jets were being blown out for much of the game, falling behind 24–0 by early in the second quarter, before making a near-miraculous comeback. A 30-yard touchdown pass from Todd to tight end Mickey Shuler and a pair of Pat Leahy field goals closed the gap to 24–13 by the start of the fourth quarter. Buffalo scored once more, and a touchdown reception by Jets receiver Bobby Jones and a one-yard touchdown run by Kevin Long brought them within four.

With the Jets on the verge of an extraordinary comeback, Buffalo's Bill Simpson intercepted a pass near the goal line in the final seconds to preserve the Bills' win. It was Simpson's second interception of the game and the fourth thrown by Todd, who completed 28 of 51 attempts for 377 yards.

At that time, no NFL team had ever recovered from that big of a deficit in a playoff game. For the Bills, who had finished behind the Jets in the AFC East (third place) during the regular season, the wild-card victory was their first postseason win since 1965.

"When the play started," Simpson said of the clinching interception, "I looked into the backfield and just read Todd's eyes. He was following the receiver all the way. I just stepped up and it was in my hands."

Todd said, "It was a bad read by me. I never saw Simpson until he caught the ball. I was looking for [receiver Derrick] Gaffney and I thought he was open."

"The Jets showed a lot of class and a lot of guts coming back the way they did," said Bills quarterback Joe Ferguson.

"The only thing I can say about us being down 24–0 and coming back was that it was like being down 0–3 at the beginning of the season," said coach Michaels. "It's just a sign of character that we never give up."

For their first postseason game in 12 years, the Jets hosted the Bills on a muddy Shea Stadium field on December 27, 1981. Mark Gastineau and the Jets rallied from a 24–0 deficit but ultimately came up short, losing 31–27. *Focus on Sport/Getty Images*

Todd took the loss hard, though.

"I'm sure that pass will stay with me for a while," Todd said the day after the game. "We were 11 yards from going to Cincinnati [for the next playoff round]. If I hit the pass, we would be sitting here talking about getting ready for Cincinnati. But I didn't, and Buffalo's going."

The quarterback echoed Michaels' sentiments about the character the team showed in rallying back, first from a 0–3 start to the season and then in the final game. He noted that, after so many years of adversity, the players simply got tired of losing and just got mad. "I think I became a leader through example," he added. "I was never a rah-rah guy. A lot of guys became leaders. A lot of guys grew up this year."

Todd believed they would be a better team the following year. "We'll all be on the same page," he said. "We'll have a year under the same offense and we'll have a year under the same defense. Our better years are coming up. I'm positive of that."

WESLEY WALKER
RECEIVER
1977–1989

DESPITE BEING LEGALLY BLIND in one eye, Wesley Walker was one of the most prolific and electrifying receivers in Jets history. As of the end of the 2010 season, he ranked fifth on the franchise's all-time receptions list (438), second in receiving touchdowns (71), and first in yards per catch (19.0).

Walker spent his entire 13-year NFL career with the Jets, earning two Pro Bowl selections (1978 and 1982) and first-team All-Pro honors in 1978. That year, he led the NFL in receiving yards with 1,168 and yards per reception (24.4) and was named the Jets' MVP. In two playoff games in 1982, Walker caught 15 passes for 314 yards and two touchdowns.

His top receiving year was 1983, when he caught 61 passes. In 1986, he logged his second 1,000-yard season and posted a career-best 12 touchdown receptions. Four of those came in a memorable 51–45 win over Miami, including the game-winning touchdown from quarterback Ken O'Brien in overtime.

The second-round pick out of Cal finished his career in 1989 with 438 catches for 8,306 yards and 71 touchdowns. In retirement, he works as a teacher in Long Island.

Wesley Walker makes a leaping catch against Detroit during a game in the late 1970s. The prolific receiver was a dangerous pass-catcher in 13 years with the Jets. *Focus on Sport/Getty Images*

NEW YORK SACK EXCHANGE

THEIR FAME WAS FLEETING, but the "New York Sack Exchange" lives on as the best of times in Jets history.

Because of injuries and other circumstances, the Sack Exchange—which consisted of the Jets' defensive front four of Joe Klecko, Mark Gastineau, Marty Lyons, and Abdul Salaam—wasn't as enduring as some of the NFL's other legendary defensive groups, such as Pittsburgh's "Steel Curtain," Minnesota's "Purple People Eaters," the Rams' "Fearsome Foursome," or Dallas' "Doomsday Defense."

The Jets' Sack Exchange was like a hot stock that made a customer a lot of money quickly and, just as quickly, went away. The four first became teammates in 1979, when Gastineau and Lyons were rookies, and lasted until Salaam departed in 1983.

"While we were together, we certainly wreaked some havoc," Klecko said.

Klecko claimed that during the 1981 season, the Sack Exchange was probably as good as the Steel Curtain and Purple People Eaters.

"We had a name, but we weren't together much longer after that," he said. "I often wonder if we had been together four or five years, what it would have been like."

In 1981, Klecko, Gastineau, Lyons, and Salaam produced 53.5 of the Jets' 66 sacks, one of the most dominant seasons a defensive unit has ever had.

Klecko, who wore No. 73, had 20.5 of those sacks. Lyons, No. 93, had 6 sacks. Salaam, No. 74, had 7 sacks. And Gastineau, No. 99, had 20 sacks.

"When we played together, something just clicked," Salaam said. "What was created here was this system of defeating opponents by the sack. . . . We would stop the run, put them in a second-and-long, third-and-long, and that would change the attitude of the offense.

"That would cause Joe and Mark to rise, because football is about intimidation. As a matter of fact, it was the fans that actually brought about the type of pressure we put on. They gave us a direction, a purpose, and a name."

The group got its nickname from Pepper Burruss, a trainer for the team at the time, although a Jets fan from Long Island named Daniel O'Connor, who won a contest to pick a name for the front four, claimed to have come up with the name first.

Joe Klecko (73), Marty Lyons (93), Abdul Salaam (74), and Mark Gastineau (99)—"The Sack Exchange"—pose on the floor of the New York Stock Exchange in June 1982. *Ronald C. Modra/Sports Imagery/ Getty Images*

Burruss recalled, "I was coming into Shea Stadium one afternoon when I looked over my right shoulder at a sign at the northeast end of the open horseshoe. It said 'Sack Exchange.' A couple of days later, I'm driving to work and listening to the stock market report on the radio, and it hit me to give these guys names and make up a stock market game."

He created what he called a "stock report" and handed it out to the players. "It used phrases like 'sack market soars' when they had a good week," Burruss said. "It was a lot of fun. It was never intended to hit the papers."

It hit more than the papers. The Sack Exchange was a craze, and it drew more publicity because of the characters involved, particularly Klecko and Gastineau, who were polar opposites. Klecko was an old-school warrior. Gastineau was a modern-day showman.

"I took a lot of heat from that dance," Gastineau said of his pioneering sack dances. "Now, if you don't dance, you'll get a fine."

Gastineau's dancing, though, rubbed some people the wrong way. His antics were perceived by many as self-centered. Klecko, Lyons, and Salaam were more about the team.

"The dance got the crowd enthused, but the team was left out," Lyons said. "People work to get you open. We would go over to congratulate him, and he would push us aside."

They learned to live with each other, but they didn't always like each other.

"You don't have to be able to socialize to go out and work with someone," Lyons reasoned. "We lived with the problems [Gastineau] created. He's beat to his own drummer for a long time."

Klecko conceded that Gastineau's antics did "drive a little bit of a stake between" them.

"We were from two different worlds," Klecko noted. "I was your lunch pail, go-to-work guy. The last thing I really wanted was to bring on the limelight. That was the difference between him and me. He liked it; I didn't like it. That was not my style."

Said Gastineau: "I was from Oklahoma, so I had no idea what I was doing. We were so competitive against one another because we were so close in sacks, and I think that was good."

Sporting News/MVP Books Collection

"We had tumultuous times," Klecko recalled. "Mark's sack dance . . . didn't sit comfortably with us from time to time. But when we came onto the field on Sunday, I don't care what was between us, there was a football game to be played, and we went out to play football and we went after other people."

"Of all the wild and crazy things that Mark did," added Lyons, "we needed him to play his best on Sundays. The one thing he could do was get to the quarterback."

Salaam and Lyons, the interior linemen in the group, did the dirty work, freeing up Klecko and Gastineau to make most of the sacks.

Salaam, analyzing the divergent group, noted, "Boy, we had some long mediations. Me and Marty had to empty our pockets so Mark and Joe could accomplish what they wanted, what we all wanted."

As for the disagreements among the group, Salaam said, "Nothing is created without polarization. There has to be negative and there has to be a positive. That's what created [the Sack Exchange], and it kept our fuel burning."

That fuel burned hottest in that memorable 1981 season, but it fizzled soon after. In the strike-shortened 1982 season, Klecko was injured and played in only two games.

Salaam appeared in one game in 1983 and was traded to San Diego following the season, although he never played for the Chargers. The other three hung around until the late 1980s, but the unit was never as effective, and the Sack Exchange never reached the peaks it had reached in 1981.

Herman Edwards, who played for the Eagles during that era and was later the Jets head coach, recalled that dominant 1981 group. "They were a wrecking crew," he said. "If they had second-and-ten on you, it was over, they were going to shut you down."

Years later, Lyons fondly recalled that season when the Sack Exchange was all the rage in the NFL.

"It was a real moment in our lives, a special moment," Lyons said. "New York opened its arms to us. When we were on the field, it wasn't a matter of, 'Are we going to get to the quarterback?' It was, 'How many times are we going to get there?'"

In November 1981, Klecko, Gastineau, Salaam, and Lyons were invited to ring the ceremonial opening bell at the New York Stock Exchange on Wall Street.

MARK GASTINEAU

THERE PROBABLY ISN'T A PLAYER in Jets history that was as much of a lightning rod as Mark Gastineau was.

The flashy defensive end, who essentially made the quarterback sack sexy and invented the sack dance, was equal parts dominating defensive player, egotistical showman, rude, immature, introspective, and laughingstock all in one intriguing package.

Gastineau once said of his show-the-opponent-up sack dance: "I like to do it a few times this week. I'm not that concerned with what other people think about it. I just do it 'cause it feels good."

Gastineau's gaudy celebrations eventually prompted the NFL to institute a rule that would be loosely called the "Gastineau Rule." It prohibited prolonged celebrations on the field after plays.

"The situation with Gastineau was a constant problem," former Jets head coach Joe Walton said.

Miami Dolphins offensive tackle Eric Laakso said of the dance: "Does the dance bother me? I can't let it bother me. If it does rattle you, it can cause you problems. The way I look at it, he's going to beat everybody once in a while."

Miami coach Don Shula, asked about Gastineau's dance, said, "As long as it's an honest thing, it doesn't bother me. And evidently it's an honest thing, but he'd have to answer that. It just bothers me that we got sacked."

When those words were relayed to Gastineau, he said, "It is honest. I'm not doing it because I'm fake. I'm just an emotional person."

Defensive end Marty Lyons disputed a *New York Post* story that stated he and linemates Joe Klecko and Abdul Salaam were critical of Gastineau's showmanship.

"That was just blown way out of proportion," Lyons said. "The *Post* ran a headline that said, 'Lyons and Klecko Abuse Team Hotdog.' That's a crock, but it did cause a lot of dissension among us, very definitely. For a week or so, there were a lot of bitter feelings.

"But then we all got together and talked about it. Went into a room at the training camp, and we didn't get out until the whole thing was straightened out. We told each other we didn't need it. You got enough problems in this league without worrying about the guys you're playing with. When we left that room, we all shook hands and, as far as I'm concerned, that's been the end of it."

One of the most amusing elements to Gastineau was his ballyhooed relationship with statuesque model Brigitte Nielsen, who appeared in the movies *Rocky IV* and *Beverly Hills Cop II*. Like everything with Gastineau, his relationship with Nielson was very public.

It was never more so than on one hot summer day in Easton, Pennsylvania, at Lafayette College, where the Jets and Washington

Mark Gastineau shows off his famous sack dance during the divisional playoff game against the Raiders on January 15, 1983. *Focus on Sport/Getty Images*

Redskins conducted an annual preseason scrimmage. During the scrimmage, a long, gray stretch limousine slowly made its way onto the field behind the Jets' sideline. The 6-foot-2 Nielson stepped out of the back seat wearing almost nothing—short shorts, a tight haltertop, and boots.

No one was watching the players on the field. They were watching Nielson preen and prance around on the sideline.

Joe Walton famously said of the incident, "Oh, my nerves."

"It was laughable," Lyons recalled. "We were all trying to figure out how she got the limo down onto the field."

Later that season, Gastineau proudly told reporters that he and Nielson both had tattoos of each other's names—on their butts. Gastineau, who loved to sashay around the locker room naked, had the word "Gitte" tattooed on his backside. Nielson bragged that she had the word "Mark" tattooed on one of her cheeks.

It all made for the typical bizarre world of Gastineau.

At one point, Gastineau's teammates all paraded around the locker room wearing fake "Gitte" tattoos on their butts.

Because of who Gastineau was and the way he conducted himself, there were plenty of less harmonious times involving him and his teammates—perhaps the worst of which was when he crossed the picket line during the 1987 players' strike. Gastineau was the

Joe Walton, the head coach at the time, admitted to the *New York Times*, "I probably didn't handle it very well. The strike probably hurt our team."

Gastineau, who had 54.5 sacks from 1983 to 1985, quit football midway through the 1988 season to be with Nielsen.

"I regret it," Gastineau later admitted of his early departure. "There's consequences to everything you do in life. My consequence is I hurt the team and I hurt me. At the time, I was in love."

Gastineau, who later started counseling teenagers, was asked what advice he gave to the youths. His response: "If a tall blonde comes through the door, I tell them don't give [football] up."

Lyons always wondered how Gastineau could have walked away so early when he was so talented and had so much more he could have accomplished.

"You almost want to call it a sin for anybody with that much God-given tools not to utilize them," Lyons said. "You want to say he shouldn't have had them at all. I see kids who can't even run who would like to be able to play football, and then you see a guy walk away because he's not interested."

Brigitte Nielsen and Mark Gastineau, 1988. *Jim Smeal/WireImage/Getty Images*

only Jets player to cross the picket line on the first day when team owners brought in replacement players to keep the season going. That infuriated teammates.

When Gastineau tried to drive his Mercedes-Benz into the team's complex at Hofstra University on Long Island, he was verbally abused by about 20 teammates at the gate. They screamed "scab" at him and peppered his car with eggs. When Gastineau rolled his window down to try to calm things, teammate Guy Bingham spat in his face, prompting Gastineau to get out of his car and charge after Bingham.

Gastineau claimed the reason he didn't want to participate in the strike was because he had just signed a five-year, $3.7 million contract and he needed the money. Eventually, other players would cross the line, fearing financial distress. But that strike season divided the team and set the franchise back.

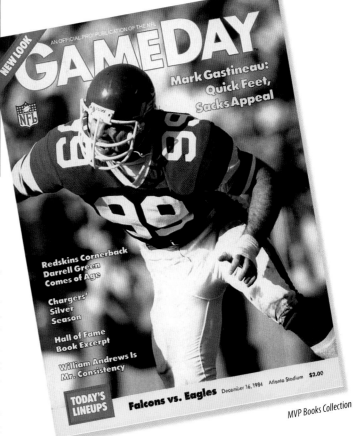

NEW LOOK AN OFFICIAL PRO PUBLICATION OF THE NFL
GAME DAY

Mark Gastineau: Quick Feet, Sacks Appeal

Redskins Cornerback Darrell Green Comes of Age

Chargers' Silver Season

Hall of Fame Book Excerpt

William Andrews Is Mr. Consistency

TODAY'S LINEUPS **Falcons vs. Eagles** December 16, 1984 Atlanta Stadium $2.00

MVP Books Collection

Wesley Walker, seen here running by All-Pro cornerback Lester Hayes, tallied 169 receiving yards and one touchdown in New York's 17–14 win over the Raiders in the divisional playoff game at Los Angeles Memorial Coliseum on January 15, 1983. The victory sent the Jets to their first conference championship game since the AFL-NFL merger. *George Long/Getty Images*

POST-STRIKE NEAR MISS

The Jets' taste of the postseason in 1981 indeed seemed to fuel their fire in 1982, when they not only reached the playoffs for the second consecutive year but advanced deep into the postseason.

The 1982 season was anything but normal, however, as a players' strike reduced the regular season to only nine games. Other than resounding losses to Miami in the season opener (45–28) and Kansas City in the finale (37–13), the Jets went 6–1, with the only midseason loss coming by one point at Miami in Week 7. The 6–3 final record was good enough for second place in the AFC East and a wild-card playoff berth.

The Jets went to Cincinnati for the opening round and crushed the Bengals 44–17. They then flew to Los Angeles to play the Raiders and, before 90,037 fans at the Coliseum, won a 17–14 decision that catapulted them to the AFC Championship Game, in which they would face the division rival Dolphins in Miami.

The Jets, after more than a decade of utter futility since their triumphant Super Bowl III victory in 1969, were one game away from the Super Bowl for the second time in their 20-year history. In Miami's cavernous Orange Bowl on that January afternoon, however, more maddening memories would be etched in the minds of tortured Jets fans.

At the end of that day, the Jets were all wet, losers of a 14–0 decision that still haunts many of the players involved in the game.

The game will be remembered for a number of things, but none more than the torrential rains that soaked the field and the exploits of Dolphins linebacker A. J. Duhe, who intercepted Jets quarterback Richard Todd three times and returned the third one for a fourth-quarter touchdown. Todd threw five interceptions in the game, and a powerful

Jets offense that had scored the third-most points in the league during the regular season was held to 139 yards by Miami's "No Name" defense.

After the game, Dolphins head coach Don Shula giddily proclaimed, "Today was the greatest day ever."

For the Jets, it was the worst day in memory.

In defeat, they not only watched Todd throw the ball to the wrong uniforms, but they watched Miami fullback Woody Bennett, a Jets castoff two years prior, run seven yards up the middle to score the only offensive touchdown in the game—and the only points the Dolphins would need to send them to the Super Bowl and send the Jets home.

Offensively, the Jets were inept. Wesley Walker, their big-play receiver who caught seven passes for 169 yards and a touchdown the previous week against the Raiders, was held to one catch for no yards. Running back Freeman McNeil, who was the NFL's rushing leader in the regular season, finished with only 46 yards on 17 carries.

As for Todd, he threw 13 interceptions all season and 10 of them were against the Dolphins—the team that handed the Jets three of their four losses that year.

"We were prepared; we just didn't execute properly," Walt Michaels said somberly after the game.

Amidst all the other drama in the game, one controversial play in particular left the Jets grumbling afterward. During the third quarter, Jets linebacker Greg Buttle appeared to force a fumble by Miami running back Andra Franklin. But the referee didn't call it a fumble, instead ruling that Franklin's forward progress had been stopped and thus the ball was dead.

Defensive end Mark Gastineau, who recovered the loose ball, said, "I think it was clearly a fumble."

Jets safety Ken Schroy concurred: "I saw it, everyone saw it. Franklin's knee wasn't on the ground. That one play didn't beat us, but it didn't help, either."

Buttle claimed that the two officials closest to the play ruled it was a fumble, but another official from across the field ruled it wasn't.

"I don't know who overruled whom," Buttle said. "But it doesn't matter. I don't think it was a fumble; I know it was a fumble. That's the drive they got the touchdown on, and that's the game."

The final dagger came 2:08 into the fourth quarter, when on third and 7 from the Jets' 48-yard line, Duhe started by rushing Todd, decided he wasn't getting enough pressure, and spotted running back Bruce Harper hanging wide for

FREEMAN MCNEIL
RUNNING BACK
1981–1992

FREEMAN McNEIL, a former star running back at UCLA, played 12 seasons for the Jets and was one of the best backs in team history, as well as one of the classiest individuals.

Through 2010, McNeil ranked second on the Jets' all-time rushing list behind only Curtis Martin with 8,074 rushing yards. His 4.5-yard average was tops among all Jets players with at least 400 attempts, and his 38 rushing touchdowns ranked him among the franchise's top five. His 144 games played were the most by a Jets running back.

During the mid- to late 1980s, he teamed with fellow running back Johnny Hector to form one of the best rushing tandems in the NFL. In the strike-shortened 1982 season, McNeil led the league with 786 rushing yards and 5.2 yards per carry and earned the only first-team All-Pro selection of his career. In 1984 and 1985, McNeil posted back-to-back 1,000-yard seasons, and his 1,331 rushing yards in 1985 were at the time the most ever by a Jets running back in a season. He is one of the few running backs in NFL history to average 4.0 yards per carry in every season he played.

A three-time Pro Bowler, Freeman McNeil was among the elite running backs of the 1980s and one of the best in Jets franchise history. *Jeffrey E. Blackman*

Quarterback Richard Todd and the Jets offense struggled mightily against the Dolphins in the AFC Championship Game on January 23, 1983. After averaging more than 27 points per game during the regular season, New York was shut out by the Miami defense on a muddy Orange Bowl field. *Ronald C. Modra/Sports Imagery/Getty Images*

a screen pass. Duhe read Todd's eyes, stepped in front of Todd's pass, and picked it off. After bobbling it twice, he ran 35 yards to the end zone to give Miami a 14–0 lead.

Afterward, the Jets were distraught.

"It's the toughest loss I've ever had in my life," Gastineau said. "It's something I didn't expect at all. Maybe we should have been more prepared for Miami's offense and defense and come down here with a better attitude."

"It's just hitting me right now," he added, "but tomorrow I'll probably start crying for three days. To be so close to the Super Bowl and yet so far, and to see the Dolphins so joyous and us staying home, is terrible. But Miami beat us fair and square, and you've got to give them credit."

Todd had little to say after the game, meekly offering only this: "I have only two things to say. They played better than we did, and we didn't play well at all. If somebody else has to go to the Super Bowl, I'm glad it's them."

With that, Todd ended his press conference and walked away.

"There are some days when you shouldn't get up in the morning," Walt Michaels said, summing it up. "Today was one of those days."

THE END FOR WALT

Michaels would not have another one of those days with the Jets because he wouldn't coach another game with the team after that loss in Miami.

One day after declining to cite the poor field conditions as an excuse, Michaels was now livid after sleeping on it. While he neglected to show up for his press conference on Monday, he ranted that the Dolphins "broke every rule in the book"—referring to Miami not using a tarp to cover the Orange Bowl field during the heavy rains.

One of the most shocking developments in the aftermath of the loss was Michaels' sudden retirement, which came just 17 days after his team got within one game of reaching the Super Bowl. Joe Walton, Michaels' offensive coordinator, was named his replacement.

"I have spent thirty-two years in this game and I've enjoyed them all," said Michaels, who was 53. "But in that time, I have never taken a vacation and have never spent enough time with my family. Now I think it's time that I should, so I am retiring as head coach of the Jets effective Tuesday, February 8, 1983.

"I wish my assistant coaches, the players, and the rest of the organization and the next head coach good luck in the future."

JOE KLECKO

DEFENSIVE LINEMAN
1977–1987

JOE KLECKO was drafted by the Jets in the sixth round (144th overall) of the 1977 NFL draft and went on to become one of the franchise's greatest players. Just four years into his career, Klecko combined with Mark Gastineau, Marty Lyons, and Abdul Salaam to form the "New York Sack Exchange," a group that terrorized opposing quarterbacks and made the sack the fashionable statistic that it's become today.

Klecko recorded a league-leading 20.5 sacks in 1981, when the Sack Exchange was named and become famous.

Klecko's greatest career accomplishment was earning his way into the Pro Bowl at every position on the defensive line. He moved from defensive end to defensive tackle in 1983 and was named to the Pro Bowl at his new position in 1983 and 1984. When the Jets switched to a 3-4 alignment in 1985, Klecko played nose tackle and become the first player in NFL history to be selected to the Pro Bowl at three different positions.

While Klecko had been nominated for the Pro Football Hall of Fame several times through 2010, he had not yet been enshrined, despite high praise from a number of players already in the Hall of Fame.

Former Miami Dolphins center Dwight Stephenson called Klecko one of the two best interior linemen he ever faced. Former Cincinnati Bengals tackle Anthony Munoz said, "In my 13 seasons, Joe is right there at the top of the defensive ends I had to block, up there with Fred Dean, Lee Roy Selmon, and Bruce Smith. Joe was the strongest guy I ever faced. He had perfect technique. He was the leader, the guy who kept that unit together."

Hall of Fame Buffalo Bills guard Joe DeLamielleure threw out some other legendary names in discussing Klecko. "I had to block Joe Greene and Merlin Olsen when I was playing, and believe me, Joe Klecko was equal to those two guys.

"If Joe Klecko had played one position for ten years, he'd have been considered one of the top two or three players at that position, whichever one it was," DeLamielleure said. "You take a defensive end and put him at nose tackle and he's just as good there—that's a great player. We need to get Joe Klecko in the Hall of Fame."

Teammate Marty Lyons called Klecko the "glue that held all of us together" on the Jets defense. "He ran the show."

Klecko's No. 73 jersey was retired by the Jets in 2004, and in 2010 they inducted him into their "Ring of Honor."

His son, Dan, followed his footsteps and played defensive tackle in the NFL for six seasons. He spent three years with the New England Patriots and won something his dad never did: Super Bowl rings. Three, in fact.

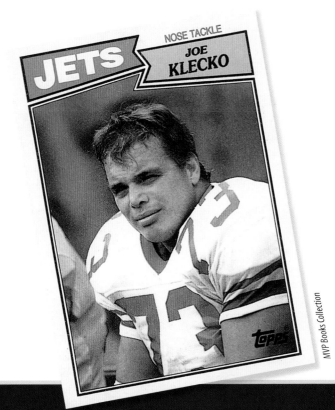

NOSE TACKLE
JETS
JOE KLECKO

In his six seasons as Jets head coach, Walt Michaels led the team to two winnings seasons, two .500 seasons, and two losing seasons for an overall record of 39–47–1. He also coached them to four postseason games, more than any Jets head coach other than Rex Ryan and Herm Edwards. *Jeffrey E. Blackman*

Michaels' "retirement" reeked of other factors being involved, considering he was a man who had always boasted that he wasn't a quitter. There were rumblings that Michaels may have been pressured by management to leave because of his occasional temper outbreaks.

To be sure, the coach's behavior at times could be described as erratic. As a Jets assistant, he was fined for trying to break down the officials' door after the infamous "Heidi Game" against the Raiders in 1968. After the 1982 playoff win over Oakland, Michaels accused Raiders owner Al Davis of calling the Jets' locker room at halftime and pretending to be Jets owner Leon Hess. It was later learned that the call came from a tavern in Woodside, New York, from a bartender who had bet on the Jets.

The final straw came when Michaels failed to appear for meetings with the media and his players at the team facility the day following the AFC Championship Game, even though he was in the building. His conduct in the aftermath of that loss to Miami, in particular, was said to have embarrassed Hess.

Michaels, whose tenure as head coach can be described as inconsistent and turbulent, finished with an overall record of 39–47–1 in regular-season games and 2–2 in the postseason.

"We're survivors," Michaels' wife, Betty, told the *New York Times* after her husband announced his retirement. "That's football. He went out with dignity."

Marty Lyons, the Jets defensive end who was drafted in the Michaels era, said he often looks back and wonders what might have been had the Jets not parted ways with Michaels, whom he described as one of the best coaches he had ever played for.

"I truly believe that if Walt had stayed, we would have won a Super Bowl, because he had already gotten us so close," Lyons said. "He was a very intimidating coach. I remembered being very intimidated by him my rookie year. He didn't care about player personalities in the locker room. He played everything straight."

Lyons recalled his first meeting with Michaels when he and Mark Gastineau were drafted.

"We both had to come in and have a picture taken with Walt, and the only thing he said to us was, 'The name of this game is get to the quarterback,'" Lyons recalled. "It wasn't, 'Great to have you. We're going to build this organization around you.' It was, 'Get to the quarterback.' I think that's the only thing he said to me my entire rookie season. I remember getting onto an elevator with him in Baltimore. He looked at me, I looked at him as we rode to the bottom floor. He got out and then I got out without a word being spoken. He was very intimidating, very demanding."

Lyons recalled the unique way that Michaels motivated his players.

Joe Walton came to training camp in August 1983 as the new head coach, and by his third year on the job he had led New York to back-to-back playoff appearances. He lasted one year longer than his predecessor, Walt Michaels, and through 2010 ranked second in franchise history for wins by a head coach (52). Nevertheless, Walton was unable to take his team past the second round of the playoffs. *Jeffrey E. Blackman*

"I remember when we were ready to make that playoff run [in 1982], we were going to play in Cincinnati, and the Friday before the game he came into the locker room with a sack of hundred-dollar bills. He had five thousand dollars in there and said, 'Hey, there's five thousand dollars in here. You want this? Win.'

"That's what the winner's share for the game was for each guy. And this was before the huge contracts were around, so that was a lot of money for everyone in that locker room.

"After we beat Cincinnati, the next week Walt came into the locker room with ten thousand dollars. That was the winner's share for the next game. He said, 'You guys want this? Win.' There's no better prop than money. There was no other speech until Sunday before we went out for the game. So that lasting impression you had before playing Cincinnati and the Raiders and Miami was your head coach holding up that sack of money and saying, 'Hey, do you want it? Win.'"

JOE WALTON ERA

Joe Walton took over for Walt Michaels after spending 14 years as an assistant. He had been passed over for head coaching opportunities by the Kansas City Chiefs, Atlanta Falcons, and Los Angeles Rams before the Jets elevated him to replace Michaels.

"Now," Walton said at the time of his promotion with the Jets, "I'm awfully glad I didn't get those other jobs."

Walton, like many, was stunned that Michaels retired. "I had no idea this could happen," he said. "Walt seemed relaxed in Hawaii [where the Jets staff was coaching the AFC in the Pro Bowl], we all were relaxed. I was hoping to talk to the Rams when we got home. Then, in twenty-four hours, everything changed."

Walton was always viewed as a strong offensive mind as an assistant. In 1981, his first season with the Jets, they averaged 337 yards per game. Quarterback Richard Todd, who had been intercepted 30 times the previous year, was intercepted only 13 times to go along with 25 touchdown passes—the most since Joe Namath threw 26 in 1967. In Walton's second season as an assistant, the Jets averaged 358 yards per game, the third-highest total in the league.

Walton hailed from Beaver Falls, Pennsylvania, the same town that Joe Namath came from. He played tight end and linebacker for three years at the University of Pittsburgh and was the second-round draft pick of the Washington Redskins in 1957. Four years later, he was traded to the Giants and was a part of three consecutive Eastern Division titles.

"Joe got more mileage out of his body than anyone," former Giants teammate Frank Gifford told the *New York Times*. "He wasn't fast. He wasn't tall. But he was a thinker. He was always the last guy [left] on the practice field. He worked hard. He had to. As small as he was [5-foot-10], Joe blocked linebackers and defensive ends. He had the initial charge. He'd come out like a bullet."

After catching 178 passes for 2,623 yards in seven NFL seasons, Walton retired as a player after the 1963 season. He scouted for the Giants and coached their farm team, the Westchester Bulls. In 1969, the Giants brought him back as an assistant to head coach Alex Webster, for whom he coached quarterbacks and receivers.

In 1974, Walton went to the Redskins as an assistant to Hall of Fame coach George Allen and started tutoring Joe Theismann.

"We became one mind in two bodies," Theismann told the *New York Times*. "I spent more time with Joe Walton than I had spent with any member of my own family."

Walton went to the Jets as an assistant in 1981 and started working with Richard Todd, who was then in his sixth season.

"When I first came here, I had a great deal of confidence, but then lost it," Todd said at the time. "Joe came in and stabilized both me and the offense. He's extremely easy to work with, but he gives you the tools, along with the discipline."

The discipline that Walton carried as an assistant sometimes didn't translate as a head coach, though. He proved to be an inconsistent leader, a trait that showed in the team's results with Walton as head coach. The Jets tended to be either really good under Walton or really bad. Most alarming, however, was the team's trend of late-season collapses during his tenure. Overall, the Jets were 17–9 in September under Walton, but they went 7–16 in December games.

After completing an up-and-down 7–9 record in Walton's first season at the helm, the Jets started off strong in 1984, winning six of their first eight games, before the bottom fell out. A six-game losing streak—with five losses coming by 10 points or more—dropped them to 6–8. A come-from-behind win over the woeful Bills followed in Week 15 before a loss to Tampa Bay concluded another 7–9 season.

Even after seven years in the NFL and five as a starter, Richard Todd was still trying to shake the shadow of his predecessor, Joe Namath. After throwing a career-high 308 passes for 3,478 yards in 1983, Todd was quarterbacking for New Orleans a year later. *MVP Books Collection*

The Jets started off even hotter in 1985, though the collapse didn't come until the postseason. They opened with a 7–2 record while notching decisive early wins against the Bills and Packers, holding them to a combined six points. The Jets stomped the Buccaneers 62–28 in Week 11, compiling 581 yards and holding Tampa Bay to 22 total rushing yards. A week later, they squeaked out a 16–13 overtime win against New England.

New York's 11–5 final record was its best mark since going 10–4 in 1969, and the Jets finished in a tie with the Patriots for the wild-card spots in the playoffs. New York hosted the postseason matchup. Although the Jets, who had the AFC's top-ranked defense during the year, held the Patriots to 240 total yards and one offensive touchdown, costly turnovers and the kicking of New England's Tony Franklin doomed them to a 26–14 defeat.

The highlight season of this era was undoubtedly 1986, even though it was also the poster child for the trend of postseason collapses for Walton's Jets. New York kicked off the year with a road win against Buffalo followed by a home loss to New England. The next game, on September 21, 1986, will go down as not only one of the greatest Jets games ever but one of the greatest in NFL history.

The Jets said farewell to Shea Stadium on December 10, 1983. Following an embarrassing 34–7 loss to the Steelers, during which the Jets committed five turnovers and fell behind 20–0 in the first half, the fans stormed the field and grabbed whatever souvenirs they could carry out—including the goal posts. *Jeffrey E. Blackman*

Freeman McNeil ran for a franchise-record (since broken) 1,331 yards in 1985. Against Buffalo in Week 2 of the season, he posted a personal career best of 192 yards on just 18 carries. He also scored twice in the 42–3 Jets romp on September 15, 1985. *Jeffrey E. Blackman*

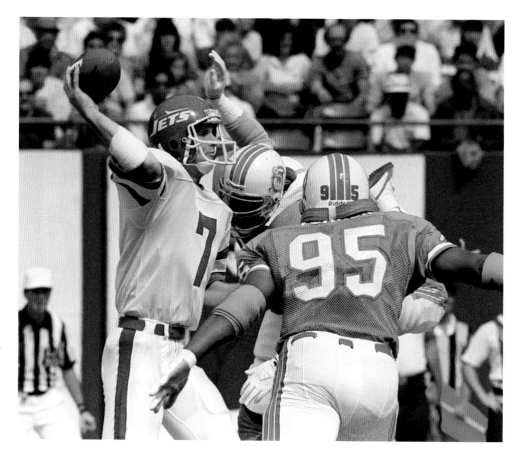

Ken O'Brien threw four touchdown passes in the Jets' legendary 51–45 overtime win against the Dolphins on September 21, 1986. The two teams combined for 1,066 total yards, including 927 yards passing—479 of them by O'Brien. *Bill Kostroun/AP Images*

Don Shula's Dolphins came to Giants Stadium hoping to extend their dominance over their division rival. The Jets had defeated Miami only once in six tries since Walton became coach. In the previous meeting between the two teams, Ken O'Brien passed for 393 yards but lost when Dan Marino threw a 50-yard game-winning touchdown pass with less than a minute left in regulation.

On this day in 1986, O'Brien would exact revenge on Marino, who had been selected in the same 1983 draft that produced O'Brien and a number of top quarterbacks. While Marino threw for 448 yards and six touchdown passes, O'Brien responded with 479 passing yards and four touchdowns on 29 of 43 passing.

With five seconds remaining in regulation and the Jets trailing 45–38, O'Brien hit Walker with a 21-yard scoring pass. Walker rolled into the end zone as time expired, and Pat Leahy's extra point tied the score at 45–45, sending the game into overtime. On the Jets' first drive in the extra session, O'Brien hit Walker with a 43-yard touchdown pass—their fourth scoring connection in the game—giving the Jets a 51–45 victory.

"It was unbelievable," said Jets left guard Ted Banker after the game. "The greatest game I've ever seen and ever played, and I was proud to be a part of it."

In what was then the second-highest-scoring overtime game in league history, the teams' combined 884 net yards passing broke by one yard the NFL record set by the Chargers and Bengals in 1982. The only overtime game in which more points were scored was when Seattle beat Kansas City 51–48 on November 27, 1983.

The wild win over Miami was one of the highlights to the Jets' 10–1 start—the best in franchise history—although that highlight would quickly be overshadowed by another colossal collapse. Beginning with a 45–3 whipping by those same Dolphins on *Monday Night Football*, the Jets went on a five-game losing streak to end the regular season, getting outscored by a staggering 183–61 margin, as they limped into the playoffs as a wild-card team.

Those playoffs provided one of the most memorable—and forgettable—plays in Jets history, involving the always-interesting Mark Gastineau.

ROUGHING THE PASSER

After stumbling hard in the season's final five games, the Jets appeared to right themselves with a 35–15 wild-card win over the Kansas City Chiefs. But it all came crashing down on January 3, 1987, in Cleveland.

The Jets built a 20–10 lead and appeared to be headed back to the AFC Championship Game, but Cleveland quarterback Bernie Kosar brought the Browns back from the deficit early in the fourth quarter. A roughing-the-passer penalty called against Gastineau in the fourth quarter enabled the Browns to keep alive a drive on which they eventually scored, cutting the deficit to three points, 20–17.

"All I know is that I've done it before and it hasn't been called," Gastineau said of the play after the game.

The Browns then tied it at 20–20 on a 22-yard field goal by Mark Moseley with seven seconds left in regulation. In the first overtime, the Browns had a chance to win it when they drove to the Jets' 5-yard line, but Moseley missed a 23-yard field goal. Later, in the second overtime, he got a chance at redemption.

Moseley, who had missed three of his previous five attempts, kicked a game-winning 27-yard field goal 2:02 into the second overtime, giving the Browns a 23–20 victory in what was then the third-longest game in NFL history (77 minutes, two seconds).

"I had a chance to redeem myself," Moseley said. "In this business, you can be a hero or a heel. For a long time, I was in the heel category."

The 38-year-old veteran kicker and former Washington Redskin had been signed by the Browns as a free agent after their regular kicker, Matt Bahr, injured his knee.

"I told him he was going to get another chance to get it done, so forget about the miss," said Cleveland coach Marty Schottenheimer. "And he did."

Gastineau would never forget the winning kick. "It's all over for us," he said. "It's like a nightmare."

Joe Walton said the loss left him with a "very empty feeling."

"Our people played very well, but you've got to give the Browns credit," Walton said. "Most of the game, our defensive line drove their running game back and they had to rely solely on their passing game. They could not get any sustained drives until the overtime periods. But then we started to wear down a little. I think our defensive line started to get tired."

The Cleveland head coach, meanwhile, explained what the game meant to his players and coaches. "This is a

KEN O'BRIEN

QUARTERBACK
1983–1992

KEN O'BRIEN was never a bad quarterback. He just never lived up to his peers from the legendary 1983 NFL draft, which produced some of the best quarterbacks in history. They included Hall of Famers John Elway, Jim Kelly, and Dan Marino, who was taken three picks later than O'Brien.

Although O'Brien never led his team to a Super Bowl—the way Elway, Kelly, and Marino did—he was the first Jets quarterback to have finished as the league's top-rated passer in a season (96.2 in 1985). He also became the first quarterback in NFL history to pass for 400 or more yards in a game and earn a perfect passer rating of 158.3, accomplished with 431 yards on 26-of-32 passing against the Seahawks on November 2, 1986.

"When O'Brien gets the time to throw the football, no one throws it any better than he does," ABC-TV analyst Frank Gifford said during a *Monday Night Football* game in 1991.

O'Brien threw for more than 25,000 yards in his 11-year career and led the league with the lowest interception rate in 1985, 1987, and 1988. He held the team record for most consecutive pass completions (17) in a game.

"I've been around a lot of tough, smart guys who won even though they couldn't throw the football that well," Joe Walton once said. "Billy Kilmer with the Redskins, Fran Tarkenton with the Giants—they didn't have a lot of physical ability; they did it by being tough and smart. But in addition to being tough and smart, Kenny O'Brien can throw the football."

Ken O'Brien spent nine seasons with the Jets, and at one time his career passer rating (80.4) was in the top 10 among retired NFL quarterbacks.
Jeffrey E. Blackman

Mark Gastineau's roughing-the-passer penalty during the AFC divisional playoff game against the Browns on January 3, 1987, proved to be the turning point in the hard-fought battle at Cleveland Stadium. The Jets ended up blowing a 20–10 fourth-quarter lead before falling 23–20 in double overtime. *Jerry Wachter/Sports Illustrated/Getty Images*

victory, a game all of us will remember the rest of our lives," Schottenheimer said. "To be honest, we all feel very fortunate to be a part of something like this."

The Jets and their fans also would remember the game, but for very different reasons. The team would never reach the postseason again under Walton, who would coach three more seasons. Those final three seasons, in which the Jets went a combined 18–28, did feature one winning year, but barely: an 8–7–1 finish in 1988 that placed them fourth in their division.

Receiver Al Toon was one of the few bright spots in the latter years of the Walton era. He earned three straight Pro Bowl selections while averaging more than 1,000 receiving yards from 1986 to 1988. He was named a first-team All-Pro in 1986 and led the league with 93 catches in 1998. After spending his entire eight-year NFL career as a Jet, Toon retired in 1992 with 517 career receptions, second (at the time) to only Don Maynard on the franchise list.

When it ended for Walton after the 1989 season—when the team posted a 4–12 record—few were surprised to see

Al Toon caught only three passes during the Jets' 45–3 win over Houston on September 18, 1988, but it was good enough for 64 receiving yards. Toon had a league-best 93 receptions that season, earning him a third straight Pro Bowl selection. *Caryn Levy/Getty Images*

A second-round draft pick in 1983, Johnny Hector remained with the Jets through the 1992 season and compiled a total of 4,280 rushing yards, fifth most in franchise history. In 1989, he posted a career high with 1,032 total yards from scrimmage. In 1987, he led the league with 11 rushing touchdowns. *Jeffrey E. Blackman*

Offensive lineman Jeff Criswell shows the frustrations of another losing season. The 38–14 loss to the Rams in Los Angeles gave the Jets their 11th defeat of the 1989 season, with one more still to come. Criswell would remain with the team for five more seasons, although it was head coach Joe Walton's last year at the helm. *George Rose/Getty Images*

him go. One of the most well-worn chants from frustrated fans at the team's Giants Stadium home in the late 1980s was "Joe must go!"

Tight end Rocky Klever, who played five seasons for Walton, said, "When people think of Joe, they'll think of all those games he lost at the end of the season. I'll never forget those Decembers and the fans chanting, 'Joe must go!'"

Joe finally did go when the Jets hired Dick Steinberg to be the first general manager they'd had in years, and he immediately cleaned house.

"I've had a lot of ups and downs," Walton said in a *Newsday* interview before he was dismissed. "Sometimes it seems like a rollercoaster."

That, indeed, was the essence of his tenure. Moreover, Walton wasn't roundly supported by many of his players when his time with the Jets finally came to an end.

"I don't think he'll be remembered too fondly by the players or the fans," said veteran center Joe Fields, who played five seasons under Walton. "He inherited a healthy patient, a team that came within one game of the Super Bowl. All we needed was a little exploratory surgery to get better, but Joe cut everything up and killed the patient."

Veteran kicker Pat Leahy added, "We had some good moments, but other than that, everything was relatively passé. . . . We made the playoffs a couple of times, but almost all the other years we were stuck in the middle of the pack."

Walton finished his Jets head coaching career with a 53–57–1 record and two playoff berths in seven years. The most common theme expressed by Jets players who played for Walton was the team's inconsistency.

"We were never consistent," receiver Wesley Walker said. "We had a lot of ups and downs. There were times when we played really well and times when we stunk up the joint."

A number of his former players expressed surprise that he lasted seven years.

"I pretty much expected him to get fired," said linebacker Lance Mehl, who retired before the 1988 season. "I'm shocked it didn't happen sooner. He did pretty well there for a while, but it seemed like he never kept it going for long. Joe was inconsistent, and inconsistency was the team's trademark."

Marty Lyons said Walton always seemed miscast as a head coach.

"He was a great offensive coordinator, but it was hard for him to make that transition from coordinator to head coach," Lyons said. "He had a difficult time relating to the

One of the most enduring and classiest figures in team history, Pat Leahy rewrote the record books for kickers in his 18 years with the Jets. The franchise's all-time leading scorer with 1,470 points, he completed 71.4 percent of his career field goal attempts and 95.5 percent of his extra points. In 250 career games, Leahy never had a kick blocked. In 1986, he set a Jets record (tied by Jay Feely in 2009) by making 22 consecutive field goals. *Rick Stewart/Allsport/Getty Images*

players. He had a personality conflict with [linebacker Greg] Buttle and Joe Klecko.

"The other thing that would happen under Walton was we'd always get close and they'd dismantle the team. They'd bring in new players. Every year we'd get close and they'd give us a pat on the ass and say, 'Don't worry, we'll get 'em next time,' and unfortunately that 'next time' never came."

Fields agreed, saying Walton's biggest mistake was "getting rid of people before he had anybody better to replace them."

"He made changes for the sake of making changes," Fields said. "He always pointed the finger at somebody else. He never pointed it at himself. He got rid of coaches, players and now he's run out of scapegoats. Finally, they're getting rid of the real problem."

Walton's final game as head coach was a rock-bottom moment—sad, really. The Jets lost to the Buffalo Bills 37–0 in front of a sparse-but-angry Giants Stadium crowd of just

21,148—more than 55,000 below capacity. The crowd was the smallest at a non-replacement Jets game since 5,826 attended a game against Buffalo at the Polo Grounds on December 14, 1963.

As Walton trotted off the field and into the tunnel after the game, he was showered with cups of beer from angry fans. Afterward, in the quiet of the locker room, he took it all in stride.

"If you stay in this business long enough, there are going to be bad times," Walton said. "I'll meet with the team tomorrow, thank them, and wish them a Merry Christmas and Happy New Year."

It was the last Jets fans would see of Walton. The next question was whom would the team get to take his place.

"What we need is someone with a lot of nasty," Leahy said. "Every club has to have a crazy."

Little did Leahy or Jets fans know just how nasty and crazy the next decade would be.

MVP Books Collection

MVP Books Collection

MVP Books Collection

THE "JOE MUST GO" CHANTS from fans demanding Joe Walton's ouster were still echoing when the franchise opted to take a new direction—one they believed would move it forward after things had gotten so stagnant.

After watching his team operate without a general manager for many years, Leon Hess hired Dick Steinberg to run his football operations. Steinberg was a respected football man around the league thanks to his work with the New England Patriots as director of player personnel and, before that, with the Los Angeles Rams as director of scouting.

Steinberg was a quiet, dignified man who had developed a reputation for building winning teams through personnel decisions and the draft—an area where the Jets, after a number of years of dubious draft choices, desperately needed upgrading. As it turned out, draft decisions would prove to be one of Steinberg's greatest weaknesses with his new club.

Steinberg's first order of business was to hire Bruce Coslet as his head coach. Coslet, who had been the offensive coordinator for the Cincinnati Bengals since 1986, had become one of the so-called hot assistant coaches in NFL circles, and Steinberg pounced.

To the credit of both Steinberg and Coslet, they would elevate the franchise from the depths it hit in Walton's latter years. But there would always be something missing. They would take the Jets only so far.

Steinberg's reputation as a terrific player personnel man took a damaging hit when he chose Penn State running back Blair Thomas with the second overall pick in the 1990 NFL draft, his first draft pick with the Jets. While everyone around the league had been high on Thomas and said, both publicly and privately, that they also would have drafted Thomas with that pick, it was hardly any consolation to the Jets when he became one of the biggest draft busts of all time. His failure to become the player the Jets hoped he'd become set the franchise back years.

Bruce Coslet, shown here in 1992, was a fiery presence on the Jets sideline for four seasons, but it didn't translate to a lot of wins for the team. His 26–38 record as head coach netted just one postseason game, in 1991, which the Jets lost to the Oilers. *Jeffrey E. Blackman*

Based on his standout career as a Penn State All-American, Thomas figured to be the cornerstone of the Jets offense for many seasons. Penn State's iconic head coach, Joe Paterno, called Thomas "the best player I've ever coached." The former Heisman Trophy runner-up was considered one of those "can't-miss" draft picks.

Yet his career went nowhere, and his work ethic was questioned by many. Thomas ended up playing only six seasons, rushing for 2,236 career yards, before quietly retiring in 1996 at age 29, still healthy. In his four years with the Jets before they decided they'd seen enough and jettisoned him from the team, Thomas rushed for just over 2,000 yards and became the poster child for the failed Steinberg-Coslet era.

Years later, Thomas told the New York *Daily News* in an interview, "As a kid, I dreamed about having the opportunity to play in the NFL. It's a one-in-a-million chance."

Every NFL draft is littered with what-if scenarios, but the 1990 draft when Steinberg took Thomas presented a number of damning coulda-beens. Among the players that the Jets passed over to draft Thomas were linebacker Junior Seau and defensive tackle Cortez Kennedy. Those two players went on to play in a combined 20 Pro Bowls, and either one could have helped change the course of the entire Jets franchise.

"I don't know how many times you want me to say it, but I've said [Thomas] hasn't been what we thought he'd be,"

After being chosen No. 2 in the 1990 draft, Blair Thomas (32) never really broke through as an NFL player. He appeared in 50 games as a Jet, gaining 2,009 yards on 468 carries. *Bernstein Associates/Getty Images*

ROB MOORE

RECEIVER
1990–1994

ROB MOORE WAS PERFECT for the Jets. He was home-grown, having been raised in Hempstead, New York, not far from the Jets' training facility at the time on Long Island. Moore went to Syracuse University and was a solid citizen, a feel-good story from a rough area of town.

Moore should have been a Jet for life, but the team traded him to the Arizona Cardinals before the 1995 draft after he played only five seasons in New York. But his five seasons were productive. Moore caught 306 passes for 4,258 yards and 22 touchdowns in 76 games as a Jet.

Moore, 6-foot-3 and 202 pounds, came to the Jets in 1990 via the supplemental draft and, as a rookie, led the team with six receiving touchdowns (tied with Al Toon) and 15.7 yards per reception. He was tops on the Jets in both total receiving yards and touchdown catches in each of the next two seasons, and he led the squad in catches and yardage in 1993.

It was after his best season as a Jet that Moore was traded away. In 1994, he caught a then career-high 78 passes for 1,010 yards and six touchdowns and was named to the Pro Bowl. Then he was promptly traded by new coach Rich Kotite.

Moore went on to enjoy five more productive seasons with the Cardinals. He finished his career with 628 catches for 9,368 yards and 49 touchdowns.

Local product Rob Moore was a Jet for five seasons and led the team in receiving yards every year from 1991 to 1994. *Joe Traver/Time Life Pictures/Getty Images*

Steinberg told reporters in April 1993. "We're not stupid and we're not blind. We see what the other guys in that draft are doing. But these things don't work in hindsight. We try to find the best value and the best fit for us. Obviously, we thought Blair was the best fit, because we took him."

Mike Allman, who was Seattle's player personnel director at the time and chose Kennedy with the third pick, told the *Daily News* that the league-wide consensus was that Thomas was the best running back in the draft that year.

"Blair Thomas had been an outstanding player in a big-time program," Allman said. "Plus, he had a great game in the Senior Bowl that year. You always take the player that you think fits the best. Obviously, Dick thought Blair was that player."

If there was one game in Thomas' Jets career that defined his existence, it was a 1991 Monday night game against the Bears in Chicago. The Jets were leading with less than two minutes remaining in the game, and Thomas fumbled deep in Jets territory. The Bears recovered the ball, tied the game, and went on to win in overtime.

Thomas' numbers that night—27 carries for 125 rushing yards—were the best of his career in a single game. He played 63 NFL games and rushed for 100 or more in only two of them.

ANOTHER ONE BITES THE BUST

Chosen 34th overall in 1991, quarterback Browning Nagle was the next big thing for the Jets in the NFL draft. He quickly became yet another torturous answer to a what-if trivia question.

At 34, Nagle was selected one spot behind quarterback Brett Favre. The man who would become the NFL's all-time passing leader with more than 70,000 yards was drafted by the Atlanta Falcons and later traded to the Green Bay Packers, with whom his legend would soon grow.

The Jets believed they had a deal in place with the Arizona Cardinals to leapfrog the Falcons in draft order so they could take Favre. But the Cardinals reneged on the deal at the last moment, and Favre went to the Falcons.

So instead of having Favre, the Jets had Nagle, who ended up just like Blair Thomas in the annals of Jets history—on the cover of their "bust file."

Typical of the team's fortunes during this era, Nagle had his best performance in his first preseason game when he wowed the Jets with big numbers against the Falcons. Those

numbers would never follow in regular-season games, and Nagle lasted with the Jets only until 1993.

Unlike Thomas, Nagle was a bit more of a reach where he was drafted and not so widely coveted by other general managers around the league. The Jets, who were desperate to find a young quarterback to replace Ken O'Brien, were seduced by the big game the 6-foot-3, 225-pound, strong-armed Nagle had produced in a surprising Fiesta Bowl victory for Louisville over Alabama.

Nagle played in only one game in his rookie year, but in his second year, 1992, he replaced O'Brien as the starter midseason, and he struggled in the role. The Jets went 3–10 in Nagle's starts as he threw 17 interceptions and completed just 49.6 percent of his passes.

The following offseason, the Jets acquired Boomer Esiason, a veteran quarterback who had played for Bruce Coslet in Cincinnati, and the short-lived Nagle era was over.

"I would be foolish to say I didn't reflect back with what-ifs or shoulda, woulda, coulda type of things," Nagle said years later. "There's a lot of great memories, but empty feelings,

too. It was cut short in New York. Could I have done some things differently that may have been more beneficial to my career in New York? Of course I could have.

"Have I played through the possibilities had I not gone to New York? Well, it would have been interesting."

After leaving the Jets in 1993, Nagle had short stints with the Indianapolis Colts and Atlanta Falcons before playing for Orlando and Buffalo in the Arena Football League and then retiring.

"I didn't retire because I wanted to retire," Nagle said. "I retired because no one was calling."

It was a stunning fall for Nagle considering the tools he possessed, with the strong arm and athleticism.

"Kenny can do a whole lot of things at the line of scrimmage," Steinberg said at the time the Jets replaced O'Brien with Nagle. "But there are some things that Browning can do that Kenny can't."

Nagle's nickname with the Jets quickly became "Nuke" for his strong arm, after the fictional character Nuke LaLoosh, the pitcher in the movie *Bull Durham*. The arm was indeed strong, but the accuracy was nonexistent. One without the other is useless.

"A great arm can turn to mush if you don't know what the heck you're doing out there," Pittsburgh Steelers Hall of Fame quarterback Terry Bradshaw observed on one of his CBS-TV broadcasts.

Year three of Dick Steinberg's reign as Jets general manager produced yet another curious pick high in the draft.

Enter tight end Johnny Mitchell, a 21-year-old sophomore out of Nebraska whom the Jets selected with the 15th overall pick in 1992. It's always risky business to draft underclassmen so high, and this was no exception. Mitchell, who had played just three years of high school football and two at Nebraska, showed a blatant immaturity that proved a disastrous mix with the big city environment of New York.

Mitchell didn't have much of a rookie season, missing five games with a shoulder injury and catching only 16 passes—all the while complaining about not getting the ball enough.

Tight end Johnny Mitchell's NFL career never really got off the ground after he was selected by the Jets with the 15th pick in 1992. Mitchell led the team with six receiving touchdowns in 1993, but he was out of the NFL by the time he was 25 years old. *Eric Draper/AP Images*

"I'm not being cocky," Mitchell said, "but I have a tremendous amount of God-given ability."

Unfortunately for the Jets, that ability never amounted to enough to justify Mitchell being picked as high as he was, and his Jets career fizzled out after four years. When it was over, he had caught 158 passes and scored 16 touchdowns in 53 games.

Mitchell played one more year after leaving the Jets, in Dallas, where he played in four games and caught only one pass before his short-lived and unfulfilled NFL career was over.

BRUCE TOO TIGHT

The failed Browning Nagle experiment that followed the Blair Thomas fiasco and preceded Johnny Mitchell were mere backdrops to what was a pretty volatile era under coach Bruce Coslet.

The fiery Coslet turned out to be too inconsistent with his behavior. There were too many high highs and too many low lows with Coslet, and his players followed suit. At the end of the day, an NFL head coach needs to be more even-keeled to have consistent success. Certainly, emotions are a good and necessary tool when dealing with players, but Coslet too often flew off the reservation with his.

Bruce Coslet's tenure as head coach proved to be a headache for all involved. He battled with reporters, opposing coaches, and even his own players. *Lonnie Major/Getty Images*

He came off as a coach who thought he invented the game, often patronizing reporters and chastising them for having no idea what they were talking about. Yet, after so often insisting how great he was, Coslet didn't win enough games to warrant or support his arrogance. He coached the Jets for four seasons and never produced a single winning year, making the playoffs once with an 8–8 record in 1991 and quickly bowing out in a wild-card loss to the Oilers in Houston.

What was most damning for Coslet in his eventual downfall was the fact that he came to the Jets as a supposed creative offensive mind—a guru, if you will—and his offenses always ended up falling woefully short.

Although the Jets scored the fourth-most points in the AFC during the 1991 season, they were fourth from the bottom in 1992, putting only 220 points on the board. Combined with a defense that allowed the fourth-most points (315) in the AFC, the Jets stumbled to a 4–12 record in '92. The defense improved dramatically in 1993, as the Jets held opponents

to just over 15 points per game, but the offense continued to flounder. In the final six games of the 1993 season, Coslet's last with the team, the New York offense managed to score a total of 36 points.

Coslet didn't help himself with his erratic behavior, either. Take, for example, the day he opted to conduct a press conference with beat reporters from his second-floor office, refusing to speak to reporters face-to-face after a 30–7 loss to the Buffalo Bills in his third game as the Jets coach. Instead of taking the one-minute walk to the first-floor press room, Coslet spoke to reporters through a speaker phone.

The first question came from Peter Finney Jr., then the beat writer for the *New York Post*. Finney asked Coslet simply, "Bruce, why are you doing this?"

Coslet said he was too busy to come downstairs for a press conference, claiming because it was a Monday night game he had no time on a Tuesday for a press conference.

"It's because I don't have time to deal with you guys today," Coslet said. "I'm in the middle of a game plan. I got my whole staff in my office, and we're working on New England, our next opponent. We're a day short, that's the reason. Next question."

Coslet's arrogance hardly endeared himself to his coaching peers around the league, either. For example, after Buffalo coach Marv Levy, always regarded as one of the classiest coaches in the league, once accused the Jets of faking injuries in an attempt to slow down his team's hurry-up, no-huddle offense, Coslet ripped Levy, calling him "an overofficious jerk."

Coslet also ripped into Dallas head coach Jimmy Johnson for continuing to let his defenders blitz in a game that was seemingly already decided between the Jets and Cowboys. Coslet was livid at Johnson for blitzing quarterback Boomer Esiason and knocking him out of the game during garbage time in the fourth quarter of a 28–7 Cowboys win.

"I was a little perturbed he would double-safety blitz leading 28–7 and try to knock Boomer out of the game,"

THE DENNIS BYRD TRAGEDY

THE BRUCE COSLET TENURE saw many low moments, but none was lower than what occurred on November 9, 1992, when Jets defensive end Dennis Byrd was paralyzed after a frightening collision at Giants Stadium.

The injury occurred when Byrd collided with teammate Scott Mersereau while trying to sack Kansas City quarterback Dave Krieg. The two linemen converged from either side of Krieg and hit each other as they reached their target.

Byrd suffered a broken neck on the play. As he lay motionless on the Giants Stadium turf, he looked up at the Jets' team of doctors and asked, "Am I going to be paralyzed?"

By the time he got to New York's Lenox Hill Hospital, Byrd had no use of his legs and only partial use of his arms.

As Byrd was carted off the field with Dr. Steve Nicholas, the team orthopedist, and assistant trainer Pepper Burruss, several teammates hurried over and gently touched him. Veterans James Hasty, Paul Frase, Brian Washington, Mike Brim, R. J. Kors, and Marvin Washington, his best friend on the team, were among them.

"I had no knowledge of what was going on initially because I was gasping for air," recalled Mersereau, who had been hit in the chest by Byrd's helmet. "It wasn't until later, when I came off on the sidelines, that I saw them take him away.

"We were both coming around the corner," Mersereau said. "The play was a stunt. When I came around the outside, I looked around and I was free. I saw Krieg, and it was me and him. I went to grab Krieg, and he stepped up and the next thing I knew—I didn't even know who hit me, but obviously it was Dennis."

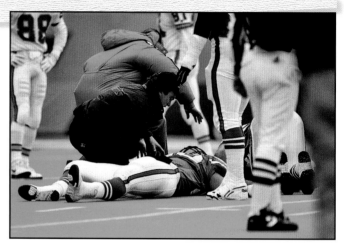

Dennis Byrd lies motionless on the Giants Stadium turf following a frightening collision with teammate Scott Mersereau on November 9, 1992. *David Drapkin/Getty Images*

The injury was particularly devastating to the Jets players because Byrd was such a popular teammate, and because it reminded them of their own mortality.

"You know it could happen to you," linebacker Mo Lewis said. "But when it happens to a teammate, it's even more scary because it could've been you."

The Byrd incident sparked his teammates to one of the most inspiring wins in franchise history the following week. With Byrd still lying in the hospital and on the minds of his teammates, the Jets upset the Bills 24–17 in Buffalo. Their spirits were buoyed by the news that Byrd had gained some voluntary movement in his legs.

Coslet said afterward. "I didn't mind him blitzing Browning [Nagle, the backup] when we were down there trying to score. But 28–7? You don't do that."

Johnson's response: "Someone needs to pass me a note or give me the rule when we are supposed to blitz and when we can't blitz. I don't know. We just try to win ballgames. When the other team tries to score, we try to stop them. Again, I haven't read the manual yet as far as what defenses we're supposed to play at the end of the game."

The Jets were 8–5 heading into the Dallas game, having won six of their previous seven, and Coslet was feeling particularly confident about his team's chances against the Cowboys. He said he had devised "the game plan of all game plans" to beat them—which only made the trouncing that much more embarrassing for Coslet.

The blowout loss to the Cowboys was such a shock to Coslet's system and such a low point that he was never able to help the team recover. It was the beginning of the end for

It was just one win in a 4–12 season, but it was memorable. The Bills had beaten the Jets in the teams' previous 10 meetings and were on their way to a third straight Super Bowl appearance.

Before the game, Jets cornerback James Hasty had a quiet conversation with linebacker Kyle Clifton.

"I told Kyle that it was in God's plan for us to win," Hasty said. "No matter what they did, we were going to win [that] game. It was destiny."

Byrd, who had undergone surgery five days before the Bills game, watched from his hospital room with his wife, Angela, and his parents.

"It was nothing but heart," defensive tackle Mario Johnson said, pointing to his chest. "You tried to keep your emotions in control, but we were all whacked out. I knew Dennis was watching and I knew if I messed up, I couldn't live with myself and I knew Dennis couldn't live with it. I was out there playing for Dennis."

After the victory, about 20 Jets players and coaches squeezed into a room adjacent to the visitors' locker room to speak to Byrd in a conference call.

"I just told him that I was happy that we won, but I was sad that he wasn't here with us," Hasty said. "He said he was here. I have to believe that Dennis' spirit was here, but it wasn't the same as him being physically here. Dennis was really happy for us. You couldn't ask for a better situation than what happened today."

Defensive end Paul Frase said he thought about Byrd throughout the entire game, adding, "Whenever I thought about him, I lifted Dennis up to God. I pray for him and I pray for God to touch his body and touch him with a miracle."

Byrd would slowly recover to the point where he was able to walk again. He went back home to Oklahoma with his family.

Byrd made an emotional return to Giants Stadium with his wife and children on September 5, 1993, less than a year after suffering a broken neck. *Jeffrey E. Blackman*

the Coslet era. The Jets lost their last three games to finish at 8–8 and out of the playoffs.

The worst loss in that final span came the week after the Dallas game. The Jets played the rival Bills in Buffalo, where a win would clinch a playoff berth and Coslet's first winning season. The Jets lost a bitter 16–14 decision in frigid Buffalo as their kicker, Cary Blanchard, missed three field goals, including a potential game-winner from 42 yards out with 53 seconds remaining in the game.

Blanchard had entered that game 12-for-12 from inside the 40, yet he also missed from 27 and 41 yards in Buffalo. All three misses were wide left. The last one looked like it was headed through the uprights before agonizingly veering off line.

"It looked like it was going right down the middle," Blanchard would say later. But alas, it drifted off course, just like yet another Jets season of hope and promise.

"I'm not going to blame anything on the wind," Blanchard said, referring to the 9-degree temperatures with 28-below-

Brad Baxter helped spark the Jets' offensive revival in 1991. The fullback, who spent his entire six-year NFL career with New York, led the team with 11 touchdowns in 1991 and teamed with Blair Thomas to give the Jets one of the most productive rushing tandems in the league. *Jeffrey E. Blackman*

The Jets didn't experience a lot of joy during the Bruce Coslet era, but veteran safety and future Hall of Famer Ronnie Lott celebrates breaking up a pass in the end zone in the final moments of the Jets' 10–6 win over the Giants on October 31, 1993. Celebrating with Lott is fellow safety Brian Washington, who led the team with six interceptions that season. *Paul Hurschmann/AP Images*

zero wind-chill factor. "The guys went out there and busted their butts, doing everything they can to get back with a win, which we needed badly. It's disappointing for me to miss three in a game. I don't think I've ever done that in my whole career."

Blanchard was stand-up afterward, and his teammates didn't blame him for the loss. But the bitterness of yet another killer defeat wasn't lost on the players.

"I've been here for four years, and I'm tired of *ifs* and I'm tired of *almosts*. *Almost* doesn't put a victory in that left-hand win column," safety Brian Washington said.

"We're missing something. Whatever it is, I don't know," Esiason said. "If you want to get to that next level, these are the games you have to win."

Under Coslet, the Jets would never get to that next level.

HOUSTON, WE HAVE A PROBLEM

The last game Bruce Coslet would coach for the Jets was on January 2, 1994, in Houston.

Earlier that day, the stars had aligned perfectly for New York. By the time the Jets took the field at the Astrodome in a late afternoon game, Miami had lost to New England in overtime, leaving open the final playoff berth in the AFC, which New York would seize with a win.

Houston was 12–4 that year with a high-powered offense, but they had already locked up the Central Division, and Pro Bowl quarterback Warren Moon did not take the field in the finale. With the Jets having everything to play for, and the Oilers not even sending in their main starters, Houston handed out a 24–0 shellacking. Moreover, the score hardly represented how bad it was, as the Jets were listless and inept in the loss.

"It was an embarrassment," cornerback James Hasty said after the game. "If anybody doesn't think it was an embarrassment, and they walk up to me and say that, I'll slap their face."

Defensive back Lonnie Young said, "It was like a nightmare. This is probably the most disappointing season I've experienced because this team has more talent than some teams in the past. It has the ability to win games but wasn't able to get it done."

"This is the first time this year that we got our rear handed to us," Coslet said. "There was no turning point, no deciding point. They handled us handily."

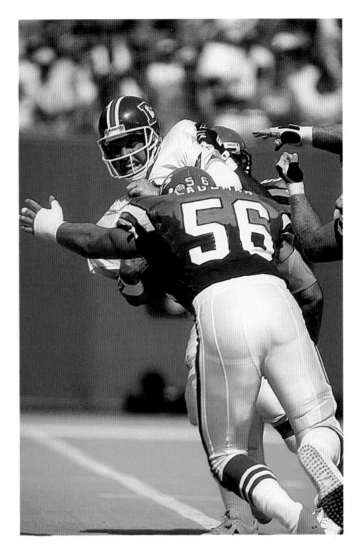

Defensive end Jeff Lageman (56) was one player who didn't appreciate coach Bruce Coslet's critical words about the team. Lageman did his part, leading the Jets with 8.5 sacks in 1993. His 34.5 sacks in 82 career games for the Jets ranked sixth on the franchise list through 2010. *Bill Hickey/Allsport/Getty Images*

According to quarterback Boomer Esiason, who went 0–7 in Houston during his career with the Cincinnati Bengals, "We didn't lose our playoff berth here at this stadium. We lost it a lot earlier in the season. There were so many games we could have won that this game shouldn't have mattered. But we probably saved our worst game for last."

An episode from earlier in the season helps to illustrate the turbulence of the Coslet era and the ways in which he lost the confidence of his players. The coach told reporters during his daily press conference that he didn't think the Jets had enough talent to make a legitimate run for the playoffs and

Ken O'Brien was soundly criticized by Bruce Coslet shortly after the coach took over in New York, but the quarterback was very productive during his nine-year tenure with the Jets. Through 2010, no Jets quarterback in history had completed more passes than O'Brien's 2,039, and only Joe Namath had thrown for more yards or more touchdowns than O'Brien. *Jeffrey E. Blackman*

beyond. The implication was that he was doing his job, but management (i.e., general manager Dick Steinberg) hadn't provided him with enough good players.

The reporters immediately went to speak to some of the veteran players, such as defensive end Jeff Lageman, who was a team leader, and relayed Coslet's words. That, of course, drew the ire of the players, who were quickly losing respect for Coslet.

Later in the day, as word got back to Coslet from some players that they were unhappy with the things he said, he realized what he'd done. He'd placed the blame for the struggling team squarely on the shoulders of Steinberg, the man who had hired him and the man who could (and eventually did) fire him.

So Coslet made an unusual early-evening trip into the press room at Weeb Ewbank Hall and begged reporters not to go with the story, to forget about his earlier diatribe. Coslet looked pathetic—stressed out, looking rattled holding a cigarette that was burned to its filter and nearly burning its way to his fingers.

Coslet explained that he was under immense pressure, and he unknowingly let on that Rob Moore, the team's best receiver and offensive threat, wasn't going to be able to play that Sunday. He said his words were not meant to tweak Steinberg and pleaded that the stories not be written the way he stated things earlier.

It was a similarly bizarre episode to the one that occurred earlier in Coslet's tenure when he went on a rant about Ken O'Brien, the quarterback he inherited from the previous regime. He told reporters, "Look, you know my quarterback sucks. I know my quarterback sucks. Everyone knows my quarterback sucks."

After that Steinberg rant and recant, reporters went with the "Coslet blames Steinberg" story anyway, despite Coslet's pleading, partly because his words were not off the record and partly because Coslet had not really built up trust with the writers along the way. He didn't have the break he was begging for coming.

It's uncertain whether that was a last straw for Steinberg or merely just another in a series of things that Coslet did to make his own bed, but a few weeks later Steinberg fired Coslet.

It finally ended for Coslet shortly after the *New York Post* ran a column imploring the Jets to make a change. The huge back-page headline read: "FIRE HIM!" The headline on the inside of the paper that accompanied the column read: "Cut Bruce Loose."

The conclusion about Coslet was simple: He had coached for four years and had produced no winning seasons and one wild-card playoff loss. It was time for him to go.

Steinberg presumably already had his mind made up about Coslet's fate long before the *Post* ran its damning column, but when the coach was fired soon after the column ran, Esiason, an ardent Coslet supporter after having played for him in Cincinnati, blamed the *Post* and other reporters for trying to bring Coslet down. But the writing was already on the wall.

"Unfortunately, we have run out of time and we have to go to the next level," Steinberg said at the time.

Pete Carroll, who was Coslet's defensive coordinator and a close friend of his, was elevated to head coach.

"We never considered anyone else," Steinberg said of Carroll, "but we know him and he knows us. It's been a four-year interview."

Unfortunately for Carroll, that four-year interview bought him only one year as the Jets' head coach.

NEW BEGINNING, QUICK END

As the defensive coordinator for four years, Pete Carroll was always a favorite among the defensive players, and he brought with him a youthful exuberance and a more easy-going outlook to the head coaching position than Coslet, his mentor.

Carroll, who emphasized the fun in the game and in work, had a mini basketball court installed alongside the practice field and held three-point shooting contests with players and coaches. He also organized bowling outings and even had a session where players took penalty kicks at a soccer goal against U.S. national goalie Tony Meola, whom the team had signed as an experiment to see if he could be an NFL kicker.

All the fun appeared to be leading to success on the field. The Jets got off to a 2–0 start under Carroll in 1994, beating the Bills 23–3 in Buffalo and downing Denver 25–22 in overtime in the home opener.

Carroll appeared ready to take his team over the top in a November 27 home game against the Miami Dolphins. The Jets entered the game with a 6–5 record and jumped out to a 24–6 lead over their division rival—a lead that would turn into a shocking 28–24 loss after the famed Dan Marino fake spike (see sidebar).

The Jets never recovered after that loss, and they never won another game under Carroll, losing the season's final five games and losing Carroll his job.

After the devastating "fake spike" loss to the Dolphins, a number of players appeared to quit on Carroll. Among the guiltiest parties were his closest confidants from his days as

Pete Carroll chats with veteran Bills coach and future Hall of Famer Marv Levy before Carroll's debut as Jets head coach in 1994. Carroll and the Jets defeated the Bills handily, 23–3, but they would win only five more games all year. *Joe Traver/Time Life Pictures/ Getty Images*

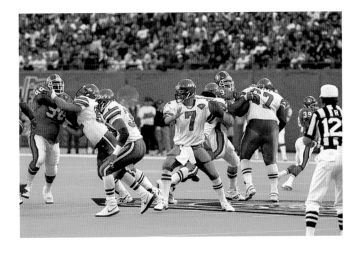

Completing 70 percent of his passes on the day, Boomer Esiason led the Jets to a 2–0 start in 1994 with a 25–22 overtime win against the Broncos on September 11. On the year, Esiason's numbers were down compared to his Pro Bowl season in 1993, but his 17 passing touchdowns helped to put points on the board for a struggling New York offense. *Tom Berg/ Getty Images*

THE FAKE SPIKE GAME

EVERY FRANCHISE has its watershed, benchmark games. The Jets had a lot of them, but unfortunately most were losses.

One of the worst in franchise history occurred on November 27, 1994, under coach Pete Carroll's watch. It proved to be the beginning of the end for his one-year reign as Jets head coach.

Facing the 7–4 Dolphins, the Jets jumped out to a 10–0 first-half lead on a Nick Lowery field goal and a 30-yard touchdown pass from Boomer Esiason to tight end Johnny Mitchell. Giants Stadium was jumping like it hadn't been jumping in years. With the win, the 6–5 Jets would tie Miami for a share of first place in the AFC East, and who knows what more good things would follow?

In the third quarter, a three-yard run by Brad Baxter put the Jets up 17–0. After a Dan Marino touchdown pass (and failed two-point conversion) put Miami on the board, Esiason again connected with Mitchell, this time on a 14-yard scoring pass, to extend the lead to 24–6.

Miami quarterback Dan Marino (13) fooled everyone with his fake spike call in the waning moments of the Dolphins-Jets game on November 27, 1994. While players on both sides stood around trying to figure out what was going on, Marino threw a game-winning touchdown pass to Mark Ingram. *Chuck Solomon/Sports Illustrated/Getty Images*

The Dolphins scored again on a Mark Ingram touchdown reception from Marino, and they converted the two-pointer to put the score at 24–14 heading into the final quarter. The Jets offense couldn't add to the lead, while the Marino-to-Ingram Miami connection continued to chip away. A 28-yard pass play made it 24–21.

With the clock winding down, Marino went into a hurry-up offense. Once he got the Dolphins to the 8-yard line and with less than 30 seconds remaining in the game, Marino instructed his teammates to get set at the line of scrimmage so he could spike the ball to stop the clock.

"Clock! Clock! Clock!" he yelled as his players got set.

With the Jets defense expecting a spike and a momentary rest, Marino took the snap, dropped two steps back, and didn't spike the ball. Instead, he threw it to Ingram in the end zone for the game-winning touchdown with 22 seconds remaining and the Jets defense standing around trying to figure out what had just happened.

Marino's fake spike faked out everyone in the stadium except Ingram, who made eye contact with his quarterback at the line in a pre-planned play that only the two of them were in on.

In the end, it wasn't simply the loss that crushed the Jets' will that season, it was the way they lost.

"I'm at a loss for words right now," left tackle Jeff Criswell said somberly at his locker after the game. "This is hard for me to believe."

Said Jets safety Ronnie Lott, a veteran of 14 NFL seasons, "This was probably the toughest loss I've ever been associated with."

"It's hard to put in words how you feel like after a loss like this," said Esiason. "You feel like your team has turned the corner and you feel like it's coming around and this kind of thing happens. You just hope we have enough character—and I'm sure we do—to bounce back."

Carroll called it "a staggering defeat," adding, "This team has to take this and not let it suck the life out of us. We have to deal with it and go on."

They would fail to do that, losing their final four games after that to finish 6–10. Carroll would never coach the Jets to another victory.

With 1,010 receiving yards on 78 catches in 1994, Pro Bowler Rob Moore had his best season in five years as a Jet. It would also be his last year in New York, as he joined the Cardinals in 1995. *Joe Traver/Time Life Pictures/Getty Images*

defensive coordinator—cornerback James Hasty and safety Brian Washington.

Hasty, for one, was tired of the losing, and he lost it in a tirade to reporters during the week leading into the last game of the season.

"Who can deal with seven years of losing?" Hasty said. "I'm at a crossroads in my career. I've had a good season that's been overshadowed by what's happened on this club. I'm a free agent after this year, and what happens is in God's hands."

Like many others who saw the team improve from 4–12 in 1992 to 8–8 in 1993, Hasty thought the Jets had the right mix of players to break out in '94, with a legitimate chance of making the playoffs. But in the end, the disappointment and frustration got to him.

"Maybe I'm supposed to deal with seven years of losing and just be the greatest guy in the world," he said. "I'm not able to be that kind of person. You see a person that's very frustrated when the games are lost. Who honestly can deal with seven years of losing? I don't know anybody who can deal with that who considers himself a competitor, who considers himself a winner.

"If my attitude is not right on the day we lose, I apologize. Seven years has taken its toll. If the Jets feel like it's time for

James Hasty to move on, or if James Hasty feels like it's time to move on, then so be it. I'm going to talk to my teammates and let them know how I feel about certain things. All I can do is hope they understand what seven years of frustration are all about."

Hasty, who had been drafted by the Jets in 1988, was a part of only one winning season—a false-hope 8–7–1 record in his rookie year. Not long after he snapped to reporters, Hasty left the Jets to play in Kansas City, where he would resurrect his career and finish with a series of playoff seasons.

It's too bad players like Hasty couldn't rebound for Carroll in 1994. Who knows what would have happened, but he surely wouldn't have been fired after only one year.

The final humiliation of the Jets' 1994 season was a 24–10 loss to the Oilers in Houston. After the game, Lageman looked back to that loss to Miami and noted, "It must have lingered with us."

Veteran center Jim Sweeney had been with the Jets since 1984, and he called the state of the team in 1994 "the worst situation I was ever in. Even worse than the 4–12 team [in 1992]. To think we were 22 seconds from first [place], and now we're in last."

Esiason said, "Going from 6–5 to 6–10 is just unbelievable. I'd tell the fans that their pain is minor compared to ours."

The finale in Houston was made even more painful by the pre-game announcement that Steinberg was suffering from stomach cancer.

"Everything that could have happened to this team has happened," said Esiason. "And then to find out about Dick, all the players looked at each other as if to say, 'What happened?'"

What happened was the team's fourth double-digit loss season and the third firing of a head coach in six years. What would happen next was even harder to comprehend.

KOTITE CALAMITY

Leon Hess was vacationing in the Bahamas when he saw a news item on television that Rich Kotite had been fired by the Philadelphia Eagles as their head coach.

Perhaps the most ill-fated phone call Hess ever made was when he got his team president, Steve Gutman, on the phone and said, "Get me Rich Kotite's number."

Hess called. Kotite answered. Kotite later said he thought the call was a prank, a joke. Little did anyone know the joke would be on the Jets.

And so days later Hess, who was otherwise highly reclusive, stood before an auditorium packed with reporters and team personnel and famously declared, "I'm eighty years old and I want results now."

That, of course, stunningly indicated that it was Hess' belief that Kotite was the man to bring him those results—winning results. Referring to Kotite's Brooklyn tough-guy boxing background, Hess called his new coach "a dese, dems, and dose" guy and deemed him the "head of the Jets family."

"I've waited twenty-five years," Hess said. "The buck stops with me. I'm just one of those fans who's been disappointed for twenty-five years. Let's make a change. If it's wrong, it's my fault. But at least I'm doing something for the fans and trying to do something for myself at eighty.

"I'm entitled to some enjoyment from this team, and that means winning."

Those ended up being sad words, looking back, because the Jets never did win a Super Bowl for Hess, who died at age 85 on May 7, 1999.

The fallout from the Pete Carroll firing and Kotite hiring was memorable. The headline on the front page of the *New York Post* read, "Dumb and Dumber," with a picture of Carroll next to the word *Dumb* and a picture of Kotite next to the word *Dumber*.

There was a glum feeling at the Meadowlands for much of the 1995 season. Rich Kotite came in as head coach and made a series of questionable decisions. The 3–13 finish in 1995 was outdone in futility by the 1–15 mark in 1996, Kotite's last year with the team. *Bill Kostroun/AP Images*

Carroll was no Vince Lombardi, but—as history would bear out with his relative success in New England and then profound success at USC—he wasn't a bad head coach, and he deserved more than one year to build his program.

Hess' knee-jerk decision to hire Kotite would, of course, set his beloved franchise in a direction toward oblivion. Maybe if Hess had not been watching television that day, he would never have hired Kotite and the Jets could have avoided one of the most futile eras in the history of all sports, not just football.

Make no mistake: Kotite was a nice man with good intentions. But being nice and having good intentions don't always translate into victories on the football field. Kotite was, simply, not a strong leader of men, and perhaps his biggest mistake at the start was not hiring a better staff of assistants.

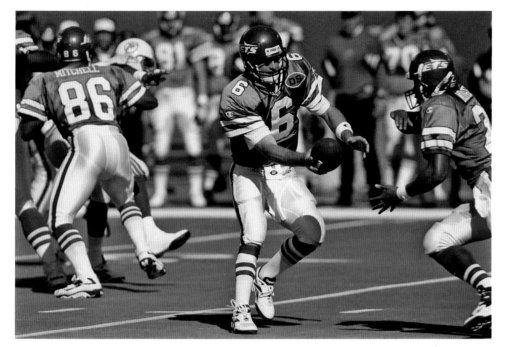

When Boomer Esiason went down with an injury, the Jets turned to veteran quarterback Bubby Brister to run the offense midway through the 1995 season. Brister led them to a 17–16 win over the Dolphins in Week 8, but the Jets lost in Brister's three other starts. He threw eight interceptions against four touchdowns for the season. *Bill Hickey/Allsport/Getty Images*

Even the best head coaches hire a strong, competent staff. Kotite, who was already guiding a rudderless ship and wasn't the hardest-working head coach who ever lived, didn't hire strong assistants who might challenge him for the sake of helping the cause. Perhaps he was too insecure to do so.

Instead, Kotite hired his buddies from around the league, those whom he had worked with before and was comfortable with—and that cost him. After a while the inmates were running the asylum, and in the NFL nothing good comes out of that.

As an example, Kotite hired Ken Rose, who had been a terrific special teams player in the league, to be his special teams coach. But Rose had no coaching experience, and the Jets special teams were awful and ended up costing them games. Once Kotite and his staff were fired, Rose never coached in the NFL again.

During his two years as the leader of the Jets, Kotite made a string of personnel decisions that were staggering in their incompetence. Jets fans will never forget when Kotite started former college quarterback Vance Joseph at cornerback against the Oakland Raiders. Joseph came to the Jets as a rookie project. They wanted to convert him from quarterback to cornerback. As if the transition from college to the pro level isn't already difficult enough, doing that while making such a drastic change in position makes it almost impossible.

In that fateful game, the Raiders blitzed the Jets 47–10 while their Hall of Fame–bound receiver, Tim Brown, schooled poor Joseph, who was making his first NFL start, by catching two touchdowns on him. The game got so out of hand that Jets fans started chanting, "Let's go Raiders!" It marked one of the most humiliating moments in Jets history.

"I'm embarrassed, the football team's embarrassed, our families are embarrassed, everybody was embarrassed," Kotite said after the game.

"I have never felt so utterly embarrassed in my football career," echoed quarterback Boomer Esiason.

Joseph took it in stride, saying, "I played this game as a quarterback. I don't blame them for going after me. You see a rookie defender out there, you throw at him."

After the game, Brown wondered aloud how the Jets could leave Joseph out there playing him man-to-man without safety help.

"It was strange out there," Brown said after the game. "I started feeling bad for the Jets."

Kotite's ill-advised decision to start Joseph in that Oakland game was trumped only by his decision to give Everett McIver his first NFL start at left tackle against the Bills in Buffalo, where he would be blocking Hall of Fame defensive end Bruce Smith, the league's all-time leader in sacks. Not long into the game, Smith blew past McIver like

ADRIAN MURRELL

RUNNING BACK

1993–1997

ADRIAN MURRELL was one of the few shining lights during the dark times of the Rich Kotite era.

Drafted out of West Virginia in the fifth round of the 1993 draft, Murrell instantly became one of the more popular players on the team. After doing mostly kick-return duty in his first two seasons, he became Kotite's featured running back beginning in 1995. That year he led the Jets in both rushing attempts (192) and pass receptions (71). The following season he ran for 1,249 yards, the most ever by a Jet until Curtis Martin and Thomas Jones came along.

Murrell remained the featured back when Bill Parcells took over in 1997, and he rushed for 1,086 yards and seven touchdowns. But when Parcells pulled off the biggest acquisition in Jets history, wresting Curtis Martin from the Patriots, Murrell's time in New York was finished.

He was traded to the Arizona Cardinals in 1998 and had his last truly productive season, rushing for 1,042 yards and a career-high eight touchdowns. His production waned in 1999, and he ended up in Washington for one season in 2000. After a two-year hiatus from the NFL, Murrell was signed by Parcells in Dallas in 2003 for the final season of his career.

In Murrell's five seasons with the Jets, he rushed for 3,447 yards and 15 touchdowns. His career totals are 5,199 yards and 23 scores.

His younger brother, Marques Murrell, is a defensive lineman/linebacker who was signed by the Jets in 2007. He played for New York until his release in 2009.

After serving mainly as a return specialist, running back Adrian Murrell emerged as the team's primary offensive weapon in 1995, amassing 1,260 total yards from scrimmage. He followed that performance with back-to-back 1,000-yard rushing seasons. *Jeffrey E. Blackman*

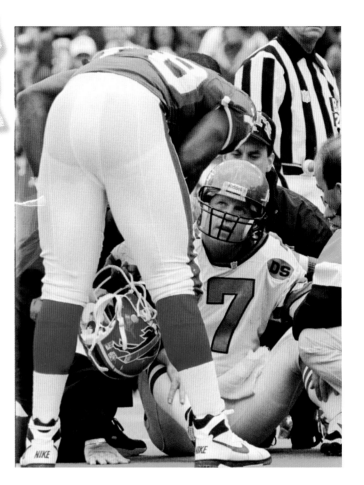

Buffalo Bills defensive end Bruce Smith checks on Boomer Esiason after the quarterback regained consciousness following a knock-out sack by Smith at Rich Stadium on October 8, 1995. Later that season, Esiason told that media that he hoped to be with a different team the next year, specifically "a team that will protect me a little better." *Bill Sikes/AP Images*

a Porsche passing a pedestrian on the side of the road and hurtled himself, helmet first, into the helmet of Esiason before Boomer had a chance to blink. The quarterback lay motionless on the Rich Stadium turf for several minutes before being helped off the field.

McIver had flinched on the play and was called for a false-start penalty, but it was so loud in the stadium that Smith never heard the whistle. After the game, not only did Esiason, who suffered a concussion, say, "I don't remember anything," but Smith was rattled.

"It was very scary," Smith said. "I have never taken part in a play that was so violent in my career. A thousand things were going through my mind. I just tried to deliver a blow and do my job, but at the same time, a part of me is saying, 'Why didn't I just push him down?' I'm just glad he's all right. I still have some concerns for him at this moment."

The Jets hoped that Neil O'Donnell was the answer for turning the team's fortunes around heading into 1996. They paid him generously, but the results were far from worth it. O'Donnell missed 10 games due to injury, and in his six starts the Jets were winless as he threw four touchdown passes and seven interceptions. *Andy Lyons/Getty Images*

Like Brown in that Raiders game, Smith openly second-guessed Kotite's decision to play McIver, saying, "I'm surprised they left me one-on-one with him so often." Jets fans everywhere wondered the same thing.

Esiason's words after that game were telling. He didn't blame Smith for the hit, and he wouldn't throw McIver under the bus. But he was clearly bewildered by Kotite's decision to start McIver.

"I do not hold Bruce Smith responsible for anything," Esiason said. "I want everybody to know that certainly I've always considered Bruce Smith one of the finest football players to play this game. I know him off the field and I've played in about ten or twelve games against him and never once have I ever felt he did anything outside the rules.

"It's important that not only he know, but everybody else know, that he's still in my book one of the best, if not the best, football players, but also the classiest in terms of playing within the rules."

In that same game, yet another personnel blunder by the Jets left their fans confounded. Dexter Carter, one of the league's best kick returners when he played for the San Francisco 49ers, turned into a mess once the Jets signed him. In that game in Buffalo, only the Jets' sixth game of the season, Carter lost a fumble for the third time that year. It was converted into a Bills touchdown and a 16–3 halftime lead for Buffalo.

When he was asked about Carter after the game, Ken Rose, the special teams coach, said, "I'm too emotionally messed up to talk right now. I'm ready to explode."

CAN IT POSSIBLY GET WORSE?

After the 3–13 debacle of Kotite's first year, Hess spent millions on new personnel that he believed was going to right the ship. The team signed free agent Neil O'Donnell, who had quarterbacked the Steelers to the Super Bowl the previous year, to a $25 million contract—the fourth-highest contract in NFL history at the time.

O'Donnell was going to be Kotite's answer to turn the bumbling franchise around. The Jets also hired Ron Erhardt as offensive coordinator. Erhardt had been O'Donnell's offensive coordinator in Pittsburgh. They signed two high-profile tackles, Jumbo Elliott and David Williams, to free agent contracts.

On top of all the high-profile acquisitions, O'Donnell was a local boy, having grown up in nearby Madison, New Jersey. So it all made such perfect sense—until the Jets began playing football in 1996, that is.

Shown with NFL Commissioner Paul Tagliabue after being selected by the Jets with the first overall pick in the 1996 draft, Keyshawn Johnson doesn't seem entirely sure of what the future might hold. *Al Messerschmidt/Getty Images*

The Jets went 1–15 in O'Donnell's first year. They were even worse than they had been the previous year, which was difficult to do.

Both Elliott and Williams promptly suffered hamstring injuries in training camp, and neither was ready to start the 1996 season, which began with a road game in Denver. Kotite decided to start Roger Duffy, who was a center and guard by trade, at right tackle. Duffy wasn't even told of his position change until shortly before game time. The Jets lost 31–6, and O'Donnell was chased, sacked, and hit by the Denver pass rushers all game.

Kotite described the Broncos' onslaught as a "flash fire in the beginning of the game and the second quarter," adding,

"I wish I could tell you how it felt for all of us. It's those kinds of ballgames where you take it right on the chin, and right now, I don't have many words for you."

After the game, Duffy offered these memorable words when asked what his reaction was to starting at right tackle for the first time in his career: "Stunned and amazed."

It's one of many quotes that will go down in Jets lore.

Another big acquisition in 1996 led to another of the many distasteful subplots of the Kotite era. When the Jets made USC star receiver Keyshawn Johnson the No. 1 overall pick in that year's draft, it forced an unlikely and uncomfortable relationship between the flashy and loquacious Johnson and low-key and quiet veteran Wayne Chrebet.

KEYSHAWN JOHNSON

RECEIVER
1996–1999

PERHAPS THE ONLY ADVANTAGE to finishing with the worst record in the NFL is that you get the top pick in the ensuing draft.

Following the Jets' 3–13 season in 1995 under Rich Kotite, the team made USC receiver Keyshawn Johnson the top overall pick in the NFL draft, with hopes that he would restore life into the sad-sack organization.

Johnson, while a terrific talent, didn't lift the franchise, but he did draw attention to the Jets—more for his chatty, cocky style and later for a book he wrote chronicling his rookie season titled, *Just Give Me the Damn Ball!: The Fast Times and Hard Knocks of an NFL Rookie.*

In the book, Johnson ripped just about everyone in the organization, highlighting his venom for Kotite, fellow receiver Wayne Chrebet, offensive coordinator Ron Erhardt, and several reporters who covered the team, among others.

Johnson never truly fulfilled the potential of a No. 1 overall pick. His numbers were solid with the Jets; he had 63 catches and eight touchdowns in his rookie year, followed by 70 catches and five touchdowns in 1997. He improved to 83 receptions for 1,131 yards and 10 touchdowns in 1998 before reaching his highest totals as a Jet in 1999 with 89 catches and 1,170 yards.

That turned out to be his final season in New York, because the organization had had enough of his selfish acts, verbal attacks on management and fellow players, and incessant self-promotion. He had become more trouble than he was worth.

So the Jets traded Johnson to the Tampa Bay Buccaneers for two first-round draft picks just before the 2000 NFL draft. They parlayed that trade into several key starters, including quarterback Chad Pennington, defensive end Shaun Ellis, and tight end Anthony Becht.

Johnson went on to have some strong seasons over the next seven years. He caught a career-high 106 passes for Tampa Bay in 2001, but he scored only one touchdown—something that irked him and eventually led to his departure there, too.

Johnson fell out of favor with Tampa Bay coach Jon Gruden and was traded to Dallas in

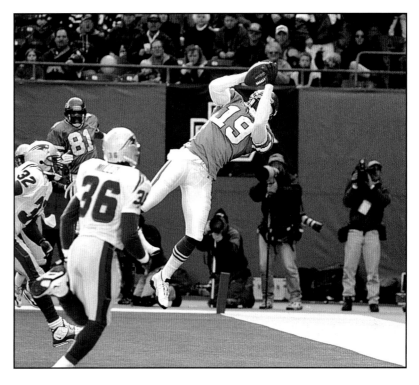

Keyshawn Johnson made some spectacular catches during his time with the Jets, but he made as many headlines with his antics. *Keith Torrie/NY Daily News Archive/Getty Images*

2004, reuniting Johnson with then-Cowboys coach Bill Parcells (who had coached him in 1998 and 1999 with the Jets) for two mildly productive seasons. Johnson finished his career quietly with the Carolina Panthers in 2006 before retiring.

Despite the controversy that seemed to follow him wherever he went, Johnson was always a tough, durable player, missing only three of a possible 145 career games (including playoffs) due to injury.

In the end, Johnson is probably better known in the NFL for his brashness and work as an author than for being a receiver that truly made a difference to his team. He finished his career with 814 receptions for 10,571 yards and 64 touchdowns—all very good numbers, but not befitting of a difference-making player.

WAYNE CHREBET

RECEIVER
1995–2005

During his 11 seasons in New York, Wayne Chrebet was not only one of the game's most reliable and productive receivers, he was also a team leader and a fan favorite. *Kevin Terrell/ Getty Images*

IN HIS TWO MISERABLE SEASONS as head coach of the Jets, Rich Kotite left the team with one shining legacy: Wayne Chrebet. The Jets signed the undrafted wide receiver as a free agent in 1995, and he went on to become not only one of the most decorated receivers in franchise history but one of its most popular players ever.

Undersized, undrafted, and under the radar, Chrebet played college ball at Hofstra University, which was located right across the street from the Jets' training facility on Long Island. At Hofstra, Chrebet set records and dreamed about making it in the NFL. He was a local boy, having grown up in Garfield, New Jersey, and he used to watch Jets practices from outside the fences of the facility.

When training camp began in 1995, Chrebet was 11th among the 11 receivers on the depth chart. He was a long shot to make the team, even a team as bad as the Jets were at the time. The coaches and potential teammates couldn't even pronounce his name. Linebacker Bobby Houston finally just nicknamed him "Q" to make things easy.

The 5-foot-9, 180-pound Chrebet looked so little like a pro football player that he was stopped and detained by the guard at the front gate of the team facility when he arrived for his first day of training camp. He became the first player from Hofstra to make an NFL roster since John Schmitt with the Jets in 1964.

Chrebet didn't just make the team in 1995, he set an NFL record for most receptions by a wide receiver in his first two seasons and launched a sparkling career. He retired as the second-leading receiver in Jets franchise history with 580 catches, second only to Don Maynard's 627. Among all-time undrafted players, he finished with the third-most receptions in the history of the league.

Chrebet was known as the best third-down receiver in the game, and 379 of his 580 career receptions resulted in first downs. In a 1996 game at Jacksonville, he made five third-down conversions and caught 12 passes for 162 yards.

Chrebet's last NFL game was on November 6, 2005, against the San Diego Chargers. He suffered a serious concussion in the game, one of nine he sustained in his career. On the play that knocked him out when his head slammed to the turf, Chrebet held onto the ball. Fittingly, the catch came on a third down and gave the Jets a first down.

Chrebet played all 11 of his NFL seasons with the Jets, catching passes from 13 different players: Boomer Esiason, Bubby Brister, Glenn Foley, Frank Reich, Neil O'Donnell, Ray Lucas, Vinny Testaverde, Rick Mirer, Tom Tupa, Curtis Martin, Chad Pennington, Quincy Carter, and Brooks Bollinger.

Although Chrebet's shy nature sometimes came across as standoffish and aloof, he always appreciated his fans, who showed their dedication by making his jersey one of the most popular of all time. Still today, years after his retirement, you see No. 80 jerseys littering the stands at Meadowlands Stadium.

"When I look at the stands during pre-game, or even in between series or walking into the stadium or driving in, and I see a father and son or family and they're all wearing my jersey, I know what that feels like and it's amazing that I've had that impact on people," Chrebet said. "I'm glad I gave them something to believe in. Everybody knew that when I got a rise out of the crowd is when I knew I made a good play. It wasn't just making the play; it was just getting the fans on their feet that made me happiest when I was on the field.

"Just to feel what it's like to drive to a game . . . and see everybody with your jersey on and hearing the 'J-E-T-S' chant and being the center of that—it's been the greatest 11 years of my life. I will always be a New York Jet."

Receivers Wayne Chrebet (80) and Keyshawn Johnson (19) had a tense relationship during their four years as teammates, and in Johnson's first season there was little reason to celebrate. By the end of the 1990s, however, the Jets emerged as playoff contenders and the two rivals could enjoy in each other's successes. *Ezra Shaw/Getty Images*

The two receivers came from completely different backgrounds and collegiate pedigrees and could not have been more opposite.

The uncomfortable part of the Johnson-Chrebet relationship came from a curious and amusing jealousy that Johnson instantly developed for Chrebet, despite the fact that the rookie was signed to a $2.5 million-per-year contract when he was drafted, at the time a record amount for a rookie. Johnson, who detested the adoration Chrebet got from the fans for his underdog status, derisively called Chrebet the "team mascot" in his book *Just Give Me the Damn Ball!: The Fast Times and Hard Knocks of an NFL Rookie*, which was released in 1997.

Later in their respective careers, after Johnson was traded to the Tampa Bay Buccaneers in 2000, the two would meet again as opponents when the Jets played the Bucs in Tampa. Before that game, Johnson told reporters that comparing Chrebet to himself "is like comparing a flashlight to a star. Flashlights only last so long and a star is in the sky forever."

In a fitting bit of theater, Chrebet ended up catching the game-winning touchdown that day—an 18-yard pass from running back Curtis Martin on a halfback option with 52 seconds remaining. Johnson had one catch for seven yards in the game.

Ironically, Chrebet and Johnson in 1998 combined to lead the NFL in receptions as a tandem with 158 catches for 2,214 yards and 18 touchdowns.

Another memorable, er, forgettable moment etched in the minds of Jets fans was the day O'Donnell popped a calf muscle while having a light toss with backup quarterback Frank Reich on the sideline. It was December 1, 1996. The Jets were sitting with a 1–11 record and were getting ready to host the Houston Oilers. O'Donnell was about to make his return to the lineup after missing seven weeks with a dislocated right (throwing) shoulder.

As he dropped back to make a throw during warmups, O'Donnell's right leg slipped on the white marking of the end zone line as he planted, and he pulled his calf muscle. Minutes before the game was to start, he was being helped back to the locker room by trainers, incredulous at how cursed he and the franchise were.

"I saw his facial expression and saw his body language and I knew something was wrong," Reich recalled. "I turned to [third-string quarterback Glenn] Foley and said, 'Here we go again.'"

"What else can go wrong?" O'Donnell asked Pat Kirwan, the team's director of player administration, as he was helped into the locker room.

"When [O'Donnell] went down, I thought, 'That's crazy.' It's so rough. We need to put this on *Unsolved Mysteries* or something," defensive end Hugh Douglas said. "It kind of makes you want to cry, man, because nothing ever goes your way. You feel like, 'What did I do to deserve this? What's going on?' That's how you feel."

Keyshawn Johnson openly speculated in his book that O'Donnell was faking the injury.

"It was supposed to be the twenty-five-million-dollar man's big comeback," Johnson wrote. "All week long, he'd been taking snaps with the first team in practice, still throwing little weak-assed two-yard routes to Chrebet, and now he was coming back as our fearless leader. How in the hell do you pull a calf muscle tossing a football around?

"Half of me says the dude was faking it so that Erhardt and Kotite could keep their jobs. It gave them a big fat

Adrian Murrell ran for 199 yards and one touchdown in the Week 9 matchup with the Cardinals in Arizona. The Jets pulled out a 31–21 victory for their only win of the 1996 season. *Stephen Dunn/ Allsport/Getty Images*

excuse as to why we were terrible. They could say, 'Hey, we haven't had the twenty-five-million-dollar man. How were we supposed to win?' O'Donnell was their boy. I think he went down, maybe not to save Kotite, but definitely to save his guru, old man Erhardt. It didn't matter, we lost without him, but I bet we would have lost with him, too."

Kotite said of the bizarre incident: "It was the first adversity we'd ever met before the game started. In my wildest dreams I wouldn't have thought it would happen. He was all by himself when it happened. Someone tapped me on the shoulder before pre-game warmups. The offensive linemen were coming into the end zone, and I saw Neil being carried off in the other end zone, and I got on a walkie-talkie and was told his calf muscle was pulled.

"I don't like the way we responded to it."

The Jets were blown out 35–10 by the Oilers in a game that only 21,723 fans saw because there were 55,985 no-shows, an NFL record that still stood as of 2010.

At the end of the game, Kotite was doused with beer by angry fans as he walked off the field and into the tunnel. It was reminiscent of Joe Walton getting the same classless treatment at the end of the last home game he coached in 1989, and it was yet another how-low-can-you-go moment in Jets history.

"I've been doused before," Kotite said. "I had a Gore-Tex jacket on. I couldn't tell."

"It's tough on him," running back Reggie Cobb said. "That's a tough position to be in. So much has happened this year. There were so many expectations and so many things have gone wrong."

The 1996 season was not a proud moment for Jets fans. *Andy Lyons/Allsport/Getty Images*

END OF AN ERROR

That ugly loss to Houston was followed by three more rather nondescript defeats—to New England, Philadelphia, and Miami—to close out not only the 1–15 1996 season but the Kotite era. And when it was done, Kotite sounded almost relieved that it was over.

"I feel I've always been a bottom-line guy, and when you're 3–13 and 1–15, that just doesn't cut it," Kotite said. "It's been a poor two years. I really don't want to lose the fans for this organization. You have to do something to show them."

"I've been very fortunate," he went on. "I'm the only guy that came out of my college [Wagner in Staten Island] who ever played in the NFL. I had two opportunities as a head coach. I'm a very lucky guy."

The Jets won four games and lost 28 in the two years Kotite coached them—and quite frankly, it seemed even worse than that, if that's possible.

Among all NFL head coaches who've coached at least 30 games, Kotite's .125 winning percentage as head coach was equaled in dubious futility as the worst in league history by only the Tampa Bay Buccaneers' Leeman Bennett (1985–1986).

Highlighting just how bad Kotite's reign was, he finished his career losing 19 of his last 20 games with the Jets. And remember, before he was hired by Hess, Kotite lost his last seven games with the Eagles before getting fired in Philadelphia. So, combining the end of his Eagles coaching career with his two flawed seasons with the Jets, Kotite lost 35 of the last 39 games he coached.

It's no wonder that, when he was mercifully fired after the 1996 season, he never went back into coaching—even as an assistant someplace, as so many fired head coaches do. Kotite, in fact, just about went into hiding after he was fired. Since his departure from the NFL, he has kept a low profile. He remains on Staten Island, where he has lived for years, but he has been so far from the spotlight that he has bordered on reclusive.

The end of the Kotite era was equal parts sad and equal parts relief. While he was a stand-up loser who was difficult to root against, the franchise had hit such rock bottom that it was hard to imagine how long it would take to be dragged from the darkness of the abyss he had led the Jets into.

When the end finally came for Kotite, he was gracious, but he never acknowledged whether he was fired, forced out, or quitting.

"I wasn't fired," Kotite said that day. "I didn't quit. I'm stepping down."

Huh?

Kotite's "stepping down" announcement took place before the Jets' final game of the 1996 season, a home game against the Dolphins that they would lose 31–28. A banner that a fan hung at Giants Stadium captured the moment perfectly. It read: "THE END OF AN ERROR."

MVP Books Collection

MVP Books Collection

MVP Books Collection

A LOT MORE THAN WINS were missing for the Jets once the Rich Kotite era came to a crashing conclusion after two years of record failure. Something even more precious and elusive than wins was missing: credibility. The Jets had not only become the bottom feeders of the NFL, but their futility had made its way into pop culture. They had become the butt of late-night television jokes on Leno and Letterman.

Only one man could save the Jets from themselves, rescue them, drag them from the abyss. Only one man could make them relevant again. Only one man could lure top players to want to play for the Jets. Only one man could bring the fan base back.

Only one man could bring credibility to the organization.

That man was Bill Parcells, whose résumé and magnetic charisma were about as impressive as the legendary Vince Lombardi's. Parcells had led the New York Giants to two Super Bowl titles and the New England Patriots to a runner-up finish for the NFL title.

Incredibly, because of an internal power struggle in the Patriots organization, he was on the outs with New England owner Robert Kraft, and Parcells was suddenly available—and he was hungry for the next challenge. Parcells being available and willing to come to the Jets was like having the prettiest girl not having been asked out to the prom and she actually wanted to go with you.

It appeared to be a perfect pairing. Parcells was a New Jersey guy with Northeast roots and he was coming back home, having already led the Giants to the promised land. Imagine where his already iconic status would rise to if he could lead both New York football teams to the pinnacle.

The Jets? Well, they needed any help they could get, and why not from someone as accomplished as Parcells?

One week before Parcells was given the head coaching job, Jets President Steve Gutman introduced Parcells' longtime assistant, Bill Belichick, as the head coach, with Parcells serving as a "consultant." The arrangement satisfied the league's decision in the battle between the Jets and Patriots, but it was really only a shell game. *Malcolm Clarke/AFP/Getty Images*

Team owner Leon Hess introduces Bill Parcells as the new head coach of the New York Jets at a press conference at the team training facility in Long Island on February 11, 1997. *Kathy Willens/AP Images*

BORDER WARS

The drama surrounding Parcells' exit from New England and return to New York was all-encompassing. The dispute between Parcells and his former employer ended up in an arbitrator's hands as things got ugly between Kraft and Jets owner Leon Hess.

In the end, NFL Commissioner Paul Tagliabue, who served as arbitrator, ordered the Jets to give the Patriots their third- and fourth-round picks in the 1997 draft, plus their second-round draft pick in 1998 and first-round pick in 1999. Tagliabue also ruled that when Parcells did join the Jets, he would have to serve as a "consultant" before he could coach the team.

In retrospect, the deal was a win-win. For the Jets, they got one of the greatest coaches in modern football history and saw a return to winning ways. For New England, those draft picks helped build their team into a dynasty. At the time, however, Kraft was ticked off, calling the arrangement a "transparent farce."

"It's like rules don't matter for the Jets and Bill Parcells," Kraft scoffed.

Kraft claimed that the Jets had tampered by speaking with Parcells while he was still coaching the Patriots during the 1996 season. Kraft told the *New York Post* that he didn't think Parcells would last in the consulting position because of his thirst for being in the media spotlight.

"Those press conferences he conducts every day, those are like a narcotic to Bill Parcells," Kraft said derisively. "He won't be able to stay away. Those are like a drug to him."

Parcells deftly and famously described the disconnect in New England between him and Kraft, whom he felt meddled in player personnel decisions. "If you're going to cook the meal," Parcells said, "you should be able to buy the groceries."

With the Jets, Parcells ran more than just the kitchen. Hess gave him the keys to the entire place and did everything Parcells asked—including building an indoor practice bubble.

The best twist of all in what would be labeled the "border war" between the Jets and Patriots was the fact that Bill Belichick, Parcells' most trusted and talented coach and defensive mastermind, was named the Jets head

coach while Parcells acted as consultant. Belichick's term as head coach lasted all of six days. He never coached a game and wouldn't until he was hired, ironically, by Kraft to coach the Patriots in 2000.

Of his short-lived head coaching stint, Belichick joked at the time that he was "stepping down with an undefeated record, untied and unscored upon."

It wasn't long before Parcells was able to take over as the head coach and move the franchise forward—from Kotite and from the tangle with the Patriots.

CLEANING UP THE MESS

When Parcells finally took the helm in New York, he announced, "This is my last job. After this, I'll ride off into the sunset."

It was not, of course, his last job—in fact, he had made a very similar statement upon taking the Patriots job in 1993, saying, "This is my last deal, no doubt about that. After that, I'm John Wayne." But in his three seasons with the Jets, Parcells was able to turn the franchise around in remarkable fashion.

His first order of business was to change the culture of the Jets franchise. One of Parcells' many gifts was how perceptive he was about everything around him. Moreover, he always had an interesting perspective of his own.

Having coached across the Hudson River for the Giants, and in the process becoming one of the most revered figures in the storied history of that franchise, Parcells was well aware of the losing culture that the Jets had been mired in essentially since Joe Namath was all the rage in Super Bowl III. Parcells would have to change the culture, change the mind-set of everyone in the organization—going well beyond finding better players to perform on the field. He cleaned out the bad seeds inside the building and changed the attitude of the secretaries, support staff, custodians, mail room and maintenance workers, security guards, everyone.

It was as if, as soon as Parcells moved his belongings into the head coach's office at the team's Hofstra University training facility on Long Island, everyone in the building began to hold their heads up higher.

Carl Banks, a former Pro Bowl linebacker with the Giants under Parcells, talked about the state of the franchise when he came to the Jets as part of Parcells' coaching staff.

"The morale was morose inside the building," Banks recalled. "Morale and everything at every phase of the organization was rotted. Secretaries, nonessential football personnel, essential personnel, everyone was kind of in a funk when we got there. Certain people had to go, because they were just bad people. There were cliques in the building, like those who were closely aligned with [team president] Steve Gutman and those that weren't."

Banks recalled how he was sitting in Parcells' office on his first day and the head coach told him, "Banksy, there's a lot of work here, but the cupboard's not bare. The first thing I've got to do is change the culture around here."

"It was a totally different culture than I had ever been around," Banks remembered. "It was very laid-back, not very football-oriented. There were just people walking around wherever they wanted to walk inside the building, doing whatever they wanted to do. Everybody just kind of had his or her own agenda."

Parcells noted that there were too many "private empires" in the organization, with everyone looking out for themselves. His first order of business was to separate the football operations people from the support staff. That meant beefed-up security all over the facility.

According to Banks, the nonessential football people were "pushed to another part of the building right away. They were no longer roaming the halls and glad-handing."

Another culture change that Parcells brought to the Jets was closing off his players and coaching staff from the media. Parcells was a believer in fostering an us-against-them mentality, and although he always was thoughtful and engaging with reporters, Parcells would tell players that the media was the "enemy" and reporters were "subversives" looking to tear the team apart.

So, at the team's Weeb Ewbank Hall training facility on Long Island, Parcells erected eight-foot-high fences barring anyone—especially media—from roaming in the player parking lots and the practice fields. The access that reporters once enjoyed to just about everywhere in and around the building was cut off. Practices that had always been open to reporters were now closed. Assistant coaches were banned from speaking to the media.

Although Parcells had not taken this approach to the media during his time with the Giants, he realized that the explosion of information on the Internet meant that more and more information from journalists' reports was available to competing teams. So he decided to shut it all down.

Early on during his Jets tenure, however, the results of this culture change were evident on the football field, and everything continued to snowball in the right direction. Consider this early statement by the Jets under Parcells: In Kotite's two season openers, the Jets were outscored 83–20 (a 52–14 loss to Miami in 1995 and a 31–6 loss to Denver in 1996). In Parcells' first game as Jets head coach, New York shellacked the Seattle Seahawks 41–3 on the road.

A statement? Indeed. As bold as they come. The Jets, so much more quickly than anyone dared to dream, were back.

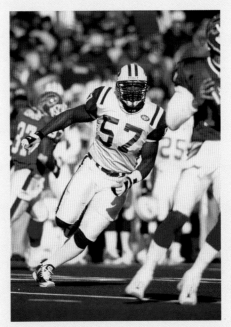

The Jets would finish 9–7 in 1997, making for one of the most dramatic one-year turnarounds not only in NFL history but in sports history. The team went from 1–15 to 9–7 in the span of a year. Unfortunately, the Jets lost three of their final four games in 1997—an anomaly for Parcells-coached teams, which historically were at their best in December—to miss out on the postseason.

Parcells, for all the good he had done so quickly, actually became the subject of some rather harsh criticism when the season ended. He was second-guessed about some questionable coaching moves he had made in the season finale in Detroit, where they lost to the Lions 13–10. A win would have catapulted the Jets into the playoffs and made the turnaround from the Kotite era even more remarkable.

Parcells pulled starting quarterback Neil O'Donnell at one point with the game in the balance, inserting backup Ray Lucas to add some run-pass dynamic to the offense. But that wasn't all. Late in the game with the Jets trying to pull out the win, he had running back Leon Johnson throw a halfback option pass into the end zone, and it was intercepted by the Lions, ending the Jets' chances.

The coach was skewered for taking the ball out of his starting quarterback's hands. O'Donnell, who had a rocky relationship with Parcells, wasn't happy about it, grumbling to confidants afterward.

The disappointment, even outrage, from both fans and the media about the team's stumbling at the end of the season and the failure to make the playoffs was evidence of how much and how quickly Parcells had raised the bar. The fact that fans were passionate enough to feel that outrage illustrated how much Parcells had changed the culture.

That, in a way, was the biggest form of flattery for where Parcells had brought the franchise in a span of less than a year. Not only had he restored hope, but he had elevated expectations.

QUANTUM LEAP FALLS SHORT

The 9–7 finish in 1997 was followed with significantly more progress, though the 1998 season didn't start out looking like the team was getting any better. The Jets lost 36–30 in overtime to the San Francisco 49ers in the season opener and then lost their home opener to the Baltimore Ravens 24–10. Suddenly, they were sitting at 0–2 in Parcells' sophomore season with the disappointment from missing out on the playoffs the previous year still lingering.

The Jets defense—specifically defensive end Hugh Douglas (99) and linebacker James Farrior (58) on this play—crushed Seahawks quarterback Warren Moon throughout the 1997 season opener at the Kingdome in Seattle. New York held Moon to 7-of-21 passing before backup John Friesz took over in the 41–3 rout. *Otto Greule/Allsport/Getty Images*

From there, though, the Jets embarked on the best stretch of winning football in franchise history. They lost only two more regular-season games, winning 12 of the last 14, and captured their first division title since the AFL-NFL merger in 1970. After losing to Indianapolis by one point on a Colts field goal with less than 30 seconds left in the game on November 15, the Jets closed out the regular season with a six-game winning streak and entered the playoffs as the hottest team in the league.

The 12–4 record meant that the Jets would host the divisional playoff game at Giants Stadium, just the sixth home playoff game in franchise history. With 78,817 on hand—at the time the largest crowd to see a pro football game in the New York region—the Jets dominated the Jacksonville Jaguars in what was, without question, their finest moment to date in that stadium.

The Jets built leads of 17–0, 24–7, and 31–14, but Jacksonville kept coming up with big plays to narrow the margin until New York sealed the deal on the 34–24 win. In the final moments of the game, receiver Keyshawn Johnson, coming in to play defensive back, intercepted a desperation pass from Jaguars quarterback Mark Brunell to clinch it.

Johnson was clearly the star of the day. In addition to his clutch defensive play, Johnson caught nine passes for 121 yards and rushed for 28 yards on two carries. He scored two touchdowns, one on a 21-yard pass from quarterback Vinny Testaverde and another on a 10-yard run on a reverse, and he also recovered a fumble at a pivotal moment by racing 60 yards in pursuit of a Jaguars player.

Running back Curtis Martin had a fine day himself, handling the ball 42 times, with 36 rushing attempts for 124 yards and two touchdowns and six receptions for 58 yards. Testaverde completed 24 of 36 passes for 284 yards with one touchdown and one interception.

After the game, Parcells said, "This was a good win for our franchise. I was happy for our fans. I'm happy about it. But there's more to do."

Vinny Testaverde celebrates after throwing one of his three touchdown passes against the Patriots in the Jets' 24–14 road win on October 19, 1998. Testaverde helped carry New York to the postseason with his Pro Bowl season, during which he threw only seven interceptions against 29 touchdowns. *Ezra Shaw/Allsport/Getty Images*

In the first quarter of the divisional playoff game against Jacksonville, Keyshawn Johnson's 21-yard scoring pass play gave the Jets an early 7–0 lead. Johnson's two touchdowns in the game helped propel New York to a 34–24 win. *Tim Clary/AFP/Getty Images*

CURTIS MARTIN

RUNNING BACK
1998–2006

The acquisition of Curtis Martin in 1998 was a coup for the Jets, giving them the most dangerous ground threat in franchise history. *Jeffrey E. Blackman*

THE MOST SIGNIFICANT transaction in Jets history came when they signed running back Curtis Martin away from the rival Patriots as a restricted free agent in 1998.

Martin went on to become arguably the best player in team history, finishing his career as the Jets' all-time leading rusher with 10,302 yards and 58 touchdowns. He ran for 100 or more yards in eight of 16 games during his first season as a Jet and led the team in rushing for eight years in a row.

Martin, who finished his career fourth on the NFL's all-time rushing list with 14,101 yards, won the NFL rushing title in 2004 with 1,697 yards. Through 2010, Martin and Hall of Famer Barry Sanders were the only two backs in NFL history to begin their careers rushing for at least 1,000 yards in each of their first 10 seasons.

A knee injury prompted Martin to officially announce his retirement from the NFL on July 26, 2007. Early in the 2010 season, he was inducted into the Jets' "Ring of Honor."

A hallmark of Martin's career was his son-and-father-like relationship with Bill Parcells.

"He's taught me many things that are invaluable as far as my profession goes," Martin said of his former coach. "If it wasn't for him, I don't believe I'd be the running back I became. He's taught me a lot of discipline. He's taught me a lot of mental toughness. He's taught me how, when you're tired, to push through it, how to be the workhorse."

Martin is open about the incredible respect he has for Parcells. "He demands what he wants, but in a proper way. His style of coaching is great for me and for most people in the NFL."

Parcells recalled testing his young running back immediately.

"In the first preseason game he played for New England in Detroit, I gave the ball to him eight straight plays, and he was hyperventilating," Parcells said. "He was so excited about the game, and now I'm running him to death. The lesson was that you need stamina to play in this league. I was trying to get him to understand what this job was going to be like."

Martin got the message.

"I was so pumped up, because this was my first game, the first time I was going to touch the ball in a real game against NFL players," Martin recalled. "I got out there expecting to run it a couple of times. He gave me the ball eight times in a row. I was so . . . hyperventilating."

Parcells developed a real soft spot in his heart for Martin.

"With my background, this kid was so nice I was almost suspicious," Parcells said. "People start talking to you like this from where I come from and you look at them funny, like 'What's this guy want?'

"It turned out that's just the way he is. I don't know why we hit it off. I was hard on him, very hard on him, but his skin was thick."

Martin once floored Parcells like the old coach had never been floored before. It took place at the end of the 1999 season, Parcells' last as Jets head coach. Martin had just been named the team's Most Valuable Player by his teammates and was given a trophy.

While Parcells wasn't around, Martin slipped into the coach's office and left the trophy. He penned a letter to Parcells telling him what he had meant to him as a player and that he wanted him to have the trophy. "I could never have won this trophy without you," Martin wrote to Parcells.

Parcells arrived at his office to see Martin's MVP trophy sitting on his desk just as the phone rang. It was his daughter, Jill.

As Jill was speaking to her dad, Parcells opened the envelope and began to read the letter.

Suddenly, there was silence on Parcells' end of the phone line. Jill could hear her father weeping.

Martin's words in that letter broke down the tough-on-the-exterior coach, who to this day cherishes that letter and trophy, both proudly displayed at his home.

Following his Pro Bowl season in 1998, Curtis Martin (28) struggled to find running room against the Denver defense in the AFC Championship Game on January 17, 1999. Martin was held to 14 yards on 13 carries as the Jets' dream of returning to the Super Bowl slipped through their fingers. *Dee Welsch/Getty Images*

The next order of business was heading to Denver to take on the Broncos in the AFC Championship Game on January 17, 1999. One more win and the Jets would return to the title game for the first time since Super Bowl III.

"I'm thrilled for the team, I'm thrilled for the fans, I'm thrilled for the coaches, and I'm thrilled for the players," Jets owner Leon Hess said in the lead-up to the game. "I'm happy about it, but there's more to do."

Unfortunately for the Jets and their tortured fans, the team couldn't complete the job, as a 10–0 third-quarter lead all-too-quickly turned into a 23–10 defeat.

Most confounding in the loss was the fact that the players who let the team down most were Parcells' most trusted men. Curtis Martin—who hardly ever fumbled—fumbled away a crucial second-half possession. Veteran fullback Keith Byars, another dependable warrior, also fumbled a ball away with the Jets driving in the second half. Finally, veteran returner Dave Meggett, who had been an integral part of the Giants' second Super Bowl win under Parcells,

muffed a kickoff. Johnson, their Pro Bowl receiver, was held to seven catches for 73 yards.

In the aftermath, the team was devastated, but also buoyed by hope.

"This wasn't baby steps," Parcells said after the game. "This was a quantum leap for this team, about as far as you can jump. I think it compares favorably with any team in history over a two-year period. I'm not saying that from an egotistical standpoint, but from an accomplishment

VINNY TESTAVERDE

QUARTERBACK
1998-2003, 2005

VINNY TESTAVERDE will forever be remembered by Jets fans for leading the team to the AFC Championship Game in 1998. It was a magical season in which he threw 29 touchdown passes and only seven interceptions.

Testaverde set an NFL record by throwing a touchdown pass in 21 consecutive seasons. He also set an NFL record by throwing touchdown passes to 70 different players. Among his dubious records was most career losses by a starting quarterback, 123.

In 1998, his first season with the Jets, Testaverde completed 61.5 percent of his passes and had a 101.6 passer rating. It was his best season in the NFL. In 1999, he suffered a ruptured left Achilles tendon in the first game and missed the rest of the season.

The following year, Testaverde authored one of the greatest comebacks of all time in the "Monday Night Miracle" against the Miami Dolphins. In that game, the Jets erased a 30–7 fourth-quarter deficit and won 40–37 in overtime on the strength of his five touchdown passes.

Testaverde was originally brought to the Jets to be a veteran backup. He had vastly different plans, though, having always been a starter in the league.

"I always reflect back on the meeting I had with coach Parcells before I signed," Testaverde said. "I knew I would be the starter. Once I had the opportunity, I felt like I was prepared enough with talent around me that I would be successful for him."

Vinny Testaverde joined the Jets in 1998 when he was 35 years old and proceeded to lead them to the conference finals with a Pro Bowl season. *Jeffrey E. Blackman*

standpoint on the players' part. I can't put aside what these players have accomplished."

Some of the players, though, were inconsolable.

"All I can think about right now is how close we were," cornerback Ray Mickens said. "We were so close. One more game to win and you go to 'The Show,' and now we have to start all over again. It's so tough to think about."

Quarterback Vinny Testaverde said, "I won't be satisfied until I win a championship. Everyone will say it's nice to close like we did, but this still hurts."

Added Martin: "We got here and didn't get the job done. It's all for naught if you don't make the Super Bowl. Hopefully, we can get back to this game and get to the Super Bowl."

Carl Banks said he'll never forget the sick look on Parcells' face as he boarded the team bus that night after the loss.

"Games like that are the ones that tear guys like Bill Parcells apart, because you fight so hard to get there and you see things start to turn for the worse," Banks said. "It was real tough to get that close and feel like you had a chance to really get it done, and things fall apart on you. When you look at the key breakdowns, they came from Byars, Curtis, Meggett. Those are the things that tear him apart, because his big thing is trust, and his go-to guys had breakdowns.

"That was absolutely one of the toughest losses on him. He'd rather get blown out and not be good enough than have the tools and be so close and have a lot of breakdowns from guys that he normally could depend on."

And with that, yet another potentially memorable moment in franchise history was nothing more than a tease.

WHAT NEXT?

That rise in 1998 and near-miss getting to the Super Bowl made the Jets instant favorites to make it to the big game in 1999. The team was intact and they were hungry. It all added up to an almost suffocating expectation.

The buildup led to the anticipated season opener against—of all teams—the Patriots. Giants Stadium was alive and buzzing with energy.

Almost as soon as the game began, though, the air was sucked from the building—and the Jets' season of promise—when quarterback Vinny Testaverde ruptured his left Achilles tendon and was lost for the year. The Patriots won that game 30–28 on a last-second field goal by Adam Vinatieri. From there the Jets would spiral, unable to wrest themselves from the shock of losing Testaverde, their leader

Third-string quarterback Ray Lucas took over the full-time starting job in mid-November 1999 and led the team to wins in six of the last eight games. He completed 80 percent of his passes (16-of-20) against the Bills in Week 10, and his nine-yard touchdown run put New York on the board first in the 17–7 Jets win at Giants Stadium. *Bill Kostroun/AP Images*

who was coming off a career year in 1998 (29 touchdown passes and only seven interceptions). The entire organization fell into a funk that lasted weeks.

"God plays in some of these games," Parcells said after the opener.

"Vinny is so durable, he's the type of player who usually gets right back up," running back Curtis Martin said. "When I saw him lying there for such a long time, I knew it was something serious. Things happen sometimes. We don't know why. But you'll hurt your brain trying to figure it out."

Following the loss to the Patriots, receiver Keyshawn Johnson cried while walking through the stadium tunnel.

"Not in a million years did I ever think I'd lose my starting quarterback for the season," Johnson said later. "Right now, I don't even know what the hell to say. . . . What can you do? You can't do shit. Nothing."

Not even Parcells, perhaps the greatest motivator of men in coaching history, could dig his players out of the funk. Parcells himself would later admit that it took him a little while to recover from the shock and that he didn't have a backup quarterback who was prepared to take over.

Rick Mirer, a disappointment in the NFL after being drafted highly out of Notre Dame, was the Jets' No. 2 quarterback, and it was clear pretty early on that Parcells had zero confidence in him. Ray Lucas, a former Rutgers quarterback and a Jersey native, was a favorite of Parcells, but he was an overachieving special teams player who wasn't really seen as an NFL quarterback.

Parcells went with Mirer, and the team won only one of its first seven games. They suffered another defeat at the wire, a 16–13 loss to the Colts at home in Week 6, and then fell to Oakland 24–23 when the Raiders scored a touchdown with less than 30 seconds left in the game.

After those two heartbreaking losses left the Jets at 1–6, Mirer led them to victory against Arizona. It was too little too late, and Parcells decided to switch to Lucas at quarterback. Lucas' passion and willingness to do anything for his team, even if it meant sacrificing his body, sparked a flame with the rest of the club.

The Jets won the first two games with Lucas under center, including a 24–17 win over the Patriots at Foxborough, and they closed out the season by winning their last four.

PARCELLS' DEPARTURE

WHEN BILL PARCELLS told his players after the 1999 season that he was retiring from coaching, he read a 1934 poem by Dale Wimbrow entitled "The Guy in the Glass." The poem, something he carried with him for years, addresses the idea of never lying to the guy you see every morning in the mirror.

When Parcells finished reading the poem, he quietly walked out of the silent locker room, leaving his players shocked, saddened, and at a loss for words.

"It was just very quiet," linebacker Dwayne Gordon said. "Everyone kind of looked at each other like, 'What do we do now?'"

"It was just like a moment of silence," safety Victor Green said. "We just sat there, maybe for a minute or so, feeling like, 'What do we do now?' It was a lot of emotions throughout the room. No one wanted to see this happen right now."

The following is the text of Parcells' version of the original poem, which he called, "The Man in the Glass":

Bill Parcells announces his retirement as Jets head coach at a press conference on January 3, 2000. *John Dunn/AP Images*

> When you get what you want in your struggle for self,
> And the world makes you king for a day,
> Just go to a mirror and look at yourself,
> And see what that man has to say.
>
> For it isn't your father, mother or wife,
> Whose judgment upon you must pass.
> The fellow whose verdict counts most in your life
> Is the one staring back from the glass.
>
> Some people may think you are a straight-shootin' chum
> And call you a wonderful guy,
> But the man in the glass says you're only a bum
> If you can't look him straight in the eye.
>
> He's the fellow to please, never mind all the rest,
> For he's with you clear up to the end,
> And you've passed your most dangerous, difficult test
> If the man in the glass is your friend.
>
> You may fool the whole world down the pathway of years,
> And get pats on the back as you pass,
> But your final reward will be heartaches and tears
> If you've cheated the man in the glass.

After telling his players of his plans, Parcells spoke to reporters. "I'm not coming back," he said. "You can write that on your chalkboard. There won't be any coaching rumors about Bill Parcells, because I've coached my last game."

Neither of those statements, of course, would be even close to the truth. Rumors of his return to coaching constantly surfaced, and in the end he did coach again, in Dallas from 2003 to 2006.

When Parcells stepped down from coaching, a number of his players knew he'd be back on the sidelines.

"He tried to stay out of Al Groh's way, but he came around to talk to certain players," defensive tackle Jason Ferguson said of the year Parcells was in the front office after he stopped coaching the Jets. "He'd get on you for bad habits, call you 'she.' You still felt like he was the head coach, really. It was like he never left when he was up in the office. You knew he was coming back. He just had to get his people together. I knew he wanted to coach again. He still had that desire."

Cornerback Ray Mickens recalled those moments while Parcells was in the front office when he'd show signs of wanting to coach again.

"He had the itch," Mickens said. "I remember him pulling me over to the side and coaching me up. Things like that and being visible were indications that he missed the game. For him to leave here and say he was never going to coach again, you really couldn't put all your apples in that basket. He really loves football and he missed it."

Speaking to the media just one day after being announced as the Jets' new head coach, Bill Belichick announces his resignation at the team facility at Hempstead, New York, on January 4, 2000. It was one of the most bizarre events for a franchise with no shortage of bizarre events in its history. *Al Pereira/Getty Images*

The 7–2 finish salvaged an 8–8 record in what was one of Parcells' best coaching jobs.

Unfortunately for the Jets and their fans, though, those were the last games Parcells would coach for the team. He opted to step away from the sideline after the 1999 season, saying he would never coach again.

"HC OF THE NYJ"

Parcells moved upstairs to become the president of the team, and he went with the obvious choice as his replacement for head coach. Bill Belichick was his top assistant dating back to their days together with the Giants, and it seemed this was his time to become a head coach.

What transpired on January 4, 2000, the day Belichick was to be introduced as the 14th head coach in franchise history, will go down as one of the most bizarre episodes in team history.

Belichick walked into the building that day, looking uncomfortable in the suit and tie he was wearing, and with something weighing heavily on his mind. Soon the whole world would know exactly what it was.

Minutes before Belichick was to step behind the podium in the Jets auditorium, which was standing-room-only packed, and be introduced as the new head coach, he quietly walked into Parcells' office and told him he was resigning. He also gave Jets President Steve Gutman a handwritten resignation note that was scrawled on a rumpled piece of paper. It read, in part, that he was "resigning as the hc of the nyj."

Belichick then went into the auditorium, stood behind the podium, and with a sheen of sweat on his brow, read his resignation note to stunned observers.

Jets fans had to deal with a lot of turmoil during the 2000 offseason, but the departure of wide receiver Keyshawn Johnson to Tampa didn't seem to upset these Jets supporters, shown at the NFL draft in April. *Manny Millan/Sports Illustrated/Getty Images*

It was magnificent theater, but it was one of the most embarrassing days for a franchise with countless embarrassing days.

"I feel like I'm making a decision based on circumstances and the situation as it is right now," Belichick said, referring to a looming change in ownership for the franchise. "The agreement that I made was with Mr. Hess, Bill Parcells, and Mr. Gutman and that situation has changed dramatically and it's going to change even further. There's going to be some point in time in the near future where the head coach would not be talking to John Hess and they may not be talking to Steve Gutman and we know they may not be speaking to Bill Parcells.

"If I'm letting anybody down I'm sorry, but the situation has changed and I have to do what's fair to everybody involved."

The fallout was, predictably, shock and anger.

"Parcells was angry," Carl Banks recalled. "That was the best word to describe it. Bill Parcells is a guy who does a lot for a lot of people. You'll never hear about it, but he puts a premium on helping people. He tries to help people that help him. He and Belichick had this relationship that was this whole Oscar-Felix thing for a while, but it probably shocked the hell out of Parcells because it wasn't discussed.

"In Parcells' mind, he said, 'Bill's a guy that deserves to be a head coach and I'm going to give him the opportunity right here.' Bill had his own way. He's not going to come up and hug you and kiss you on the cheek and say, 'Hey buddy, I love you and I'm going to make you my next head coach.' It was kind of unspoken in saying, 'You're the next guy.'

"But in the end, it was one of those deals where Belichick did his own soul-searching and decided he didn't want to do it. There were things about the organization that Belichick didn't like."

Cornerback Aaron Glenn said at the time, "Not that the situation is funny, but it is kind of funny. I think everyone has to wonder about themselves. A new owner is coming in now and no one knows what's going to happen. I don't think much stuff is crazy, but this is about the craziest thing I've seen."

Few were kind to Belichick, but the headline writers for the New York papers were vicious.

"Belichicken: Jets Better off without Quitter," was the *New York Post* headline. Another read: "Belichick Arnold."

Perhaps the harshest jab of all came from Gutman, who bordered on slanderous when talking about Belichick.

"Bill's conversation certainly tells me we should have some feelings of sorrow and regret for him and his family as he's obviously in some turmoil and I have to wish him the best with whatever the future holds for him," Gutman said. "I'm not a psychologist, but I think I just listened for an hour to a person who is in some turmoil and deserves our understanding and our consideration."

Belichick, who would eventually become the Patriots' head coach and forge record-setting success, kept his mouth shut about the situation for years until finally revealing his thoughts to the *New York Post* in 2004.

"I'm going to make one comment and we can close the book on it," Belichick said that day. "I can't think of anybody in professional sports—and certainly in my thirty years of professional football—who has said more and won less than Steve Gutman."

Belichick, explaining his decision not to take the Jets job, said the uncertainties that surrounded the franchise were a concern to him.

Selected fourth overall in the 1993 draft, linebacker Marvin Jones was one of the Jets' best high draft picks. Although he had some injury issues and never became a dominant force, Jones had a solid NFL career, playing 142 games for New York from 1993 to 2003. Nicknamed "Shade Tree," he had his best season in 2000, when he recorded a career-high 135 tackles. *Mitchell Layton/Getty Images*

"I knew I did the right thing and I didn't know where my career was going to go," Belichick said.

As shocking as Belichick's decision was, there were some in the organization who praised him for having the guts to make it.

"You've got to give him credit," said Banks, "because he was his own man, and a lot of coaches would never have stepped down on faith to say, 'Okay, I'm not working in the shadow. I've got to blaze my own trail.'"

Defensive end Rick Lyle said, "I remember being at the facility and watching the press conference and being

Jumbo Elliott, a 6-foot-7, 305-pound lineman, makes a lunging catch in the end zone with less than a minute to go in regulation against the Dolphins on October 23, 2000. The touchdown sent the game into overtime and catapulted the Jets to victory in the "Monday Night Miracle" at the Meadowlands. It was Elliott's first and only touchdown of his 14-year NFL career. *Bill Kostroun/AP Images*

shocked when he made the announcement that he was leaving. I remember saying, 'Good for him.' He knew he was going to face a lot of criticism from it, but he did it because it was best for his career and his family."

Linebacker Roman Phifer, who was watching the press conference from home, admitted to having reservations about the uncertainty of what would come next, but he too credited Belichick for making the tough decision. "You've got to take your hat off to him," said Phifer. "Maybe he had been under the shadow of Parcells for so many years, and sometimes you've got to spread your wings and go your own way. I felt like that's what he was doing."

ENTER AL GROH

Once the chaotic fallout from the Belichick resignation settled down, Al Groh, one of Parcells' most trusted assistants dating back to his days with the Giants, was hired as the hc of the nyj.

On the surface, it was a perfect transition. Groh was not only a good coach, but he was a people person, an intelligent man with terrific perspective, and he was from Long Island.

Hopes for a postseason berth in 2000 went out the window with the disappointing 34–20 loss to Baltimore in the season finale. Here tight end Anthony Becht (88) and guard Randy Thomas (77) leave the field after Chris McAlister's 98-yard interception return in the waning seconds of the first half gave the Ravens a 20–14 lead. *Doug Pensinger/Allsport/Getty Images*

It all looked good at the start of that 2000 season. The Jets won their first four games and six of their first seven. A year before, they were 1–6 and heading nowhere. Now they were 6–1 and a virtual shoo-in to make the playoffs.

That 6–1 start was punctuated by a stirring 40–37 overtime victory over the Miami Dolphins on a Monday night at Giants Stadium. The game, in which the Jets trailed 30-7 at halftime before engineering one of the greatest comebacks of all time, would become an instant classic. It was dubbed the "Monday Night Miracle."

Given the history of the teams and the heated Jets–Dolphins rivalry, it was somewhat fitting that the amazing comeback against Miami was followed by new drama for New York.

Six years earlier, the famous Dan Marino "fake spike" game marked the beginning of the end of the Jets' 1994 season. The "Monday Night Miracle" of 2000 was followed

by three straight losses for the Jets, putting their season of promise in peril. But they recovered to win three in a row after that, including another victory over the Dolphins and a 27–17 win over the Colts. With three games left to play, New York was 9–4, seemingly a lock for the playoffs.

You know what happens to the Jets and supposed locks, right?

The Jets proceeded to lose their next two games, to the Raiders and Lions, setting up a win-and-they're-in matchup in Baltimore on Christmas Eve in the regular-season finale. New York jumped out to a quick 14–0 lead on two first-quarter touchdown passes by Vinny Testaverde, but the Ravens rallied with 20 points in the second quarter. Baltimore eventually wrapped up the 34–20 victory, leaving the Jets at 9–7 for the year and out of the postseason picture.

The unraveling of the organization continued shortly after the end of the season. Just six days after the loss in

2000: A TURBULENT YEAR

HERE'S A LOOK at the unsettling series of events that took place with the Jets from January 2000 to January 2001:

- January 3, 2000: After three seasons and one division title, Bill Parcells retires from coaching but stays on as director of football operations. His retirement makes Bill Belichick the new head coach.

- January 4, 2000: The Bill Belichick era is over within 24 hours. In a bizarre press conference, Belichick resigns, citing a "number of uncertainties that would affect the head coach of the team."

- January 6, 2000: Belichick files a formal grievance against the Jets in an attempt to have his contract voided.

- January 11, 2000: Woody Johnson purchases the Jets from the estate of Leon Hess for $635 million.

- January 18, 2000: NFL owners unanimously approve the sale of the Jets to Johnson.

- January 21, 2000: NFL Commissioner Paul Tagliabue denies Belichick's grievance. Legally, Belichick is still an employee of the Jets.

- January 24, 2000: Al Groh is named head coach after three seasons as the Jets linebackers coach.

- January 24, 2000: Belichick's attorney, Jeffrey Kessler, asks for a temporary restraining order against the NFL in the hopes of allowing Belichick to become head coach and general manager of the New England Patriots.

- January 25, 2000: A federal court judge dismisses Belichick's motion for a temporary restraining order.

- January 27, 2000: Belichick is released from his Jets contract and signs a five-year deal with the Patriots that is worth some $15 million and includes autonomy on personnel decisions. The Jets receive a first-round draft pick in exchange.

- April 12, 2000: Groh trades wide receiver Keyshawn Johnson, arguably the team's best player, to the Tampa Bay Buccaneers for two first-round picks (13th and 27th overall in the 2000 draft).

- April 15, 2000: The Jets use their four first-round draft picks to select defensive linemen Shaun Ellis and John Abraham, quarterback Chad Pennington, and tight end Anthony Becht.

- September 3, 2000: The Al Groh era begins with a 20–16 win over the Packers in Green Bay.

- September 11, 2000: The Jets beat New England 20–19, leaving Groh 2–0 and Belichick 0–2.

- October 23, 2000: The Jets rally from a 23-point fourth-quarter deficit and beat the Dolphins 40–37 in overtime in the "Monday Night Miracle."

- December 24, 2000: The Jets blow a 14–0 first-quarter lead and lose to the Ravens 34–20 in Baltimore, capping a three-game losing streak that eliminates them from the playoffs. A win in any of the team's three losses to end the season would have qualified the Jets for the playoffs.

- December 30, 2000: Groh resigns from the Jets to take the head coaching job at Virginia.

- January 1, 2001: The Jets search for a fourth head coach in one year.

Baltimore, Groh announced that he was leaving the Jets to become head coach of his alma mater, the University of Virginia.

Groh's downfall as Jets coach was that he tried to become like Parcells rather than simply being himself. Groh's tough-guy act grew tired on players, who began to see through it and resent it.

It seemed that Groh, too, became tired of the rigors of being a head coach in the NFL. He entered the job as a very amicable man, always ready with an intelligent and pithy analysis or analogy or story for reporters, and he left beleaguered and beaten down by the relentless volume of media he had to deal with on a daily basis.

Bill Parcells' passion and fire—here directed at sideline judge Mike Pereira following a game in November 1997—provided a much-needed lift to a slumping organization. The Jets had posted a combined record of 22–58 in the five seasons prior to Parcells' arrival. They went 38–26 under Parcells and his protégé Al Groh from 1997 to 2000.
Hans Deryk/AP Images

THE PARCELLS LEGACY

For all the good things that Bill Parcells brought to the New York Jets organization, it is almost fitting that so much unrest took place under his watch, because Parcells has always been a restless soul of sorts, wandering from job to job all his life.

He had quit as head coach of Air Force after one year and took an assistant coach's job with the Giants in 1979. Then he quit after a few weeks because his wife didn't want to leave Colorado. He returned to football in 1980 (after selling real estate for a year) as an assistant with the Patriots. He rejoined the Giants in 1981 as an assistant and became head coach in 1983 after Ray Perkins resigned to take the University of Alabama job.

After he won his first Super Bowl in 1987, his agent, Robert Fraley (who later died in a plane crash with PGA Tour golf pro Payne Stewart), negotiated a deal for him to go to the Atlanta Falcons. Then NFL Commissioner Pete Rozelle stepped in and blocked the move because Parcells was still under contract with the Giants. Four years later, after winning another Super Bowl, Parcells quit the Giants on May 15, 1991, resigning for health reasons (he would later have three heart procedures).

After spending a year as a TV analyst, Parcells seemed ready to return in 1992 when his agent negotiated a deal for him to coach the Tampa Bay Buccaneers. At the last minute, Parcells backed out, leaving Tampa Bay's owner, Hugh Culverhouse, to say, "I was left at the altar."

Parcells went back to TV for a year and then took the Patriots' job in 1993, saying at the time that it would be his last career move. After his third season with New England, Parcells' relationship with Kraft became so strained that he wanted out. That's when he orchestrated his way to the Jets, whom he would eventually jilt before his contract was up by "retiring" again.

Following his three years as head coach of the Jets and another two as the team president, Parcells was lured out of "retirement" by the Dallas Cowboys, whom he would coach from 2003 to 2006.

One could argue that by leaving the sidelines after only three years without getting the team to the Super Bowl, Parcells didn't finish the job he started with the Jets. That perception bothered Parcells, because he took pride in where he left the franchise compared to where it was when he took over.

"It depends on what the expectations were," Carl Banks said. "I think he did as good a job as he could have done. . . . To say he didn't finish the job is one thing, but if he left the team in bad shape and then walked away from it, then you'd have a reason to be upset.

"You're probably better off celebrating the good times than dwelling on the moment that he left, because when he leaves he's got his own internal things that precipitate that."

What makes Banks' perspective unique is that he played under Parcells with the Giants and he worked under Parcells with the Jets coaching staff, so he had a keen knowledge of what it was like on both sides of the Hudson River.

"The Jets were always second-class citizens in New York," Banks said. "If we'd all be out in New York City at the same club, there was tension. You could see those guys [Jets players] had chips on their shoulders any time they were in the same place as us. It never got escalated to a brawl or anything like that, but you couldn't coexist with those guys without evil looks. I really don't think we had an arrogance about us, but any time we ran into those guys, we knew we owned the town."

Speaking of his impression of the Giants once he was with the Jets, Banks said he sensed the jealousy from the Jets.

"I'll tell you this much, the people in that [Jets] organization, excluding our [coaching] staff, hated the Giants," Banks said. "Anything that they could do that was different or better than what the Giants were doing, they wanted to do it. They were bent on being better than the Giants at something. There were some things that were so little, they probably didn't even cross the Giants' radar screen, but those were victories for those guys. Oh, I could see the jealousy."

That jealousy abated once Parcells came to the organization and restored pride and credibility.

"We didn't feel like second-class citizens as Jets then only because we had Bill Parcells and he was Mr. New York," Banks said. "Everyone that worked in the Jets organization

Although the Jets failed to achieve the ultimate goal of reaching the Super Bowl during Parcells' tenure, they did have three straight seasons without a losing record for the first time in three decades. Here the coach receives an ice-water dousing after clinching the AFC East title on December 19, 1998, the Jets' first division title since the merger. *Kevin Rivoli/ AP Images*

who was there before we came in with Bill and his coaching staff had more of a sense of pride than they had in the past.

"I'll tell you this much, the one thing that Bill Parcells brought to that organization that was certainly not there— and I can unequivocally say this—was a sense of pride. He never gave speeches to the non-football staff, but the way he went about his business, he led by example of how things should be run. Everyone in the organization started to walk around with a little more sense of pride and probably didn't feel as much like a second-class citizen the way they did before."

That, as much as anything, underscores the Parcells legacy with the Jets.

MVP Books Collection

MVP Books Collection

MVP Books Collection

"HELLO," HERMAN EDWARDS bellowed as if he were yelling through a forest of trees.

"You . . . play . . . to . . . win . . . the . . . game," Edwards ranted to reporters on an otherwise quiet October day in 2002 at the Weeb Ewbank Hall training facility, every word measured for affect.

Those six words might be what Herman Edwards, the 13th head coach in Jets history, is best known for during his five-year tenure with the team. But there was so much more to Edwards and what he did for the Jets. Leading them to the playoffs in three of his first four seasons is the most important thing. It might also be his most forgotten accomplishment, considering the way things ended for Edwards and the Jets—an ugly divorce following the 2005 season.

The detractors will say that Edwards won with the players the Bill Parcells regime left him. That, of course, is unfair because every new head coach inherits the players from the previous regime, and in fact, Edwards won with many players that he brought in.

Nevertheless, there will always be an all-too-large faction of Jets fans who will never give Edwards the respect he deserves. These fans conveniently forget that in each of the two seasons that the Jets failed to make the playoffs under his watch, they lost their starting quarterback for the year. In fact, the second time that happened, in Edwards' final season with the team in 2005, the Jets lost both their starter and backup in the same game in the third week of the season.

But back to "You play to win the game."

That fall day in late October 2002, the Jets were mired in last place in the AFC East Division with a 2–5 record, and they were about to embark on a road trip to San Diego to play the high-flying Chargers, who were 6–1 at the time. The team was also fresh off a 24–21 home loss to the Cleveland Browns in which the Jets blew a 21–3 lead. So nerves were frayed, and a reporter stirred a pot Edwards felt didn't need to be stirred.

Shown here in December 2002, Herman Edwards was an outspoken leader from the moment he took over as Jets head coach in 2001. Although he often doesn't receive full credit for the success, Edwards led the team to three postseason appearances—more than any coach in franchise history (through 2010). *Corey Sipkin/NY Daily News Archive/Getty Images*

The questioner innocently asked Edwards if he was concerned that one more loss might cause his players to lose their focus on the "carrot"—the prize at the end of the season of a playoff berth. Ten wins in an NFL season is somewhat of a magic number to make the playoffs. A loss in San Diego that upcoming Sunday would mean six losses, and that would mean the Jets would need to win out to get to 10 wins—a nearly impossible task.

Edwards took the reporter's question about the carrot to mean if he was worried that his players would quit on him, and it set him off.

"Oh no, they're not going to do that," Edwards said, beginning to show the angriest side of himself he had ever shown as Jets coach. "Not on my watch. It's inexcusable. Don't even think about it. It's called being a professional.

"They're going to conduct themselves that way [as professionals]. When I see they don't, everybody will know about

that. I will make that decision. That's unthinkable for me to even think that."

Edwards grew up as a perennial underdog, and he was not a quitter. He was not recruited as a player out of high school, and he signed with the Eagles in 1977 as an undrafted free agent before going on to have a long productive playing career. Edwards also was never afraid to express himself, to showcase his emotions. The mere suggestion that his players would quit on him if they lost the motivation of making the playoffs came as a personal affront to the coach.

"That's unthinkable to me, that you have an opportunity in your lifetime to be a professional, that you would think about quitting," Edwards said. "You don't quit in sports. You retire. You don't get to quit. It's not an option. I don't need to relay it to them. They know who their coach is. They know they've got no choice. When you lose, people start assuming they quit. This team ain't doing that.

The Jets got off to a rough start in 2002, and the fans didn't stick around long to watch. New York fell behind New England 37–7 and ultimately lost 44–7 in the home opener, kicking off a four-game losing streak. Coach Edwards led the team to a dramatic turnaround, as the Jets reached the playoffs despite a 1–4 start. *Al Bello/Getty Images*

Retirement? Yes. Quitting? No. You don't do that in sports. It's ridiculous."

This is where Edwards hit his crescendo.

"This is the greatest thing about sports—you play to win the game," he said. "Hello? You play to win the game. You don't play to just play it. When you start telling me it doesn't matter, then retire, get out, because it matters. This whole conversation bothers me big-time."

Edwards' words fired up his players, led by quarterback Chad Pennington.

"There's no way on the face of this earth this team is going to quit," Pennington said. "There's no doubt in my mind that we're going to keep fighting. Like I've said all year long, it's not over by any stretch of the imagination.

"I'm aware of the Jets' history, but that's what it is, history. We have to make our own history and we are going to make some of our own. I am really focused on putting our name on something and to do whatever it takes to make

people remember this team and how we turned it around. Until the door is totally slammed on us, doubt will never creep in. This is a free ticket for us to go out and have fun and play to the best of our abilities."

The unbridled passion Edwards showed that day may or may not have made a difference to the team's performance the rest of the season. Those kinds of intangibles are always impossible to measure. That's why they're called intangibles.

But the results on the field cannot be questioned. The Jets went to San Diego that Sunday and dismantled the cocky Chargers 44–13. They would lose only two more games the rest of the regular season, finish 9–7, and win the AFC East.

They routed the Colts 41–0 at home in the wild-card game and then lost to the Raiders in Oakland 30–10 in the divisional round. But the fact that the Jets got to the playoffs at all remains one of the most remarkable turnarounds in franchise history.

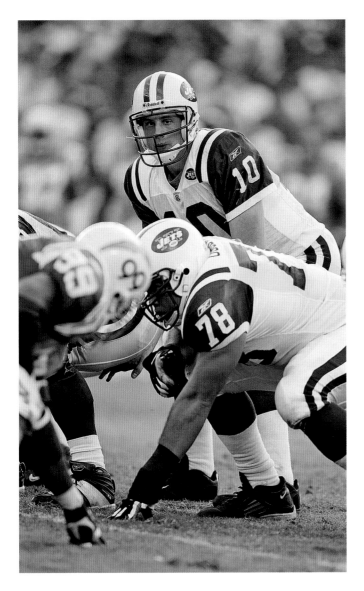

Chad Pennington helped rally the Jets behind their embattled coach, beginning with a decisive win over a dangerous San Diego Chargers team in Week 9 of the 2002 season.
Al Bello/Getty Images

A NEW BEGINNING

Bill Parcells and his disciples had led the Jets since 1997, so the hiring of Edwards on January 18, 2001, marked a major shift for the organization.

Edwards had no ties to Parcells. This was a fresh start, a new approach, and it was coming with not only a first-time NFL head coach, but a first-time head coach, period. Edwards, who had previously worked as an NFL scout, in personnel, and as an assistant coach, hadn't even been a head coach on the high school or college level.

Yet here he was, the fourth head coach in four years for a franchise that was starved for some stability after Al Groh had quit on them, Bill Belichick ran from the job, and Bill Parcells left the sidelines too early. All Edwards did was lead the Jets to a 10–6 record in his rookie season, a record good enough to earn the Jets a wild-card playoff berth—their first trip to the postseason in three years.

Edwards seemed to be the perfect package as a head coach for a number of reasons. A former NFL player, Edwards had been an undrafted cornerback who went on to play 10 seasons with the Philadelphia Eagles. He was highly disciplined, often talking about how his father, Herman Sr., an army man, would insist on "doing the corners" when preaching attention to detail.

Edwards had also been an assistant coach in the NFL, working his way up through the ranks with the Kansas City Chiefs, so he knew how every aspect of the NFL business worked. He also had terrific mentors, including Schottenheimer and Dick Vermeil, his former coach in Philadelphia.

"He has a personality that I think will play very well in New York," ESPN's Ron Jaworski, a former teammate of Edwards with the Eagles, said when Edwards was hired. "People want a guy that's dynamic. Herman is dynamic. Dom Capers [another candidate for the Jets job at the time] is a tremendous football coach, but his personality wouldn't have fit in New York. Herm is the kind of guy New Yorkers are really going to enjoy. What you see is what you get. His personality is right on his sleeve. . . . That's the beauty of Herman Edwards."

Jaworski also praised Edwards' ability to relate to people.

"Herm was always one of those guys who was the consummate team guy," Jaworski went on. "He was an overachiever as a player. He was never the quickest, never the fastest, never the strongest, never the smartest. But no one was going to outwork him. He made himself a player. And I think he's going to make himself a fine head coach."

Marty Schottenheimer, the Chargers head coach at the time and a mentor of Edwards, had endured a similar slump while coaching the Washington Redskins the year before, when they started 0–5 but finished 8–8. He heard Edwards' words the week leading up to their game together and knew where they were coming from—Edwards' heart.

"I always thought Herman had a good pulse of the players and did an excellent job of teaching," Schottenheimer said. "I know Herman is as tough-minded and strong-willed as any coach I've been around. He is a great communicator. Herman knows what works and will continue to be patient."

FENCE CLIMBER

BILL PARCELLS HAD MADE his presence felt right away when he arrived at Weeb Ewbank Hall for the first time and saw reporters hanging out in the parking lot. Parcells cursed and scowled at the handful of ink-wretched scribes and snoopy television reporters and promised that he was going to change things around there.

He wasn't kidding. Parcells had fences with locked gates built all around the facility, precluding anyone from gaining access to the team parking lot through the press room or from the outside unless they were let in by his security personnel.

He also brought in a director of security named Steve Yarnell, a former FBI agent with a supposedly intimidating 24-hour scowl on his face. Yarnell was in charge of locking the world out. Reporters and employees in the building often half-joked that Yarnell had rooms bugged and that he sat in his eye-in-the-sky office upstairs watching everyone's move on a series of television monitors.

Yarnell was also Parcells' personal bodyguard, like a secret service agent attached to the president of the United States, never leaving Parcells' side when he roamed in public. The whole thing was quite a bit over the top.

When Herman Edwards arrived as the new head coach, he must have looked at Yarnell in an odd way, certainly not needing a bodyguard but still tolerating Yarnell's presence. Edwards was a much more grounded regular-guy type than Parcells, who had become somewhat a caricature of himself as his success built.

One day, however, Yarnell's high-tech, intricate security system got under Edwards' skin.

An early riser who was often inside the team facility by 4 or 4:30 in the morning to work out and begin his day, Edwards arrived early one rainy morning in September 2003, the opening week of that regular season, and found himself locked out. He punched his personal code into the keypad that controlled the front gate, and nothing happened. The gate did not move.

Edwards, annoyed, got out of his car and climbed the six-foot-tall, barbed-wire-topped fence.

"I came to work and I thought, 'That's odd. Did they fire me already? They didn't let me get to the season yet,'" Edwards joked. "It's the first place I ever came to that they didn't want me to come to work. That's how the day started."

After the incident, Edwards decided he would boycott the reserved lot for coaches, players, and team personnel and instead park several hundred yards away in one of the Hofstra University student lots.

Edwards had one of the maintenance people remove the "Reserved, Head Coach" sign that stands in the parking space right in front of the players' and coaches' entrance. (Edwards joked that the Jets never personalized that parking sign because they've had so many head coaches over the years.) He later told his players that the spot was open for whoever arrived first each day.

Once the players arrived, Edwards told them in a fiery team meeting of the inconvenience he experienced that morning. With both reporters and players in attendance, Edwards never named Yarnell by name, but he was clearly annoyed by the over-the-top Stalag 17 security that he felt was unnecessary.

"Parcells would have probably just run his car through the fence," cornerback Ray Mickens said. "He seemed mad, but what he was saying was funny. I didn't know whether to laugh or be serious. Now you're keeping your own people out. I'm glad it happened to the head man. It's happened to me a couple of times, but with the little guy nobody cares."

"He was pretty upset," center Kevin Mawae said. "It's a shame when you can't come to work. There used to be a time around here when they didn't let you leave."

Vermeil, the man whom Edwards credited most for mentoring him, knew exactly what the Jets were getting in Edwards.

"He'll give it everything he's got . . . and then just a little more," Vermeil said. "People will respect him and care for him, because he will respect them and care for them. He was very special then [as a player] and has never stopped being very special. What you see is what you get; what you hear is what he is. He's not going to fill you full of baloney."

Wayne Chrebet, who was driving in his car somewhere in New Jersey listening to Edwards on the live broadcast of the press conference announcing his hiring, said he was ready to suit up in his pads right then and there.

"I was listening to it on the radio in my car, and he made me want to strap on my helmet, stop the car, get out, and start hitting things," Chrebet recalled. "He's definitely motivational."

Edwards was, indeed, highly motivational. That, above all, was his best gift. But he was also very perceptive. Although few knew much about him when the Jets hired him, Edwards was very in tune with the Jets and their tortured history.

Herman Edwards addresses his team at training camp at Hofstra University before the 2001 season, Edwards' first as head coach. *Ed Betz/AP Images*

"When you look at the history of the Jets, you always knew they had some good players," Edwards said. "You fall back into the Joe Namath era and the Sack Exchange and when John Riggins was here. Then you look back at what they've done and you go, 'Whoa.' Their history was more a series of snapshots and vignettes than it was of winning championship after championship, because when you look at the history, that hasn't happened around here a whole lot."

He noted that, when he was a player, the Jets were a good team but not consistent playoff contenders.

"The perception of the organization's success or lack thereof is a little bit larger than the reality," Edwards went on, "and it's due to the fact that they're in New York. Everything you do [in New York] is either very, very good or very, very bad. There's no in-between."

Edwards also recognized that he was coming into a situation where Parcells had instilled a winning attitude with the Jets, and the burden was on him to keep that tradition alive while establishing his own approach and philosophy.

"The first thing I tried to do was make people understand that teams win, individuals don't," he said. "I wanted to establish my philosophy and let everyone in the building know that they're all needed for us to win. I really didn't want to go back into the past a whole lot.

"My philosophy is to learn from the past but live in the future. I don't dwell on the past. I know the Jets have felt like second-class citizens in New York for years. The Jets were the team that came out of the AFL, so you knew they were going to be the red-headed stepchild of the NFL."

The challenge for Edwards and anybody in the Jets organization looking to overcome that inferiority complex was to win. "Winning solves all the problems," he said. "That's what it does, and we all know that."

Edwards said he could feel the pressure the Jets players were under because the only championship in franchise history had been all the way back in 1969.

"Every year without a championship, you know the pressure mounts, and it's really unfair at times to the younger

Laveranues Coles dives into the end zone with one of his two touchdowns against the Dolphins on October 14, 2001. In addition to adding to his team-high eight receiving touchdown for the year, Coles helped the Jets rally back from a 17–0 halftime deficit to defeat Miami 21–17 at Giants Stadium. *Keith Torrie/NY Daily News Archive/Getty Images*

Defensive end John Abraham tallied 13 sacks in 2001 and earned selection as a first-team All-Pro. He also made three Pro Bowl appearances in four years on a steadily improving Jets defense in the early 2000s. *Chuck Solomon/Sports Illustrated/Getty Images*

players that come into this organization," he said. "They're forced to deal with the history of the franchise and it's not their history. I try to tell players, 'Our history is our history and what we're going to try to do when we're here.'

"Every season is a microcosm of other seasons the Jets have had in the past. It's people's mind-set, what people think is going to happen.

"As a coach here in New York, you're constantly fighting that and trying to make the players in the locker room realize, 'Guys, that has nothing to do with us. If you listen to it and you believe it, it'll have something to do with you, but it really doesn't have anything to do with you.'"

Edwards did win with the Jets, but he never won that elusive championship for them.

9/11/2001

Almost immediately into Edwards' tenure as Jets head coach, he and his team faced significant adversity: September, 11, 2001, the day the World Trade Center and Pentagon were attacked.

The attacks came two days after Edwards' first game as the Jets head coach, a 45–24 loss to the Indianapolis Colts. The thought of conducting sporting events in the immediate aftermath of the attacks was unthinkable, and the NFL did the right thing by canceling the games the weekend afterward. The league's decision to cancel the games had a lot to do with Edwards and the Jets as well as the Giants, Yankees, and Mets.

Jets quarterback Vinny Testaverde, whose late father, Al, a mason, had helped build the World Trade Center, was

Defensive tackle James Reed (93), quarterback Vinny Testaverde (16), and punter Tom Tupa (7) observe the pre-game ceremony honoring those who died during the terrorist attacks of September 11, 2001. In their first post-9/11 game, the Jets defeated the Patriots at Foxboro Stadium on September 23. *Ezra Shaw/Allsport/Getty Images*

resolute about not playing the following weekend. He held a team meeting and found complete support. The Jets were not going to play even if the games weren't canceled.

"I think all the games should be canceled this week; I don't think anyone wants to play this week," Testaverde said. "We've never, in our lifetimes, seen anything like this in this country. What happened is a threat to everybody in America. We've been violated.

"For me being a New Yorker, I'm still waiting on calls that I know I'm going to get that family of friends were in those buildings. Playing football is not what you want to be doing. You want to be mourning the loss of those people and be with your family."

Jets center Kevin Mawae, another leader in the locker room, supported Testaverde's stance.

"It's hard to say we should be playing," Mawae said. "People in this locker room have neighbors missing. Our children's friends don't have moms and dads anymore. As far as this locker room is concerned, it's going to be hard to have us play. It's hard to concentrate. Football is probably the least important thing in the world right now."

The Jets had no intention of playing regardless of whether the games were canceled. Fortunately, the league canceled the games.

"I would've lost respect for anyone who tried to force us to play," running back Curtis Martin said. "It would've been disrespectful. There's nothing they could've said to me that would've legitimized it. That would've been one time you saw Curtis Martin rebel."

"This is America," Testaverde said. "We mourn, we comfort, and we come together. After a period of time, we get back to a normal way of life. It would be hard for us to fly out of LaGuardia and look at that smoke and rubble as we take off, knowing there's people buried in there and people dead in there."

Another shaken player was Chrebet, who lost a friend who was working on the 104th floor of the North Tower. Offensive guard Kerry Jenkins witnessed the horror up close, from the roof of his girlfriend's East Village apartment building in Manhattan.

"I saw more than I needed to see," Jenkins said.

The emotional Edwards, his eyes moistening, said, "We're not robots. You can't plug us in and say, 'Go play.' These players are human beings just like everybody else."

Paying homage to his father, Testaverde visited "Ground Zero" and spoke to firefighters and rescue workers who were still trying to dig out possible survivors.

"I felt their pain," Testaverde recalled. "It was just amazing to see a group of people, men and women, come together from across the country, but mostly from our area right here, and see how committed they were trying to save lives. You

The tragedy of 9/11 brought together even the bitterest of enemies on the football field. Following their game on September 23, members of the Jets and Patriots gathered at midfield for a prayer. *Ezra Shaw/Allsport/Getty Images*

could see their heads were hanging, their morale was low. They hadn't saved anybody and that was their purpose for going down there. I just wanted to go down and tell them, 'Thanks for all your efforts and thanks for being so brave. Stay healthy, stay strong, and keep hope alive.'"

Three days after Testaverde made his own visit to Ground Zero, Edwards took the entire team there to do some volunteer work, helping the Red Cross unload tons of bottled water and other beverages.

"After witnessing some of the things I saw, you can't understand or get a feel for the magnitude of the destruction down there and what it's done, not only to the buildings but to the people and their way of living," Testaverde said.

Testaverde told a story of a man coming up to him in church and informing him that his brother had died in the building. "He asked me if I could get him an autographed football from the team because his brother was a big Jets fan

and he wanted to leave something to his daughter in memory of him," Testaverde said. "It's just chilling."

Testaverde, Edwards, and the rest of the Jets would resume their season the following week, returning to the field in New England to play the Patriots on September 23, but the memory of 9/11 was still fresh, the emotions still raw.

The Jets beat the Patriots 10–3 that day. As they filed into the visitors' locker room, they were greeted with hugs and high-fives from team owner Woody Johnson. Once the entire Jets family was together in the locker room and the doors were closed, Edwards emerged with the game ball in his hands and told the players it was going to the city of New York.

"It was pretty quiet and there were some pretty teary eyes," Jets linebacker James Darling recalled. "Everyone was just sitting there thinking about what that meant. It was pretty deep."

The patriotism and emotion continued at the Jets' first post-9/11 home game. Wayne Chrebet came out of the tunnel for introductions wearing an FDNY cap and waving an American flag. *Howard Earl Simmons/NY Daily News Archive/Getty Images*

BAY AREA DRAMA

It can only be viewed as coincidence, but for some odd reason, the Jets—during the Edwards era—seemed to play the Oakland Raiders an inordinate amount of times for a team not in their division.

Edwards grew up in the Bay Area, some two hours south of Oakland in Seaside, California, and he went to the University of California-Berkeley. He was even a Raiders fan growing up.

The Jets not only played the Raiders six times in Edwards' five years as their coach, but the matchup factored in some of the most dramatic moments of his time in New York. Two of the games were playoff games, and one was a regular-season finale that determined the Jets' playoff hopes.

The teams' first meeting was perhaps the most dramatic.

The Jets were coming off a terrible 14–9 home loss to a struggling Buffalo Bills team the week before, and they went to Oakland on January 6, 2002, needing to beat the Raiders to qualify for the playoffs. The Jets won the game 24–22 on a 53-yard field goal by kicker John Hall in the final seconds to earn a wild-card playoff spot. Their opponent for the playoff opener the following week? The Oakland Raiders.

"We shocked the world today," right guard Randy Thomas yelled throughout the locker room after the season-finale win.

Edwards said he asked Hall before the field goal attempt, "Can you make it?"

Hall said, "I can make it."

"When he hit it, he hit it," Edwards said. "That thing looked like it was going to go out of the stadium when he hit it."

Testaverde told Hall it was the biggest kick he had ever been around in his career.

A few days before the game, the *New York Post* had run a column saying they had no chance to win in Oakland after the bad loss to the Bills. The back page headline read: "Stick a Fork in Them."

In the locker room after the game, as the jubilant players were getting ready to fly back to New York, backup quarterback Chad Pennington—who hadn't started a game that year, much less played a down that counted—burst from the shower and instigated his teammates in a rant against me in the locker room over the reporter who wrote the column in the *Post*.

"Stick a fork in them, stick a fork in them," Pennington yelled, mimicking the headline. "What do you have to say about that now?"

Chrebet called returning to the field "the first step in getting back to our normal lives," adding, "This touches a lot of people. If you don't feel it, you don't have a heart."

Edwards said, "We needed this for a lot of different reasons. We needed a win like this, one that was in doubt, that was a struggle. This tests your will and belief. This team accepted the challenge."

Edwards then looked at the football he was clutching in the air and said with emotion, "This is going to the city of New York, for all of those people that have worked to try to save lives and all of those who lost their lives. It's only fitting that this ball goes to them."

The game-winning, 53-yard field goal by John Hall in the waning seconds of the 2001 season finale at Oakland carried the Jets into the playoffs and heated up the brewing rivalry between the Jets and Raiders that developed during Herman Edwards' tenure. *John G. Mabanglo/AFP/Getty Images*

The Jets returned to Oakland a mere six days after their dramatic 24–22 win. This time, the result was quite different, a 38–24 beating at the hands of the Raiders. Oakland's veteran receiving corps, led by Jerry Rice, schooled the Jets defense. Rice caught nine passes for 183 yards and a touchdown.

"It was like volleyball—back and forth, back and forth—and we couldn't stop them," Edwards said.

"This is the worst way to end the season," said Curtis Martin, who ran for more than 1,500 yards during the regular campaign. "You don't come to the playoffs just to come to the playoffs. You come to get to the Super Bowl. And when it doesn't happen, you have to deal with the bitter end. That's what we're dealing with now."

LAVERANUES COLES

RECEIVER

2000–2002, 2005–2008

A THIRD-ROUND PICK in 2000, Laveranues Coles was somewhat of an afterthought that year since the Jets drafted four players in the first round. Coles had gotten into trouble as a student-athlete at Florida State University, which caused his stock to drop.

But Coles grew into one of the Jets' most respected and dependable players. He finished his career with 674 catches, 8,609 yards, and 49 touchdowns. He went to the Pro Bowl in 2003 as a member of the Redskins, for whom he played between two stints with the Jets.

A multi-sport star in high school in Jacksonville, Florida, Coles was recruited to play football at FSU, where he would eventually run into trouble. In September 1999, during his senior season, Coles and teammate Peter Warrick were arrested for shoplifting. The following month, he pleaded guilty to misdemeanor petty theft and was kicked off the football team.

Coles had many memorable plays and games for the Jets, but perhaps the most memorable was his first career touchdown catch, which came in the "Monday Night Miracle" victory against the Dolphins on October 23, 2000.

He was released by the Jets in February 2009 and signed with Cincinnati, where he played one season. The Jets brought him back for training camp in 2010, but he was released.

"I think I'm done," Coles said after the release. "I don't want to become one of those journeyman football players. I don't need the money. I had fun, though. I was able to finish my career as a Jet. That was the main thing. That means a lot to me."

In his second season as a pro, Laveranues Coles emerged as the Jets' go-to receiver, compiling a team-best 59 receptions and 868 receiving yards in 2001. In the wild-card playoff loss to the Raiders, he caught eight passes for a season-high 123 yards. *Harry How/Getty Images*

The fans were back in full force at Giants Stadium when the Jets took on the Colts in the wild-card playoff game on January 4, 2003. New York's 41–0 victory gave the sellout crowd plenty to cheer about. *Al Bello/Getty Images*

New York couldn't get much going against Oakland in the second round of the playoffs in January 2003. The Jets' only touchdown was a one-yard pass to backup fullback Jerald Sowell, his only catch in the game. Two interceptions and two lost fumbles didn't help the Jets' cause, as they lost 30–10. *Howard Earl Simmons/NY Daily News Archive/Getty Images*

Incredibly, the Jets would play the Raiders twice again in the 2002 season, once in the regular season and once in the playoffs.

New York started the 2002 season 1–4, with the only win coming in overtime against a mediocre Bills team. But after a bye in Week 6, the Jets won five of the next six, including the inspiring win over the dangerous Chargers following Edwards' "You play to win the game" speech. The 6–5 Jets then headed to Oakland with a chance to seize first place in the AFC East with a win. The Jets fell to the Raiders 26–20, forcing them to make a serious late-season run to make the playoffs.

"It gets to the point where we really can't breathe," tight end Anthony Becht said. "We're in a do-or-die situation every week. It's to the point of the year where we've got to win every game. We've got to overcome everything."

The Jets won three of their last four games in the regular season and earned a second consecutive playoff berth under Edwards. In their final six wins, the Jets outscored their opponents by an average score of 30–14, this after giving up an average of more than 32 points through the first five games of the season.

They rolled to a 41–0 win over the Indianapolis Colts in the opening playoff game, as Pennington went 19-of-25 for 222 yards and three touchdowns while the Jets defense held the Colts' Peyton Manning to 14-for-31 passing and two interceptions. Jets running back Lamont Jordan compiled 102 yards on the ground compared to a total of 52 yards rushing by the entire Colts team.

Eight days later, they went back to Oakland for a divisional playoff showdown exactly one year to the day—January 12—after their playoff game the previous season. This time, they lost 30–10 to the Raiders, ending yet another season in Oakland.

The Jets gained a bit of revenge on the Raiders the following season, beating them 27–24 in overtime, though this was a regular-season game during a season in which the Jets went 6–10 with no hope for a playoff berth.

The teams faced each other once more in the Edwards era, a 26–20 Jets win on December 11, 2005, at Giants Stadium. It was Edwards' second-to-last win as New York's head coach.

CHANGING OF THE GUARD AT QUARTERBACK

Chad Pennington, who was one of four first-round draft picks for the Jets in 2000, became the starting quarterback in

Veteran Vinny Testaverde didn't much appreciate getting benched in favor of the young Chad Pennington back in 2002, but Pennington's frequent injuries gave Testaverde ample opportunity to show he still had it, even in his 40s. *Bill Kostroun/AP Images*

2002. After three consecutive dreadful losses—44–7 to New England, 30–3 at Miami, and then 28–3 at Jacksonville—Edwards decided to take a chance, benching Vinny Testaverde in favor of Pennington.

"We're all held accountable, but I think the quarterback is the guy that always takes the hit first, and Vinny understood that," Edwards said. "It's not on Vinny at all. I think it's just the way we've performed."

Players were torn about the decision because Testaverde was such a popular figure.

"Everybody was shocked and some people probably were disturbed," nose tackle Jason Ferguson said. "We've been behind Vinny all this time and now he gets sat down. It wasn't really him. It's the whole team. He's just the first one to take the blow."

Testaverde didn't like the move, feeling that he could still help the team win games, but because he prided himself on being the good soldier, he didn't complain.

"I'm not going to sit here and tell you I'm getting a raw deal, because that will be the headline," Testaverde said.

CHAD PENNINGTON

QUARTERBACK
2000-2008

BORN JAMES CHADWICK PENNINGTON in Knoxville, Tennessee, to a football coach father named Elwood, Chad Pennington was destined to play football.

Resilience defined Pennington's career, as evidenced by his two NFL Comeback Player of the Year Awards, won in 2006 and 2008. He also finished second in the league MVP voting to Peyton Manning in 2008.

Pennington went to college at Marshall, where he started out as the fourth-string quarterback in 1995 and was slated to be red-shirted. He went on to lead the team to the NCAA Division I-AA Football Championship Game. Pennington set school records in several passing categories, finishing his career at Marshall with 1,026 completions, a 63.4 completion percentage, 13,423 yards, 115 touchdowns, and only 45 interceptions.

After his standout collegiate career, he was drafted by Bill Parcells and the Jets in the first round, 18th overall, in 2000. Pennington made only three appearances during his first two seasons, but he finally took over for Vinny Testaverde in the fifth game of the 2002 season, and he never looked back.

Pennington helped turn the 1–4 Jets into division champs with a 9–7 record. Despite playing less than a full season in 2002, he threw for 3,120 yards with 22 touchdowns and six interceptions, earning him a league-best 104.2 passer rating, which set a team record.

In every season that Pennington stayed healthy and was able to play at least most of the year, he led the Jets to the playoffs. In the years he was injured (2003, 2005, and 2007), the Jets failed to make the playoffs.

Pennington returned from his 2005 shoulder injury to become Eric Mangini's starter, and he started all 16 games for the first time in his career. He took advantage by setting then-career highs in completions (313), pass attempts (485), and passing yardage (3,352) and leading the Jets to a 10–6 record and another postseason trip.

When he led the Jets to a wild-card playoff game in New England after that season, he became the Jets' all-time leader in postseason starts by a quarterback with five.

The 2007 season was a difficult one for Pennington, and it ended up being his last in New York. In the first game of the season, against the Patriots, Pennington suffered a high ankle

Chad Pennington assumed the starting quarterback job in Week 5 of the 2002 season and went on to lead the NFL in completion percentage while carrying the Jets to the postseason. *Ron Antonelli/NY Daily News Archive/Getty Images*

sprain that kept him out of the next game and nagged him for a while.

Mangini benched Pennington after the 1–7 start and went with Kellen Clemens. After Mangini announced entering training camp of 2008 that there would be a competition for the starting quarterback job between Pennington and Clemens, the Jets acquired Brett Favre and released Pennington.

Although he was often criticized for his lack of arm strength, Pennington, when healthy, was able to consistently lead his team to success because of his highly accurate arm and brilliant game-management skills.

MVP Books Collection

Offensive coordinator Paul Hackett (left) took the brunt of the fan and media abuse about the team's offensive shortcomings in the early 2000s. On one particular morning after an injury to Chad Pennington forced Vinny Testaverde into the starting role, Hackett was greeted by the following voicemail message: "Hey Hackett, I hope you learned something last year. Testaverde can't run the West Coast offense. Get yourself a new offense." Then the person hung up. *Mike Albans/NY Daily News Archive/Getty Images*

HERMAN EDWARDS COACHING CHART

HERMAN EDWARDS is the only Jets coach to reach the playoffs in each of his first two seasons. Here's a look at how Edwards' two-year mark compares to other Jets coaches:

Coach	Years	Regular-Season Record	Playoff Appearances
Bill Parcells	1997–1998	21–11 (.656)	1
Herman Edwards	2001–2002	19–13 (.594)	2
Sammy Baugh	1960–1961	14–14 (.500)	0
Bruce Coslet	1990–1991	14–18 (.438)	1
Joe Walton	1983–1984	14–18 (.438)	0
Weeb Ewbank	1963–1964	10–16–2 (.393)	0
Walt Michaels	1977–1978	11–19 (.367)	0
Rich Kotite	1995–1996	4–28 (.125)	0

"Anybody in my position isn't happy about it. Understand that I don't want to be a distraction for this football team. I understand how the process works.

"When I was in Cleveland, I asked [head coach Bill] Belichick, 'Why are you making me the scapegoat in all this?' His words were: 'I can't change the left guard and get a spark. I have to change the quarterback to get something going.' That's the reality of the situation."

The young Pennington talked tough when he got the job, surely an effort to gain the respect of the locker room.

"Talk is cheap," Pennington said. "We're going to get the ball into the end zone. I'm not focused on how pretty it looks, how many completions I have, how many touchdown passes I throw. It's about putting points on the board and helping the Jets win."

He did just that. After losing his first game as the starter—a 29–25 loss to Kansas City when the Chiefs scored in the final minute—Pennington led the Jets to eight wins in their last 12 games and into the playoffs. He threw 22 touchdown passes and only six interceptions in his first starting duty while completing a league-best 68.9 percent of his passes. He would remain the starter until the Jets released him before the 2008 season after they acquired Brett Favre.

Unfortunately for Pennington, his career was as defined by all the injuries he suffered as by all the good things he did on the field. Before his career was over, he had undergone three shoulder surgeries. Pennington's string of injuries began when he shattered his right wrist while being tackled by Giants linebacker Brandon Short in a 2003 preseason game following his eye-opening first season as a starter.

"All of our hearts stopped," Martin recalled about the injury. "Chad is an integral part of this team, and for him to go down scared everyone."

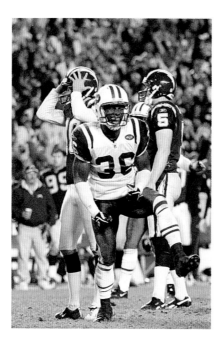

Cornerback David Barrett celebrates after Chargers kicker Nate Kaeding—in the background holding his head in disbelief—missed a potential game-winning field goal in overtime of the Chargers-Jets playoff game on January 8, 2005, in San Diego. The Jets went on to win 20–17 on Doug Brien's 28-yard kick—although he would face a very different fate the following weekend in Pittsburgh. *David Drapkin/Getty Images*

Doug Brien yells with frustration after missing a field goal in the closing minutes of the AFC divisional playoff game against the Pittsburgh Steelers at Heinz Field on January 15, 2005. He missed another one less than two minutes later, and the Steelers went on to win 20–17 in overtime. *Ron Antonelli/NY Daily News Archive/Getty Images*

With the game still in progress, Pennington was rushed to Lenox Hill Hospital in Manhattan, where he was operated on by Jets orthopedists Dr. Elliott Hershman and Dr. Ken Montgomery. Pennington missed the first six games of the 2003 season. The Jets, who went 2–4 in his absence, never recovered, finishing 6–10.

Although he would suffer a season-ending shoulder injury in 2005, Edwards' last season as coach, Pennington was healthy enough in 2004 to lead the Jets to a 6–1 start. He was sidelined during a subsequent loss to the Bills and missed the next three starts, but he returned to the field for the final five games of the season. They went 2–3 in those games—including losses to the 15–1 Steelers and 14–2 Patriots—but the team's 10–6 final record was good enough for a wild-card spot in the playoffs, the Jets' third postseason appearance in Edwards' first four years on the job.

That season was the closest Edwards would get to the promised land of a championship game as head coach.

AIN'T THAT A KICK?

After a scintillating 20–17 overtime wild-card victory over the favored Chargers in San Diego, the Jets went to the 2004 AFC divisional playoff in Pittsburgh, where they would face the top-seeded Steelers, who were a nine-point favorite.

Few outside the New York locker room gave the Jets much of a chance to upset the powerful Steelers. Yet the Jets not only played the Steelers toe-to-toe, they dictated the action in that January 15, 2005, game, and they should have won and advanced to the AFC Championship Game had it not been for kicker Doug Brien, who was uncharacteristically errant that day.

Brien missed two field goals he usually would have made, and the Jets lost to the Steelers by the exact 20–17 overtime score by which they had won the previous week, when Brien made the game-winning 28-yard field goal in San Diego.

Brien had two chances to win the Steelers game in the final two minutes of regulation and put the Jets one game away from only their second Super Bowl in franchise history,

In the second quarter of the playoff game against the Steelers, Santana Moss' 75-yard punt return for a touchdown tied the game 10–10. Moss returned five punts and caught four passes in the game. He left New York after the season and became a Pro Bowl receiver for the Redskins in 2005. *David Drapkin/Getty Images*

and he missed both. The first miss came from 47 yards out with 1:58 left when the ball hit the crossbar and bounced back. The second came from 43 yards away as time expired at the end of regulation. The kick went wide left.

Steelers kicker Jeff Reed ended the Jets' third consecutive overtime game (they had defeated the St. Louis Rams in OT in their regular-season finale) when he kicked a 33-yard field goal 11 minutes into overtime.

Brien, an 11-year veteran, had converted 24 of 29 field goals that season and had been virtually automatic from inside 45 yards. He entered that game in Pittsburgh having missed only two field goals between 40 and 50 yards over the previous two seasons. In fact, he had entered the game as the 10th-most accurate kicker in NFL history, having connected on nearly 82 percent of his career field goal attempts.

None of those statistics mattered by game's end that day in Pittsburgh, where Jets dreams died hard.

"I thought it was in," Brien said after the game about his first field goal attempt. "I was really surprised. I thought I hit it really well. It must have been the wind. The second one, I tried to over-kick it. I tried to hit it too hard. The second one I missed. The first one didn't go in.

"I just feel bad for the team. I'll be fine. I feel bad for the guys who played so well and played so hard and we came up short."

There was a feeling of devastation inside the Jets locker room, but the players didn't blame Brien.

"It's like somebody just ripped something out of you," defensive end Shaun Ellis said. "It was right there. We were ready to come in the locker room. We knew he was going to make it [both times]."

Martin said, "There is blood out there on the field that's ours. We played our hearts out. I've never been this angry. You realize it's more than a game. You take it personal. This is the worst way to end the season."

But Martin, the spiritual leader of the team, found himself feeling for Brien despite the bitter disappointment.

"You hear stories about how people carry around a burden like this all their life," Martin said. "I heard about some guy who had been retired for 40 years and was still thinking about a kick or something like that. I feel for the guy [Brien]. I really feel for him. It wasn't his fault. Just like we win as a team, we also lose as a team."

Edwards praised his team.

"I thought our guys battled," he said. "I told my players not to put their heads down. I thought they competed and had some shots to win the game and we didn't do it. It'll be a long offseason and we will have to deal with that.

"Doug has been a good kicker for us," Edwards went on. "It was just a tough day. We had our shots to win, and we didn't do it."

Brien said, "This is hard. It's going to take a long time to get over it."

He described the moment as "being at the wrong place at the wrong time," adding, "Everything kind of came together in about as bad a way as it can. The hard thing is to end the season on that. Normally, you get a chance to go out the next week and make up for it—and I always have.

"But now there won't be a next chance. I wish I would have gotten a chance to redeem myself to Jets fans and my teammates."

Brien would never get a shot at redemption, because that second miss in Pittsburgh proved to be his last NFL kick. Three months later, the Jets drafted Ohio State's Mike Nugent in the third round, making him the fourth-highest picked kicker in NFL draft history.

Brien, who had an 83.6-percent field goal success rate (51-of-61) in his two seasons with the Jets, was released a short time later. It's unfair that Brien will forever be remembered by Jets fans for those two misses inside the final two minutes in Pittsburgh. As Brien himself said after the game, "I'm not as bad as those last two minutes."

On the positive side, Brien said he'll never forget the support he got from teammates in the aftermath of the loss to Pittsburgh. He remembers walking into the locker room the following day and seeing Jets center Kevin Mawae calling him over to his locker and embracing him in a big hug.

"That sticks out in my mind the most," Brien said. "It was an almost overwhelming show of support, more than anything I've ever had in my career. That's the biggest reason I wanted to come back so badly, because I wanted to help the team make it to the next level and say thanks to all those guys.

"I hope I'll have another opportunity," Brien went on. "If not, I've been blessed to be doing this for 11 years and I have no regrets. It's been a great ride."

Brien tried to hook on with another team in 2005, but no one signed him and he never kicked again.

ALL GOOD THINGS MUST COME TO AN END

It's difficult to believe, but a year after nearly making it to the AFC Championship Game, the Jets fell to 4–12 in 2005.

Why?

Simple. In a span of mere minutes, the Jets lost starting quarterback Chad Pennington as well as his backup, Jay Fiedler, for the season in the third game.

That left inexperienced third-stringer Brooks Bollinger as their only option, and the results were predictable. The Jets lost eight of their next nine games after losing quarterbacks Pennington and Fiedler as well as the game in which they were injured, 26–20 in overtime to the Jacksonville Jaguars at home.

Pennington and Fiedler suffered their respective shoulder injuries on consecutive offensive possessions, a real-time span of about 15 minutes. Those 15 minutes doomed the Jets' season and, remarkably, signaled the beginning of the end of the Edwards era, even though Vince Lombardi likely wouldn't have won more than six games with Bollinger (one career game before his insertion into the lineup) at quarterback.

As the Jets' season spiraled downward, their fans became restless and so did team owner Woody Johnson. Tensions arose between Johnson and Edwards, and it finally came to a head after the 2005 season was over.

Edwards, who had led the Jets to three playoff berths— more than any coach in team history—in five years, was unceremoniously pushed out the door in a bizarre few days of embarrassing miscommunication on the part of Jets management and ownership.

Edwards, just months removed from nearly leading the team to the AFC Championship Game, was suddenly being painted as a bad guy who was trying to shoot his way out of

A rare bright spot for the Jets during the 4–12 campaign of 2005 was cornerback Ty Law's league-best 10 interceptions, including this 74-yard return for a touchdown against his former team, the Patriots. Law went to Kansas City after the season and returned to New York as a backup in 2008. *Jim McIsaac/Getty Images*

Though they appear cordial in this 2004 photo, things ended badly between Jets owner Robert Wood Johnson IV and head coach Herman Edwards in 2005, leading to Edwards' departure one year after he took his team within a few feet of the AFC Championship Game (if not for Doug Brien's missed field goal). *David Drapkin/AP Images*

New York and go to Kansas City to work for one of his long-time mentors, Carl Peterson, the Chiefs' general manager.

"I can tell you that no one in the front office—not Woody Johnson, not [team president] Jay Cross, not [general manager] Terry Bradway—ever said to Herm, 'Do you want to be here?'" a highly placed team source said in an interview with the *New York Post*. "They assumed he wanted out and it kept on snow-balling from there. For him to go from hero to goat in a span of eight months, that amazes me."

This, apparently, is how much the Jets thought of Edwards once he was released from his contract and allowed to go to Kansas City: The Jets settled for a mere 2006 fourth-round draft pick as compensation.

By comparison, when the Chiefs hired Dick Vermeil out of retirement in 2001, they had to pay the St. Louis Rams (who owned his rights) second- and third-round picks. When Jon Gruden went to Tampa Bay, the Buccaneers had to cough up two first-round picks, two second-rounders,

and some $8 million to the Oakland Raiders, who owned his rights at the time.

Said a Jets source familiar with the compensation negotiation between the Jets and Chiefs: "The thing had gotten so ugly that there was no way Edwards was coming back, and Woody got so pissed off that the Chiefs could have thrown in a couple of jockstraps and a towel and it was going to happen."

"All Woody had to do is say, 'Herm's my coach and no one's talking to him,'" a team source told the *New York Post* shortly after Edwards' departure. "But Woody got his feathers ruffled. Herm did nothing wrong. That's the amazing thing. Woody got mad two days ago, saying, 'He wants out of here and he thinks we're second-class.' Herm never said he wanted out of here."

Long after Edwards went to coach the Chiefs and the dust settled from all the controversy, Bradway, the Jets general manager at the time, put Edwards' run as the Jets head coach in the best perspective when he said, "I don't think Herm ever got the credit he deserved in this town. He won games. He won playoff games. The only years he didn't win, it was because our quarterback got hurt. Say what you want: Herm knew how to win games."

FROM ONE JETS COACH TO ANOTHER

There was an interesting back-and-forth between Herman Edwards and Bill Parcells in the days before Edwards' Jets played Parcells' Cowboys in an early-season game in 2003. Discussing the topic of coaching, Edwards was asked if he could envision himself coaching into his 60s, like Parcells had done.

"No . . . no way," Edwards, who was 49 at the time, said. "No. I promise you. That's a promise. I won't do it to myself. I won't, because I literally couldn't do it. I don't have enough energy to last that long. I put too much energy into it. I sleep three, four hours a day. I give everything I can give to this football team, to these players.

"Sixty years old? No way. Ain't no way, ever. If I dream [about coaching beyond 60], I wake up and slap myself. When I wake up my wife and she asks, 'Why did you slap yourself?' and I tell her, then she slaps me and says, 'Are you crazy?' There is no way. No, no, no.

"I like it, but I don't like it that much," Edwards went on. "In New York, New York is like dog years, where one year is three. I've been here two years already, which is six. And, when you start off like we've started off, it seems like it's been ten."

Parcells, 62 at the time, was amused by Edwards' response.

"Herman said there's no way he'll be coaching when he's 60?" Parcells asked. "Well, you tell Herman I made that statement, only it was fifty [years old]. You get into where the game beats you down and eats you alive and then you find out [that you feel differently later].

"Here's the best way to describe it: At some point in time the game ceases to be a job and it becomes your life. At some point in time you no longer are ashamed of that. Tell Herman that I have the advantage of a retrospective view, and if he keeps winning like he's been doing, there's a good chance he might keep doing it."

Parcells, explaining why he went back into coaching again and again after publicly vowing several times he was retiring, said, "I know some cynics will laugh, but I really didn't think I was ever going to coach again. But then all of

Herman Edwards and Bill Parcells, now the head coach in Dallas, have a chat before the Jets-Cowboys game at the Meadowlands in September 2003. Edwards and Parcells, along with Weeb Ewbank and Rex Ryan, rank among the most successful coaches in Jets franchise history. *Julie Jacobson/AP Images*

a sudden something happens that gets you going and wakes you up and it rekindles what you think and then you don't remember all the crap and the times you're beat down and how this game kills you. It's like your body not remembering pain. Well, your mind doesn't remember the pain either, and you say, 'I can do that.' Then you go and you do it."

Edwards insisted that he understood why Parcells came back after promising everyone when he left the Jets that he'd coached his last game.

"Competitive," Edwards said of Parcells. "He's very, very competitive. That's why guys get out and come back. There's nothing that fulfills that void. Whether you're a player or a coach, that's the void you lose. Some guys can do it when they get out. Some guys do it for a while. Dick Vermeil is the same way. He came back. You don't get the same adrenaline rush."

Edwards, after three years as the head coach in Kansas City, was fired in 2008. He went into television, working as an analyst for ESPN. He was out of coaching at age 54.

6 MANGENIUS
2006–2008

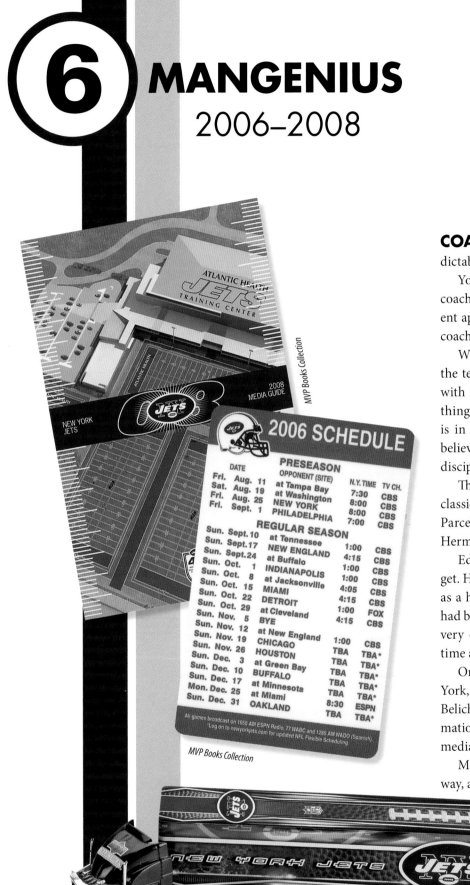

MVP Books Collection

JETS 2006 SCHEDULE

DATE	PRESEASON OPPONENT (SITE)	N.Y. TIME	TV CH.
Fri. Aug. 11	at Tampa Bay	7:30	CBS
Sat. Aug. 19	at Washington	8:00	CBS
Fri. Aug. 25	NEW YORK	8:00	CBS
Fri. Sept. 1	PHILADELPHIA	7:00	CBS
	REGULAR SEASON		
Sun. Sept. 10	at Tennessee	1:00	CBS
Sun. Sept.17	NEW ENGLAND	4:15	CBS
Sun. Sept.24	at Buffalo	1:00	CBS
Sun. Oct. 1	INDIANAPOLIS	1:00	CBS
Sun. Oct. 8	at Jacksonville	4:05	CBS
Sun. Oct. 15	MIAMI	4:15	CBS
Sun. Oct. 22	DETROIT	1:00	FOX
Sun. Oct. 29	at Cleveland	4:15	CBS
Sun. Nov. 5	BYE		
Sun. Nov. 12	at New England	1:00	CBS
Sun. Nov. 19	CHICAGO	TBA	TBA*
Sun. Nov. 26	HOUSTON	TBA	TBA*
Sun. Dec. 3	at Green Bay	TBA	TBA*
Sun. Dec. 10	BUFFALO	TBA	TBA*
Sun. Dec. 17	at Minnesota	TBA	TBA*
Mon. Dec. 25	at Miami	8:30	ESPN
Sun. Dec. 31	OAKLAND	TBA	TBA*

All games broadcast on 1050 AM ESPN Radio, 77 WABC and 1280 AM WADO (Spanish).
*Log on to newyorkjets.com for updated NFL Flexible Scheduling.

MVP Books Collection

MVP Books Collection

COACHING CHANGES IN THE NFL go in predictable cycles.

You can almost guarantee that when a team fires one head coach, the next one they hire will have a completely different approach. Almost invariably, teams go from a "players' coach" to a classic disciplinarian and vice versa.

When a disciplinarian is in charge and things go awry, the team's ownership and management believes it must go with a looser, more approachable players' coach to make things right or risk a player revolt. When a players' coach is in charge and things go awry, the team's management believes it must go in a "different direction" and hire a more disciplined head coach to get things in order.

The Jets hiring of Eric Mangini in January 2006 is a classic example of that. Mangini, who came from the Bill Parcells/Bill Belichick coaching tree of discipline, succeeded Herman Edwards.

Edwards was as players' coach as a players' coach could get. Having played 10 years in the NFL, he built his strength as a head coach on relating to his players as someone who had been in their shoes as a former player. Edwards also was very outward with the media—highly accessible with his time and the information he gave out.

Once Edwards was fired after his five-year reign in New York, it came out that New England Patriots head coach Bill Belichick was often amused by how much pertinent information he would learn from Edwards' openness with the media, seeing it as a weakness of Edwards.

Mangini, by contrast, approached the media the Belichick way, and he immediately ruffled some feathers.

Mangini's strengths as a head coach were not in his press conference demeanor or rah-rah speeches to his players. His strength was in his work ethic and preparation. Terry Bradway, the general manager at the time, said of Mangini, "I think the 'wow' is in his work. He's a good teacher. He wants smart, hardworking players. He's very detailed, very confident. He knows what he wants to do."

The 34-year-old Mangini, always the realist, said, "Obviously, my age is a question. I read recently where Bill Walsh said you are never quite ready for your first head coaching job regardless of how old you are. I think that's true. I am not naive to think that there won't be bumps along the way. We're going to grow together. I'm confident in my experiences."

"I've got tremendous mentors," Mangini added. "I worked with some of the greatest coaching minds in the NFL. I am not Bill Belichick and I am not Bill Parcells. I am Eric Mangini, and I'm going to approach it my way."

Mangini was part of Belichick's staff in New England and saw how Belichick ridiculed Edwards for his openness with reporters. When he was hired as the Jets head coach, Mangini was damned if he was going to offer up any information that might give his mentor a competitive edge.

It should be noted that when Mangini was hired by the Jets to succeed Edwards, he took the job without Belichick's blessing. Belichick had his own problems with the Jets organization in the past and had a lack of respect for the team's ownership. He flat-out told Mangini not to take the job, that he could do better than the Jets.

Mangini, whose lifelong goal was to become an NFL head coach, knew that second chances don't always come in life. He wanted the Jets job and he took it. Mangini's decision to take the job immediately estranged him from Belichick, his friend and mentor, and so began yet another fascinating chapter of the Jets-Patriots "Border War."

Not more than hours after Mangini accepted the Jets job, his keycard to get into the Patriots' building—and his office—had been deactivated; he was locked out. His belongings were withheld for weeks before they were finally boxed and sent to him.

The way this unfolded was highly unsettling and puzzling to Mangini, who had been under Belichick's wing since about the time he started shaving.

Mangini had been a public relations assistant and then a ball boy and a gopher with the Cleveland Browns when Belichick was the head coach there. Because of his obvious smarts as well as his drive and hunger, Mangini was eventually given some football assignments by Belichick.

And so began his coaching career.

The two became close friends. Mangini and his wife, Julie, would socialize with Belichick and his family, exchange

Thirty-five-year-old Eric Mangini addresses the media at the team complex at Hofstra University after being announced as the new head coach of the New York Jets on January 17, 2006. Mangini had up-and-down success during his three years on the job, but there was no shortage of drama. *Jim McIsaac/Getty Images*

The Jets brass at the time of Mangini's hiring as head coach (left to right): general manager Terry Bradway, Eric Mangini, CEO Woody Johnson, President Jay Cross, and assistant general manager Mike Tannenbaum. A week later, Tannenbaum would take Bradway's spot as GM. *Jim McIsaac/Getty Images*

Shown here in July 2005 holding his 16-month-old son, Eric Mangini had a close relationship with his former boss Bill Belichick while he was an assistant in New England. Once Mangini made the decision to go to the Jets, however, things changed forever between the two. *Chitose Suzuki/AP Images*

Christmas gifts, and even go to Bruce Springsteen concerts together. Suddenly, with one crucial career decision that Mangini made to better himself, he was dead to Belichick.

Mangini's eventful three-year head coaching career with the Jets was defined by several dramatic subplots: his relationship with Belichick, his quick success at such a young age, Brett Favre, and his unceremonious firing.

"TANGINI"

When Eric Mangini was 16 years old, his father, Carmine, died of a heart attack while playing racquetball with Eric's brother Kyle. It was a life-changing moment for Mangini, who embraced his father's work ethic and realized he needed to seize every opportunity in life.

"He was amazing in terms of whatever I was involved in, he'd be there watching," Mangini said of his dad. "He helped me learn how to throw a football and baseball. He was just a real special person. I remember one time in downtown Hartford, there was a homeless man, and he took off his jacket and gave it to this guy. I never really asked him why that was the cause he felt so strongly about. He was generous with a lot of people."

After he graduated from Bulkeley High School in Hartford, Connecticut, Mangini went to Wesleyan and starred as a defensive end at the same school that Belichick had attended a few years before. After graduating from Wesleyan, Mangini moved to Australia with his older brother, and he coached a club team that played American football. That lit his fire to coach, and when he returned to

The Jets enjoyed a 10–6 season in Mangini's first year on the job, which earned him an icy Gatorade bath from his players after they clinched a playoff berth with a 23–3 win over the Raiders in the final regular-season game of 2006. *David Drapkin/Getty Images*

the United States, he wrote letters to every NFL team looking for work. The Browns were one of the few teams to respond, and he took an unpaid position as a ball boy.

Kevin Byrne, then the Browns public relations director, noticed Mangini's work ethic as ball boy and offered him a job as a public relations intern. Mangini spent a lot of time doing menial tasks, such as buying the beat writers lunch and making copies. He was also tasked with picking up barbecued ribs for the players, earning him the nickname "Rib Boy."

Mangini eventually was noticed by head coach Belichick, who gave him some responsibilities after the PR internship ended. From there, Mangini's ascent was steady. Belichick took Mangini with him when the Browns moved from Cleveland to Baltimore, and Mangini later joined Belichick on Bill Parcells' staff with the Jets as a quality control coach.

When Belichick left the Jets to be the head coach in New England, he hired Mangini as his defensive backs coach. When Romeo Crennel left the Patriots to become Cleveland's head coach, Mangini was elevated to defensive coordinator.

From there, the Jets hired him—much to Belichick's dismay.

Bill Belichick wasn't the only important connection that Mangini made in his early years with the Browns in the 1990s. While Mangini was getting his toe in the door as a low-level assistant in the PR department, a Tulane law school graduate named Mike Tannenbaum was a young up-and-comer in the front office.

The two forged a relationship at the office's old copy machine, affectionately nicknamed the "Queen Mary." They would talk long into the night dreaming about running

JERRICHO COTCHERY
RECEIVER
2004–

HERMAN EDWARDS always said one of his biggest mistakes was not playing Jerricho Cotchery more as a receiver. Cotchery played mostly on special teams during his first two seasons, catching only 25 passes and starting just one game under Edwards.

When Mangini arrived in 2006, he made Cotchery a starter, and he flourished, averaging averaged 78 catches and 983 yards from 2006 to 2008.

When Rex Ryan took over for Mangini, he knew about Cotchery from having to defend against him as an opposing defensive coach.

"I've said from day one [that he's a No. 1 receiver]," Ryan said. "I remember him when he scorched me when I was in Baltimore. . . . I know he's a talented guy. I never knew he was this hard a worker. He's a leader."

The low-key Cotchery is the anti-diva at a position filled with attention-grabbers.

"People just don't give him his due," former Jets safety Kerry Rhodes said of Cotchery. "He is not flashy, doesn't talk, doesn't complain like a number-one receiver. He just goes out and does his job. He is a boring guy, but I give him a little love."

Cotchery said he's always been low-key after growing up as the 12th of 13 kids. He also said he's used to critics expecting little from him, starting when he came out of North Carolina State as a fourth-round pick in 2004. He was either too slow or destined to be a third or, maybe, second receiver at best.

"I've been dealing with this my entire life," Cotchery said. "It is just déjà vu for me."

Jerricho Cotchery became the Jets' number one receiver under coach Mangini. He caught 82 passes for 961 yards and six touchdowns in 2006, then logged another 82 catches for a career-high 1,130 yards in 2007. *Al Bello/Getty Images*

Mangini learned a lot about football from Bill Belichick, whom he worked for in Cleveland, Baltimore, New York, and New England. Mangini would later be accused of trying to be like Belichick in his approach to coaching and to the media. *Robert E. Klein/AP Images*

their own NFL team together one day. Twelve years later, they would be together again, running the Jets, Mangini as head coach and Tannenbaum as general manager.

The relationship between Mangini and Tannenbaum, linked by both business and a close friendship, seemed like it would last forever. Merging their names together, they were known collectively as "Tangini."

Growing up just outside of Boston, Tannenbaum always knew that he was not going to be a professional athlete or coach. However, he had been obsessed with sports since he was old enough to read. He read the newspaper sports pages religiously and vowed he would be the general manager of a pro sports team some day.

"Most kids dream of making the big shot, as Larry Bird always seemed to do," Tannenbaum said in an interview with the *Boston Herald*. "I idolized Red Auerbach growing up. I felt Red was always a half step ahead of the competition. He pulled off one great trade after another. . . . The

Like Mangini, Mike Tannenbaum worked his way through the football ranks before landing a job leading the Jets in 2006. Here the general manager (left) chats with running back Curtis Martin and team owner Robert "Woody" Johnson at training camp in Hempstead, New York. Martin had been one of Tannenbaum's key acquisitions when he was assistant GM in 1997. *Ed Betz/AP Images*

Celtics were the iconic brand in Boston when I was growing up, and they were led by one guy [Auerbach].

"I loved basketball but I knew I wasn't going to be 6-foot-11 and play in the NBA. I was Mike Tannenbaum from Needham [Massachusetts], so I looked at a different part of the game. My mom always gave me the sports section first every morning at breakfast, but she'd say, 'There's more to life than sports. At some point you'll have to get a real job.'"

As a student at the University of Massachusetts, Tannenbaum wrote a term paper about putting together a sports team, choosing the San Francisco 49ers as the team he would build and emulating the head coach and team architect, Bill Walsh.

Tannenbaum went to Tulane and studied sports law, and while he was in New Orleans he landed a low-level job with the Saints. Bill Kuharich, then the team's player personnel director, gave him a job of similar importance to Mangini buying barbeque ribs for the Browns players. For the first six months, Kuharich had Tannenbaum shredding paper.

Tannenbaum, who never complained, later said he knew what was going on.

"He was trying to see if I would hang in there, so I was committed to being the best shredder in the country," Tannenbaum said. "I graduated from that to getting his dry cleaning. It went from that to getting people from the airport. It was just paying my dues, and they weren't going to break me. I was not going to be broken because I had a dream and I wasn't going to lose it."

On someone's recommendation, Belichick hired him to study contracts for the Browns in an ever-changing NFL landscape where a salary cap would soon be implemented. Tannenbaum would later be hired by Parcells with the Jets on Belichick's recommendation, and it was with the Jets that he became known as one of the league's most knowledgeable people about the complicated salary cap.

He became one of Parcells' most trusted advisors, and the two would meet every night at about six o'clock for what Parcells used to call "family business"—to talk about the players on the team and available players either on other teams or on the street.

Tannenbaum truly made his name on February 19, 1997, when he executed the intricate plan to sign restricted free agent running back Curtis Martin from the Patriots. That move changed the course of history for the Jets, as Martin became the best player the team ever had.

Tannenbaum was 37 years old when he was elevated to general manager of the Jets, succeeding Terry Bradway and becoming the youngest GM in the NFL. Mangini was the youngest head coach in the NFL by nearly six years, getting hired by the Jets two days before his 35th birthday.

"Whether we're trailblazers or not, it's more about taking the opportunity and making the most of it and putting the best Jet team on the field," Tannenbaum said at the time of his promotion.

Mangini, aware that critics were wondering aloud about how young he was, joked that he'd rather be viewed as too young than too old. Always self-deprecating, he then took a shot at himself, saying, "Age has always been a question. I've always been a young guy. The only time I was an old guy was when I was a 23-year-old ball boy."

As much as the focus was on the age of the cherub-faced Mangini, who looked even younger than his years, Tannenbaum ran into some funny age issues of his own. One day before a Jets preseason game in 2006 at Tampa, Tannenbaum, who like Mangini was always baby-faced, was stopped by some young kids who noticed the Jets shirt he was wearing.

"What do you do for the Jets?" one of the kids said.

"I'm the general manager," Tannenbaum answered.

"No, no, really," the kid pressed, "what's your job?"

"Really," Tannenbaum said, "I'm the general manager."

The youth of the head coach and general manager wasn't lost on the Jets players.

"It's a little unique," said guard Pete Kendall, who's just three years younger than Mangini. "I think we have these preconceived notions of what our coach is supposed to look like. My kids are older than his kids, but I don't think he's coming up to me asking for parenting advice."

In the first game under Mangini, wide receiver Laveranues Coles piled up 153 yards on just eight catches, including this 38-yarder to set up the game-winning touchdown pass to Chris Baker late in the Jets' 23–16 victory over the Titans. Coles had the third 1,000-yard season of his career in 2006 while tallying a career-best 91 receptions. *Stephen Dunn/Getty Images*

FROM MINI-BELICHICK TO MANGENIUS

For a very young, first-time head coach, Mangini had a lot on his plate when he came to the Jets and the largest media market in the world. Not only had he never been a head coach, but he never had to deal with the media before, since Belichick forbad his assistants from speaking to reporters.

His lack of media experience was immediately evident. From the moment he was introduced by Jets management, Mangini appeared nervous, and his subsequent press conferences were the same. His defense mechanism was to offer little to nothing to the media, just like his mentor did. And God forbid he offer any information that might make its way up Interstate 95 to New England, where Belichick could ridicule the rookie head coach.

Mangini's Jets took on the rival New England Patriots in his second game on the job. This acrobatic catch by Jerricho Cotchery was one of six receptions for 121 yards by the receiver. Fellow receiver Laveranues Coles had six catches for 100 yards, and each scored a touchdown, but it wasn't enough as the Jets fell 24–17. *Corey Sipkin/NY Daily News Archive/Getty Images*

So Mangini, who's a very personable man with a great sense of humor, conducted his press conferences essentially in a shell. He was universally disliked by reporters who were used to the charismatic and accessible Edwards, a walking sound bite machine. Mangini was ripped for trying to be like Belichick, and the criticism came down on him as a Belichick wannabe with nothing on his résumé to warrant that kind of arrogant behavior.

Mangini didn't mean for it to be that way. He was merely trying to survive the best way he knew how—by following the formula of his mentor, for whom it worked.

"Prior to my first press conference as a head coach, I'd had one press conference during training camp [in New England] and there were about six people in there and it went for about eight minutes," Mangini reflected years later. "That was my experience talking in front of the press prior to becoming a head coach in the biggest market in the world.

"So what do you do? You look at people that have done it and you know that system has been successful and you've gone through years of not giving out information. It's all you know.

"I don't think it's trying to be like one person, like Belichick or [Bill] Parcells. Those are my football fathers. That's who I watched in that role for multiple, multiple years—six years in New England, three years in New York, two more years in Cleveland. That's what I saw, the one year with Ted Marchibroda.

"That way has won a lot of Super Bowls. It's been very successful, so as a thirty-four-year-old young guy going into

Justin Miller (22) set a new franchise record with his 103-yard kick return for a touchdown against the Colts on October 1, 2006. Indianapolis kicker Martin Gramatica (7) was the last obstacle for Miller, who had two return scores in his Pro Bowl season. Despite Miller's efforts, the Jets lost to the Colts 31–28. *Bill Kostroun/AP Images*

a new environment, it's hard to look at this extreme body of work that's produced results after results and say, 'Yes, I'm going to do it totally differently.'"

For Mangini, it was a matter of taking the good stuff he had learned from his teachers and doing it in his own style.

Mangini later said he tried to learn to "maintain your competitive edge without having an edge," saying, "You can do both, but you've got to learn how to do both. It's not the easiest thing in the world."

The attitude among both reporters and fans was that Mangini better win if he was going to try to be like Belichick, and he did pretty quickly.

Mangini's rigid style took some time for his players to adjust to, and there was opposition inside the locker room.

"I was informed there's no light at the end of the tunnel," receiver Laveranues Coles said, mocking Mangini's comment from the start of his first training camp. "You'll see the light before we do," Coles mused to reporters. "When y'all see the light, come tell me."

After a rigorous first training camp and preseason, the Jets won their first game under Mangini—a 23–16 victory over the Tennessee Titans—and that quick success eased the tension. It was an important win for Mangini, who needed immediate success to convince skeptics in the locker room that his hard-driving style could work.

"For any guy to go from a Herm Edwards system to a Belichick-tree system, it's dramatic," said linebacker Matt Chatham, who won three Super Bowl rings in New England before joining the Jets with Mangini. "For a young guy, it's like a baseball bat to the side of the head. It's like high school again. I think that's what a lot of guys were experiencing. Once you get into the regular season, though, you realize you did it for a reason and it wasn't just punitive."

Defensive lineman Bobby Hamilton, who won two Super Bowls with the Patriots, said: "The system works. It shows up. Just look at the history."

The Jets went 10–6 in Mangini's rookie season and made the playoffs, playing a wild-card game against—who

It's always explosive when the Jets play the Patriots, and the rivalry took on even greater magnitude after Mangini left New England to coach in New York. Mangini lost his first game against his old team on September 17, 2006, and after winning in their next encounter eight weeks later, Mangini and the Jets lost the next four meetings with New England, playoffs included. *Al Bello/Getty Images*

else?—Belichick's Patriots in Foxborough, Massachusetts. The Jets lost the game 37–16, but a new era had dawned, and the same Mangini who had been ridiculed for being a "mini-me" to Belichick when he first arrived in New York was suddenly being called "Mangenuis."

His success landed him a cameo role on the hit HBO series *The Sopranos*, so he was now a part of national pop culture. In his scene, Mangini is dining with his wife at the New Jersey restaurant owned by Artie Bucco, who says to Tony Soprano, eating at a nearby table, "Hey, Tone. You know who's in tonight? Mangenius."

Pretty heady stuff for the youngest coach in the NFL.

BILL AND ERIC

Mangini's relationship with Belichick, his mentor, was a constant theme throughout his reign as Jets head coach. It was an issue when he took the job, and the subplot only got juicier once the Jets and Patriots started playing each other.

The first meeting was September 17, 2006, in Mangini's second game as head coach of the Jets. New England managed to hold off a late Jets rally after taking a 24–0 lead. Jets receivers Jerricho Cotchery and Laveranues Coles each caught touchdown passes, and Mike Nugent kicked a 42-yard field goal to cut into the New England lead. But in the end, it was the first loss of the Mangini era.

LEON WASHINGTON

RUNNING BACK
2006–2009

Leon Washington was a threat both on special teams and out of the backfield. In 2007 he ran back three kickoffs for a touchdown, including on a 98-yard return against the Giants on October 7. *David Drapkin/Getty Images*

LEON WASHINGTON, who was selected in the fourth round (117th overall) of the 2006 NFL draft, played himself into one of the most popular and productive Jets players during his time in New York.

He developed into a dynamic weapon on both offense and special teams. He finished his Jets career with 1,782 rushing yards on 370 carries for a 4.8-yard average and 13 touchdowns. As a receiver, he caught 123 passes for 969 yards and two touchdowns. As a kickoff returner, he was one of the best in the NFL, averaging 25.5 yards in four years with the Jets and returning four kicks for touchdowns.

Washington had his best season in 2008, when he led the NFL in all-purpose yards with 2,332 and was voted to the Pro Bowl. But just one year later, Washington's Jets career ended horrendously when he suffered a compound fracture to his fibula during a 38–0 win over the Oakland Raiders in Week 7.

"Things happen for a reason," Washington said at the time. "I'm a firm believer in that because I'm strong in my faith. You have to have faith that the right thing is going to come out of this. I'll be fine. I'm reasonably optimistic I'll be good to go by the start of the 2010 season."

Because 2009 was a contract year for Washington, it was a severe blow to him financially. The Jets and Washington had failed to come to terms on an extension before the 2009 training camp, and Washington turned down a sizable contract offer. Once he got hurt, he lost all his leverage.

"I knew the risks going into the season," Washington said about not signing the extension. "The reason we didn't come to an agreement is a lot of details in the contract I just didn't agree with. We had an offer, they had an offer, it didn't match up, so we moved on. That's the business side of it. All business is risk and reward. I'm not down about it."

The loss of the productive and popular Washington hurt the Jets on the field.

"You can't replace him," head coach Rex Ryan said at the time. "You try your best. We got like three or four guys trying to do his roles now. His personality and everything else, the competitiveness, you just love being around the guy. The great thing is, he's still around here in the facility getting treatment [for his injury]. He's still a big part of our football team.

"He's clearly a guy that you wish there were more than one, but we're happy we have the one, Leon Washington. But, wow! You wish you could clone him."

The Jets in the end didn't clone Washington. Instead, they traded him to the Seattle Seahawks for a fifth-round pick on draft day in 2009. He made a triumphant comeback from the injury, returning two kickoffs for touchdowns in his third game with Seattle.

The Patriots won the game 24–17, but the lead-up was more intriguing than the game itself because of the obvious disdain Belichick had for Mangini.

In a midweek conference call with New York reporters, Belichick barely acknowledged Mangini's existence. The by-play between reporters and Belichick was like pulling teeth.

Question: "Can you see Eric's stamp on the Jets already?"

Answer: "I don't know. I'm sure there are a lot of people, a lot of forces that work down there."

Question: "Was there a point when you thought Eric could be a head coach?"

Answer: "I don't know. That's not any kind of decision I have to make."

Question: "When he worked for you, did you see him as a coach one day?"

Answer: "Again, that's not my decision to make. I see coaches as coaches."

Question: "Are there things in particular that were special about Eric when he worked for you?"

Answer: "He worked hard."

Asked if he'll root for Mangini to do well in his career, except when he faces the Patriots, Belichick said, "I'm more concerned about us doing well. Really, I don't sit around cheering for everybody else."

The Jets and Patriots met again, on November 12, and this time the Jets got their revenge, beating the Patriots 17–14 in New England. New York built a lead and held off a late comeback by the Patriots. Chad Pennington led two long scoring drives, one covering 16 plays that led to Kevan Barlow's touchdown and a 7–3 lead. The other drive was 15 plays and was capped by Mike Nugent's 34-yard field goal. The Jets made it 17–6 on Pennington's 22-yard pass to Cotchery.

Again, in the pre-game conference call, Belichick was as icy as ever when asked about Mangini. At one point, in an effort to divert reporters' attention from the Mangini topic, Belichick rambled on, naming some 16 Jets players on the roster without mentioning Mangini's name.

Asked about his relationship with Mangini, Belichick said, "We're two head coaches in the same division, playing a big division game this week. That's how I would characterize it."

Asked what kind of job Mangini has done with the Jets, Belichick said, "I think the Jets are a very good football team. They're a very talented team, and they're a very explosive team in all three phases of the game. They play that way on a weekly basis."

Asked again if he saw any particular stamp that Mangini had put on the Jets in his first season as a head coach, Belichick said, "The Jets have been a strong, competitive football team ever since I've been here."

That's when Belichick went on to name 16 Jets players in a 352-word answer that acknowledged nothing Mangini had brought to the Jets.

There weren't exactly hugs and smiles going around when head coaches Eric Mangini and Bill Belichick met for their post-game handshake at midfield following New York's 17–14 win in November 2006. *Winslow Townson/AP Images*

Belichick was asked specifically why, when he asked about other former assistants of his, including Nick Saban, Romeo Crennel, and Charlie Weis, he offered insightful, complimentary commentary about them but was reticent about even mentioning Mangini by name.

After a long pause, Belichick's answer was: "I think the Jets are a good football team. He's the coach; I think he's done a good job with them. I have a lot of respect for them. What do you want me to say?"

Mangini, meanwhile, was unwavering in his admiration for his mentor.

"My feelings on Bill haven't changed," Mangini said. "I talked quite a bit last time [before the September 17 game] how important he was to my career, and how much I appreciate that. So nothing has changed for me in that sense."

Some players who played for both Mangini and Belichick found the entire soap opera rather curious.

"I'm not into all that drama," Patriots linebacker Tedy Bruschi said. "I don't get myself involved with it. I don't care to comment about it. How I feel about Eric Mangini is I believe he was a great coach when he was here and I'm going to leave it at that."

Jets linebacker Matt Chatham, who played in New England from 2000 to 2005 before signing with the Jets as a free agent in 2006, downplayed the feud.

"I think Bill is good at keeping things close to his vest and this is another example of that," Chatham said. "They both have a ton of respect for each other regardless of who's saying what. They wouldn't have spent that many years together if they didn't respect each other. What they're letting on to this point doesn't really matter. It is odd, but what are you going to do?"

Belichick's disrespecting of Mangini, though, stirred his players, who were bent on beating the Patriots for their new head coach.

"Great coaching from Mangini on down," defensive end Kimo von Oelhoffen said after the game. "Hell, yeah, we wanted to win this for Eric. He busts his ass more than anyone else in the NFL."

Receiver Laveranues Coles said he felt Belichick's public ignoring of Mangini was an effort to "belittle" his former assistant.

"Eric is probably the smartest coach I've ever been around," Coles said. "He wouldn't want me saying this, but

The Jets and Patriots met for a third time in the span of five months when they faced off in the wild-card playoff game in New England on January 7, 2007. Here, safety Kerry Rhodes (25) and linebacker Jonathan Vilma (51) wrap up running back Kevin Faulk, but they couldn't stop the Patriots from winning 37–16. *Al Messerschmidt/Getty Images*

yeah, you wanted it a little bit extra for Coach [Mangini]. You know how much hard work and time he put into it. Guys were saying that Belichick refers to him as 'the other guy.' Any time you come out and you disrespect our coach, of course guys want to step up and play a little harder for him."

Chatham said: "Eric has all the respect in the world for [the Patriots] organization and has a lot of respect for the players on that team, so it's hard when you feel like all those people have turned their backs on you—at least that's the perception. So for him to kind of justify what he's doing down in New York was great for him."

And, of course, bad for Belichick, who saw up-close why he didn't want his talented assistant to take a job with his hated division rival.

The teams met for a third time on January 7, 2007, in the AFC wild-card playoff game at Gillette Stadium, where the Patriots blew out the Jets to put an end to Mangini's rookie season.

Before that game, Belichick, who had received widespread criticism and ridicule for his pettiness regarding Mangini prior to the previous meetings, changed his tact slightly. This time in the pre-game conference call, Belichick quickly referred to Mangini as "Eric" with some bland praise.

From there, Belichick called Mangini by name four times during the call. Most of his praise was phrased like this: "Eric and his staff have done a great job with their team."

When asked specifically where his relationship with Mangini "soured," there was such a long pause that reporters could have left the room, cooked a three-course meal, done the dishes, and returned in time to hear the answer.

"I made comments about Eric when he was hired and I still feel that way; nothing has changed there," Belichick said at last. "This game is about these two teams this week playing to keep their season alive. That's really what my focus is and that's what our team's focus is."

Asked why he was so cold to Mangini during the post-game handshake in November, Belichick repeated three times, "I never said anything negative."

Mangini said this to New England reporters about his relationship with Belichick: "I can't tell you how much I appreciate what he has done for me and my family, how kind he's been throughout our relationship, and the opportunity that he's given me. I care about him deeply, and I respect him as a person and as a coach."

Some of the highlight moments from the three games the Jets and Patriots played during Mangini's rookie season as coach were centered around the post-game handshakes

THOMAS JONES

RUNNING BACK
2007–2009

THE JETS ACQUIRED running back Thomas Jones from Chicago in the spring of 2007 hoping to fill the void left by the departure of Curtis Martin in 2005. The previous year Jones had rushed for 1,210 yards and six touchdowns while helping the Bears reach the Super Bowl.

From the start, Jones was ready to fill those star-studded shoes of the Jets' No. 1 back.

"Curtis Martin is one of the best backs of all time in the NFL," Jones said upon his arrival. "I followed him for a long time, but I'm just excited about being here in New York and having the opportunity to help this team win. They have an exciting team; they have a lot of great players. I'm just one of the guys here on the team. That's my mentality coming in."

Jones, the No. 7 overall pick out of the University of Virginia in 2000, was coming off back-to-back 1,000-yard seasons with Chicago. But despite having seven years in the NFL under his belt, Jones came to New York with just 1,349 career carries, mostly because he shared the workload early in his career.

With the Jets, he ran like a 25-year-old, and his performances got better with each season. In his first year in 2007, he rushed for 1,119 yards but scored only one touchdown. In 2008, he rushed for 1,312 yards and scored 13 rushing touchdowns, good enough for a Pro Bowl selection. In his last season with the Jets, 2009, he posted career highs with 1,402 yards and 14 touchdowns before going to the Chiefs in 2010.

Running back Thomas Jones had a monster game against the Rams on November 9, 2008, rushing for 149 yards on 26 carries and scoring a career-high three touchdowns. *David Bergman/Sports Illustrated/Getty Images*

between the two head coaches—an exercise that took on comedic proportions.

After the Jets' Week 2 loss to the Patriots, Belichick barely acknowledged Mangini when Mangini approached him for the customary congratulatory handshake at midfield. After the Jets won the second meeting, Belichick didn't even look at Mangini and gave him essentially a brush-off. After the playoff game, having created such attention around the handshake, Belichick angrily shoved a photographer as he made it a point to meet Mangini at midfield for the handshake.

When asked about it afterwards, Belichick reacted with typical disdain.

"Do you want to talk about the game?" he said testily. "I'm not going to get into a post-game analysis here. Really, I've had enough of that."

Mangini said that Belichick told him "good luck" after the playoff loss.

Mangini continued to show his strong appreciation for what Belichick had done for him despite Belichick holding a grudge.

"I can't say enough about what I learned from Bill Belichick," Mangini said. "Bill has always been very supportive of the things I've done, and has helped me throughout my career. I can't thank him enough for the opportunities he's given me.

"There are so many things you can learn from him. He's incredibly smart, he's extremely hard-working, and it doesn't matter how much success he's had, he approaches things the same way week in and week out. His focus is amazing."

Years after Mangini was fired from the Jets and hired by the Cleveland Browns, he tried to thaw the chill between himself and Belichick, and it never took.

"It hasn't really warmed at all," Mangini said in 2010 after his Browns defeated the Patriots. "I've put it out there that I'm open to it. His daughter, Amanda, even e-mailed me to congratulate me [on the Browns' win]. We were close to the family. A lot of stuff is just bullshit things that happened."

For the record, in the seven games they coached against each other, Mangini went 2–5 against Belichick.

THE FAVRE EXPERIMENT

The disappointing playoff loss to New England after a surprising 10–6 finish in 2006 was nothing compared to the disappointment Jets fans would face in 2007. The two losses to the undefeated Patriots wasn't the worst of it. It was the

Wearing a throwback-style uniform from the old New York Titans days, second-year quarterback Kellen Clemens had his best game as a pro on December 2, 2007. He completed 15 of 24 passes for 236 yards and one touchdown in the Jets' 40–13 win over the Dolphins in Miami. *Al Pereira/Getty Images*

10 other losses the Jets suffered, pushing the final record to 4–12 for the second time in three years. Indeed, of the Jets' four victories, two were at the expense of the 1–15 Dolphins, and two were accomplished in overtime in games they had led early on, first against Pittsburgh and then, in the season finale, against Kansas City.

The quarterback duties in 2007 had been split between Chad Pennington and Kellen Clemens—the duo combining for 15 touchdowns and 19 interceptions—and Mangini was working with them throughout the 2008 offseason as well. Then, suddenly, Jets owner Woody Johnson and Mike Tannenbaum wooed Brett Favre and executed a trade with the Green Bay Packers in August to bring Favre to the Jets.

And just like that, all the offseason work Mangini and offensive coordinator Brian Schottenheimer had put in with Pennington and Clemens was tossed aside. Favre had to be brought up to speed with only a couple of weeks to go before the start of the regular season.

Mangini, who was never for the Favre trade, dutifully jumped on board, and he even helped recruit Favre to New Jersey by researching places for Favre to hunt in his free time. But Mangini had a feeling all along that the move had the potential to blow up in everyone's face. Favre, after all, was at the end of his career and had almost no time to learn the system.

"I believed in what we were doing there," Mangini recalled. "The goal was to build an organization for the long term, not the short term. That was the goal: to make sure there was a solid process in place in all different areas, to make sure we could compete at the highest level—not just for one year, but year in and year out."

Mangini said making an acquisition like Favre "really wasn't the plan."

"The plan was to grow organically—with draft picks, free agency, build long term, and get better each year and ideally compete year in and year out," he said. "Then when Favre

The acquisition of Brett Favre in the 2008 offseason created quite a stir in Jets country, and the veteran quarterback helped get the team off to a strong 8–3 start before the bottom fell out on the season. In Week 4 against the Arizona, Favre tore apart the Cardinals defense, going 24-of-34 with a career-high six touchdown passes in the 56–35 Jets triumph. *Chris McGrath/Getty Images*

came along, I was asked, 'Would you be interested?' I said 'No. That's not really what we're trying to do.'

"Then when we agreed to talk, it was sort of a one-off type thing, and I went through in detail the pluses and minuses in detail with everybody. And I said, as long as we collectively were going to live with the minuses . . . then I got what the positives were—building a new stadium, the excitement, and all that stuff."

Indeed, the Favre experiment was as much a maneuver by Johnson to try to win a championship as it was to generate excitement and interest among fans who were being asked to pay public seat license (PSL) fees to be season ticket holders for the new stadium, which would open in 2010.

Mangini understood there were more powerful forces at play and that he needed to make the best of his owner's fascination with Favre.

"Brett was great for a lot of reasons, and there are other things that happen that aren't always great," Mangini continued. "You're not going to change him. He's not going to be different wearing our uniform than he was wearing another

Although Leon Washington's 92-yard kickoff return staked New York to a 17–6 lead in the second quarter against New England on November 13, 2008, it took a 34-yard field goal by Jets kicker Jay Feely in overtime to pull off the 34–31 win. A first-team All-Pro, Washington led the NFL with 2,337 all-purpose yards in 2008. *Damian Strohmeyer/Sports Illustrated/Getty Images*

The Jets and Favre stumbled badly in the last five weeks of the 2008 season, capped off by a 24–17 loss at home to the Dolphins. This hit by Miami safety Yeremiah Bell ended Favre's night and his Jets career. *Ron Antonelli/NY Daily News Archive/Getty Images*

uniform. With all the good there comes some downside, and you've got to live with both. You've got to be honest about what it is. That's where I thought things were."

Despite how it all ended with Favre, Mangini, who gave his third child the middle name of Brett because of Favre, discounted the many reports that he and Favre didn't get along.

"There was a lot made that we didn't get along and that's so untrue," Mangini said. "We get along fine—better than fine. I liked the guy. When I say I didn't want him, it didn't mean I didn't want the person; it was just not the way we said we were going to build the organization."

Favre led the Jets on a thrill ride that included winning seven of eight games in the middle of the season—a streak that concluded with a wild 34–31 overtime victory in New England and then a rugged win over the Tennessee Titans, at the time the best team in the league. That win over the Titans got the Jets to 8–3, and New York was buzzing about Super Bowl possibilities.

Little did anyone know that the Jets wouldn't even make the playoffs. Favre's production declined dramatically, and the Jets lost four of their last five games to finish at 9–7, missing the playoffs for the second straight year.

Brett Favre congratulates former Jets quarterback Chad Pennington after Pennington's Dolphins defeated the Jets 24–17 in the 2008 season finale, capping New York's monumental collapse and ending Favre's Jets career. *David Drapkin/Getty Images*

THE FATEFUL FINAL STRETCH

HEAD COACH ERIC MANGINI'S three-year run with the Jets came to an unceremonious end after the 2008 season collapse. After jumping out to an 8–3 start, the Jets lost four of their last five games to miss the playoffs.

That stretch included excruciating losses to the Denver Broncos at home (34–17), the San Francisco 49ers on the road (24–14), the Seattle Seahawks on the road (13–3), and finally the Miami Dolphins at home (24–17).

Here is the anatomy of the Jets' unraveling:

Denver 34, Jets 17

One week after the Jets beat the league-best Tennessee Titans, they were ready to take off. Instead, Broncos quarterback Jay Cutler shredded the defense on a rainy, windy day at Giants Stadium, throwing for 357 yards and two touchdowns.

It was a sobering loss for the Jets, who entered the game as the AFC's hottest team.

"We just didn't show up like we were supposed to today," running back Thomas Jones said.

"We realize we're not as good as we thought we were," added Leon Washington, offering the most honest assessment.

"I was really disappointed with the way that we played today," Mangini said after the game. "We've established a certain way to play football around here. We've established a certain identity, and this wasn't even close to that."

Brett Favre struggled in the sloppy conditions, finishing 23-of-43 for 247 yards and an interception.

"We got outplayed," Favre said.

49ers 24, Jets 14

The Jets were unable to rebound the next week at San Francisco. Making matters worse, the loss came against a 49ers team that had little to play for and was nowhere near playoff contention.

With the second straight defeat, the Jets' playoff chances were suddenly in peril. At 8–5, New York had dropped into a three-way tie for first place with the Dolphins and Patriots in the highly competitive AFC East.

For the second week in a row, the Jets struggled on offense, managing only 182 total yards. Brett Favre (20-of-31, 137 yards) was unable to take advantage of a mediocre 49ers defense.

"It's another wake-up call," receiver Laveranues Coles said after the game. "I don't know how many of these we're going to need."

"We're not playing to the best of our potential," nose tackle Kris Jenkins said. "We know what's wrong. We just have to find the answer to it."

They never would find that answer.

Seahawks 13, Jets 3

Following a 31–27 win over the Bills, the loss in Seattle marked a low point for the 2008 Jets. They had gone from a five-game winning streak to a free-fall.

Brett Favre was simply awful in this game, throwing two more interceptions, while the Jets scored a season-low three points against one of the league's lowest-ranked defenses.

"We knew what was at stake. We didn't take advantage of it," Favre said afterward. "It's not good enough. That's the bottom line."

The loss left the Jets at 9–6. They needed to beat AFC East co-leading Miami at home the next week and have either New England or Baltimore lose in order to get into the playoffs.

"There is no such thing as a shoo-in," Jets receiver Laveranues Coles said in reference to the Jets' 8–3 record before the slump. "The situation we're in now says that."

Dolphins 24, Jets 17

This game was the end for Mangini and Favre and tasty revenge for Chad Pennington.

Pennington, whom the Jets had released the previous August to make room for the aging Favre, was having a fabulous season. He led the Dolphins to the playoffs, while Favre's one-and-done New York tenure fizzled in the December chill of crunch time.

"It's always a sweet feeling to be a champion," Pennington said after throwing two touchdowns in the 24–17 win over the Jets. "That's what we are: AFC East champions. It's a great feeling. This organization has been unbelievable. They accepted me from the get-go. This has been an unbelievable ride.

"It's not a revenge factor," Pennington said. "This week . . . it was strictly focused on winning the championship, knowing that we controlled our own destiny. It just so happened that it had to come through New York. That's the only way fate would have it."

After an 8–3 start and being mentioned as possible Super Bowl contenders with an NFL-high seven Pro Bowl selections, the Jets completed their tailspin.

"The hardest part is the finality of it," Favre said, "especially when you expect to go on."

Cornerback Darrelle Revis emerged as a Pro Bowl caliber defensive back for the Jets in 2008. His five interceptions on the year led the team, and his tumbling one-handed pickoff in the end zone preserved New York's 20–14 win over the Dolphins in the season opener.
Al Pereira/Getty Images

BREAKING UP IS HARD TO DO

For Mike Tannenbaum, living the dream of running his own sports team also meant making some very difficult decisions. The toughest one he ever had to make was firing Mangini after the 2008 season.

After the Jets missed the playoffs with a 9–7 record and Brett Favre at quarterback, Woody Johnson, who was clearly affected by the fan unrest following the collapse from 8–3, decided it was time for a change at head coach. Tannenbaum had to do the dirty work. He called Mangini late at night and told him of the decision.

"Those were painful days, but that comes with the job," Tannenbaum said. "Eric is a great coach and a great friend. . . . It was bumpy, but ours is a long-term relationship. My responsibility was to do what was right for the Jets, not what was easiest for me.

"Eric's a guy I deeply care for," Tannenbaum went on. "That was the hardest thing I've had to do."

Tannenbaum recalled meeting with Woody Johnson in New York City the night after the Jets' season finale against Miami.

"We came to the conclusion that we had to go in another direction," he recalled. "That was not a referendum on whether we thought Eric was a good coach or not. We got a lot accomplished in three years, and Eric deserves a lot of credit for the foundation that he helped build."

Mangini recalled being "sick as a dog with a stomach virus" when he got the late-night call from Tannenbaum, who had been such a close friend. He said the firing "hurt," but he was philosophical about it.

"You can't appreciate and be thankful for the friendship when it works well for you and then be angry for the friendship when it doesn't work well for you," he said. "That's not right. It's hard when you hear it from a friend, and it's hard for that friend to deliver it. But it's the reality of what we do. Mike was a friend throughout the whole time I was there. I don't think he cared about me any less afterward."

Mangini recognized that football is a business where scapegoats are sacrificed when things don't go as planned, but he also didn't run from his own culpability about the collapse that ended the 2008 season. "I'm not by any means saying I couldn't have done better that stretch run," he said. "I'm not absolving myself from accountability. But when you throw a lot of touchdowns, you throw a lot of [interceptions]. Sometimes that leads to wins, sometimes it leads to losses."

Still, Mangini did express surprise about getting fired, saying, "Maybe I was the only one that didn't anticipate it, but I didn't think that was going to happen."

Mangini said he was going by what Woody Johnson told the *New York Post* in an interview at the 2008 NFL owners meetings. Citing his desire to build the kind of continuity that franchises like the Pittsburgh Steelers and New York Giants had, the Jets owner said both Mangini and Tannenbaum would be back regardless of the results of that season.

Mangini believed, from what Johnson said at the owners meetings, that he was going to be the head coach and Tannenbaum was going to be the GM. "Then we had a

It was a somber occasion for general manager Mike Tannenbaum (right) when he announced the firing of his longtime friend Eric Mangini as head coach of the Jets. Owner Woody Johnson sits to Tannenbaum's right. *Al Pereira/Getty Images*

winning season and it wasn't what we hoped it would be at the end, but it was the same result as when they went 9–7 [in 2009 under his replacement, Rex Ryan]. But 9–7 one year gets you in the playoffs, and 9–7 another year gets you fired."

Even if he believes he was wrongly fired by the Jets, he knows that it was Johnson and Tannenbaum who brought him into the NFL head coaching world and gave him his first opportunity at age 34, which led to where he is now.

"There are two sides to that," Mangini said when asked if he felt betrayed by Tannenbaum. "He's also the guy that gave me a chance when nobody else would. I've had to let go of guys I really like and cared about, but if you think it's what's best for the greater good, then you do it.

"When I was there, he supported me every day. He gave me the first opportunity. I respect all that stuff, because that wasn't easy for him to do, but he did it. When you make tough decisions, then you have to accept the fact that other people have to make tough decisions about you. You may not agree with them or like them, but it's their right."

Mangini was hardly the abject failure with the Jets that many Jets fans perceive him to be. This perception was largely projected by the media, to whom he rarely endeared himself with team access, information, or witty sound bites.

But Mangini did succeed in moving the Jets forward. He led them to the playoffs in his first season, suffered through a poor second season with quarterback injury issues, and finally was fired after finishing 9–7 following an 8–3 start with an aging Brett Favre.

Within a few days of his firing, Mangini got a call from the Cleveland Browns about their head coaching position. The fact that the Browns called so quickly was, for Mangini, "an indication to me that the good things that we'd done [with the Jets] had been recognized."

When Mangini was fired the day after the 2008 season, he met with his players and delivered one final message.

"I told them I've been across the table and told other people they have to go home, and it sucks," he recalled. "It's not a fun part of the job at all, but [it's] part of what we all do, part of what we all have to live with. What I asked them to do was, whoever the next coach is, embrace him and don't waste time fighting the system, fighting his philosophy."

Enter Rex Ryan.

7 KING REX
2009–2010

THERE WAS LITTLE LEFT to the imagination when Rex Ryan stood at the podium at his introductory press conference upon his hiring in February 2009.

It took only seconds for Ryan to tell the world in his own unique way what he was about. Ryan gazed around the auditorium at the crowd of reporters and said, "With all the cameras and all that, I was looking for our new president back there."

After a perfectly placed pause, Ryan then added, "You know, I think we'll get to meet him in the next couple years anyway."

So the new Jets coach made a big splash, predicting a team visit to the White House as Super Bowl champions.

Give this to Ryan: He aims high.

"I'm not afraid of expectations," Ryan said. "My goal is to win a Super Bowl. It's not to just win X number of games."

Jets owner Woody Johnson had just weeks before fired Eric Mangini, who was too close-to-the-vest and rigid for Johnson's liking. Now Johnson was squirming in his seat listening to Ryan's bravado, and he couldn't wait to back up his new coach.

"Why else are we here?" Johnson asked, wearing a look of delighted anticipation on his face.

Ryan, who came to the Jets after four years as the Baltimore Ravens' defensive coordinator, backed down from nothing in his first visit with the New York media.

"We want to be known as the most physical football team in the NFL," Ryan said. "The players will have each other's backs, and if you take a swipe at one of ours, we'll take a swipe at two of yours."

Ryan didn't seem daunted at all to be taking over a team that had just let an 8–3 start melt into a playoff-less 9–7 finish in 2008.

"We expect to win," Ryan said. "We have a lot of talent here that's already in place."

Rex Ryan caught the attention of his players, the media, and Jets fans everywhere at the very first press conference following his hiring as head coach. He wasn't the first member of the Jets organization to make a Super Bowl prediction, of course, but Ryan put his confidence and outspoken nature on full display from day one. *Andy Marlin/Getty Images*

Highlighting the excitement surrounding the Ryan hire, several players attended the press conference, including cornerback Darrelle Revis and wide receiver Jerricho Cotchery, who wanted to get an up-close look at their new coach.

What the incumbent players experienced while listening to Ryan was culture shock after three years of Mangini.

"He's relaxed and he's not tense," Revis said. "He's exciting, and you can just tell he's going to bring a lot of stuff over here that we'll like."

Ryan, who signed a four-year deal worth a reported $12 million, brought with him from Baltimore the Ravens' outside linebackers coach, Mike Pettine, as his defensive coordinator, and defensive backs coach Dennis Thurman. Along with Ryan, those guys were like the Three Musketeers, all for one and one for all.

Bill Callahan, the offensive line coach, and special teams coordinator Mike Westhoff were retained from the previous staff, as was offensive coordinator Brian Schottenheimer.

Football, of course, is in Ryan's blood. His father, Buddy Ryan, was the head coach of the Philadelphia Eagles and Arizona Cardinals and before that was the architect of the 1985 Chicago Bears defense. The elder Ryan also worked as a linebackers coach on Weeb Ewbank's Jets staff when they won Super Bowl III.

"I know my dad is known as one of the best defensive coaches in the history of this league," Ryan said. "I want to be a better head coach than my father."

Buddy Ryan couldn't have been more proud to see his son take over his old team, but he offered this zinger: "I told him the Jets were my team; just don't screw them up."

Rex Ryan's father and coaching legend Buddy Ryan was at Rex's side during the first mini-camps in the spring and summer of 2009. *Michael J. LeBrecht II/Sports Illustrated/Getty Images*

"He's qualified and certified," Buddy Ryan said of Rex. "They did theirselves a good favor by hiring him."

Ironically, Buddy tried to discourage both Rex and his twin brother, Rob (a longtime defensive coordinator in the NFL), from coaching. "They worked food services for the Air Force in Philadelphia when they were younger," Buddy said. "I tried to get them into management. Neither one wanted it. They wanted to coach."

Both Rex and Rob Ryan were ball boys on the 1969 Jets Super Bowl team and caught the bug.

"Rex was six years old when we won that ring," Buddy said. "He wanted to be a football coach since he was seven."

When Rex Ryan was hired by the Jets, it was a long time coming for him. He had been passed over numerous times for head coaching jobs, and Ryan always believed his brash attitude and appearance (he's overweight and not the sharpest dresser) scared teams away.

Ryan had interviewed for head coaching jobs with the San Diego Chargers, Atlanta Falcons, Miami Dolphins, St. Louis Rams, and Ravens in the two years before the Jets called. Ryan has been vocal about how grateful he was to Johnson for hiring him "because he wanted the best football coach."

"I'd like to thank Woody Johnson and [general manager] Mike Tannenbaum for this once-in-a-lifetime opportunity," Ryan said. "It's been a dream of mine to become a head coach in the NFL. Coming here to the New York Jets, where my father once coached and was part of the Super Bowl III staff, is fantastic. I look around at the facilities and the people they have in place and see a first-class organization. I'm just proud to be part of it."

Ryan, a former player at Southwestern Oklahoma State, had no previous head coaching experience, but he had been an assistant at the pro and college levels for more than 20

In his 10 seasons as a member of the Baltimore coaching staff, Ryan built one of the most fearsome defenses in the league while also building the respect and admiration of his players. Here he addresses his charges during the 2008 playoff game against the Steelers, which proved to be Ryan's last game with the Ravens. *Damian Strohmeyer/Sports Illustrated/ Getty Images*

THE REX RYAN FILE

COACHING HISTORY		
College		
Years	*School*	*Position*
1987–1988	Eastern Kentucky	Defensive end coach
1989	New Mexico Highlands	Asst. head coach/ defensive coordinator
1990–1993	Morehead State	Defensive coordinator
1996–1997	Cincinnati	Defensive coordinator
1998	Oklahoma	Defensive coordinator
Pro		
Years	*Team*	*Position*
1994	Arizona Cardinals	Defensive line coach
1995	Arizona Cardinals	Linebackers coach
1999–2004	Baltimore Ravens	Defensive line coach
2005–2007	Baltimore Ravens	Defensive coordinator
2008	Baltimore Ravens	Asst. head coach/ defensive coordinator
Named 2006 NFL Assistant Coach of the Year by *Pro Football Weekly* and the Pro Football Writers Association.		

years. His Baltimore defenses were consistently among the top ranked in the league, and Ryan's defense was instrumental in the Ravens' championship season in 2000, when they held the Giants to seven points and 152 total yards in the Super Bowl.

Ryan is such a keen Xs and Os coach that he was nicknamed "The Mad Scientist" by his players for his aggressive and unpredictable game plans.

"I'm not a one-hit wonder," Ryan said. "When you look at my background, I think I've been successful at all stops along the way. I know the kind of responsibility it takes to be a head football coach. Again, you got the right guy and I plan on proving that each and every week."

Ryan added that the message to the rest of the league was, "Hey, the Jets are coming, and we're going to give you everything we got, and I think that's going to be more than you can handle."

After the press conference, Johnson described Ryan as someone who was "very comfortable in his own skin."

"Rex is revered by his players and respected by his peers around the NFL for his innovative schemes," Johnson continued. "There is no doubt in my mind that Rex has the expertise and instincts to build on the foundation that we have in place and take this franchise to the ranks of the NFL's elite. He will bring an aggressive, physical brand of football that will captivate our fans and ignite their passion."

That reverence and respect by his players was illustrated by the comments from those he had coached in Baltimore, who had mixed feelings about him taking the Jets job; they hated to see him leave, but they were ecstatic for him to be getting the opportunity to be a head coach.

"I think it's a gain for [the Jets] and a loss for us," said linebacker Bart Scott, "but it's well deserved and a long time coming."

"He will bring his personality and his passion for the game," safety Jim Leonhard told reporters. "They're getting a hell of a coach, and he will make them a better football team."

Leonhard spoke of the strong relationship that Ryan had with his players in Baltimore. "Guys would run in front of a

Known as a "players' coach," Rex Ryan works closely with his players from the first mini-camp all the way through the season and postseason. In the words of safety Jim Leonhard, Ryan "understands the game from a player's perspective. He understands what you go through on a day-to-day basis and what players need to be told." *Al Pereira/Getty Images*

bus for Rex," he said. "We'd do anything for Rex. You could tell he loves this group of guys. He's been around this group of guys for a long time, a number of them. They mean a lot to him. You can tell guys respect him for that."

Showing their respect and loyalty, both Scott and Leonhard soon followed Ryan to the Jets as free agents.

MIDNIGHT RUN

Ryan wasted no time putting his stamp on the Jets.

His first order of business was to secure the assistant coaches he wanted to bring from Baltimore. His second order of business was bringing the players he wanted in from Baltimore.

That's why Ryan was sitting in a rental car in the driveway of Bart Scott's Maryland home at midnight at the opening of

the NFL's free agent signing period. Ryan, along with Pettine and Thurman, the Three Musketeers, weren't leaving Scott's house until he would agree to be a Jet.

"I thought it was the most hilarious thing in the world," Scott recalled. "I am happy that they did not get out of the car and get bit by my dogs. When I heard my dogs barking, I thought they were out chasing deer or something. When Coach Thurman called me and said, 'Come on out, man, and get these dogs,' it was the funniest thing in the world."

Ryan, as part of his pitch to Scott, said he wanted Scott to become a centerpiece of the Jets defense. Scott had always played in the shadow of Ray Lewis in Baltimore.

Aside from playing for Ryan again, the thought of being an integral part of what Ryan wanted to build with the Jets was too good for Scott to pass up. The six-year contract worth $48 million wasn't a bad recruiting tool, either.

After seven seasons with the Ravens, linebacker Bart Scott signed with the Jets in 2009 to join his former defensive coordinator, Rex Ryan. Scott emerged right away as a leader on the New York defensive unit. *Al Pereira/Getty Images*

"To be able to have the opportunity to kind of move from the passenger's seat to the driver's seat is very flattering and it comes with a great sense of responsibility," Scott said. "I'm ready to take on the challenge."

Scott, whose nickname is "Mad Backer," immediately backed up Ryan's bold talk. "We won't back down from anybody," he said. "You guys can expect to see a very physical, violent defense. I don't know if this division has ever seen a violent defense. It's one thing to make a tackle; it's another thing to be violent. Violence makes guys stay on the sideline when they get hit."

Scott was first signed by the Ravens as an undrafted free agent out of Southern Illinois in 2002 and began his career as a backup and special teams player, always considering himself an underdog and wearing the label proudly.

"What better place for the underdog than the original underdog from Super Bowl III?" Scott said.

Another example of how much players want to play for Ryan is the case of Jim Leonhard, who played safety for one year in Baltimore under Ryan. Leonhard, who like Scott was a free agent after the 2008 season, took less money from the Jets than the Denver Broncos were offering him so that he could play for Ryan.

"We were very close to having everything signed, sealed, and delivered out to New York when all of a sudden the Denver Broncos came out of nowhere and threw out a really big number at me," Leonhard said. "So, I took a few hours to consider it, and we ultimately decided that regardless of the money situation, the Jets were the place to be."

Another former Raven that headed to New York to play for Ryan, Jim Leonhard brought his multiple talents to the Jets. In addition to his 54 tackles as a safety, Leonhard returned 21 punts in 2009, including a 51-yarder against the Tennessee Titans on September 27. Both teams donned throwback uniforms in honor of the 50th anniversary of the American Football League. The Jets won the game 24–17. *Al Pereira/Getty Images*

Like Scott, Leonhard, at 5-foot-8, is an underdog type. These are the kinds of hungry players Ryan surrounded himself with.

"Everyone has that chip, and with the underdog role and being undersized, everyone telling me that you can't do something, I've dealt with that my whole life," Leonhard said. "I do like to prove those people wrong. It's definitely something that drives me, but it's not the only thing that drives me. I've never had a lack of confidence in my ability."

Leonhard didn't receive any scholarship offers from Division I schools and walked on to the team at Wisconsin. He signed with the Buffalo Bills in 2005 as an undrafted

free agent, and he was allowed to walk away from the Bills and sign with the Ravens before the 2008 season. Even after the '08 campaign, Ravens general manager Ozzie Newsome made it clear it was unlikely the team would re-sign him because of Baltimore's depth at the position.

Settling into his new team, where he was wanted, Leonhard quickly became the quarterback of the Jets defense and, along with Scott, was the bridge between the returning Jets players and the new coach.

"THE SANCHISE"

As splashy as the Jets' moves were to get Scott and Leonhard, nothing beat the aggressive move they made to land Mark Sanchez as their franchise quarterback. The Jets traded up 12 spots in the 2009 NFL draft and took USC's Sanchez with the No. 5 overall pick.

In a nice twist, the Jets' dance partner in the blockbuster draft-day deal was none other than Eric Mangini and the Cleveland Browns, who owned the fifth pick in the draft. The Jets traded their first-round pick (No. 17 overall) and their second-round pick (No. 52 overall), along with defensive end Kenyon Coleman, safety Abram Elam, and quarterback Brett Ratliff.

The acquisition of Sanchez answered the question everyone already knew the answer to: Brett Favre was a goner. The Favre experiment had lasted for one season and probably cost Mangini his job.

As for Sanchez, he came in with high expectations. When the Jets selected him, the fans at the draft went wild with approval.

"I can't promise we're going to win the division," Sanchez said upon his arrival. "I can't promise we're going to win the Super Bowl and I'm going to be the MVP of the league. All I can promise is that I'm going to work hard."

Sanchez's only obstacle between him and the starting job was Kellen Clemens, a career backup whose agent, David Dunn, also happened to be Sanchez's agent.

"The only thing I can say to that is I've never grown up dreaming of being a backup," Sanchez said. "That's what it's all about, and I'm sure Kellen Clemens feels the same way and that's what this position is all about . . . . [It is about] competing for your job, and that's all I know how to do. It'll be a great matchup for us."

Sanchez had Rex Ryan and the Jets at "hello." When they visited with him in California for a workout, Sanchez blew them away with his personality and skill.

"We saw the great feet, the poise, and how confident he was," Ryan said. "Brian [Schottenheimer] put him through every workout known to man, and he passed every one of them with flying colors. We knew, I think, right then that this was the guy we really wanted."

Much of the attention at Jets training camp in 2009 was centered around first-round pick Mark Sanchez. He was tasked with filling the shoes left by Brett Favre and playing for a head coach that was talking Super Bowl before even coaching a game for New York. *Al Pereira/Getty Images*

MARK SANCHEZ
QUARTERBACK
2009–

THEY CAME IN TOGETHER as the new faces of the franchise, Rex Ryan and Mark Sanchez.

Ryan, who made it clear he wanted no part of Brett Favre returning to the Jets after his 2008 season in New York, was a rookie head coach who wanted his new start to have a fresh face at quarterback.

That face was Sanchez, for whom the Jets traded up to draft as the fifth overall pick in 2009. Sanchez had started only 16 college games at USC and was forgoing his senior year against his coach Pete Carroll's advice. But he would become an immediate starter for the Jets.

There were growing pains in the form of 20 interceptions and three lost fumbles in his debut season, but Sanchez quickly proved himself to be a tough player and a winner.

After the rocky start, he helped lead the Jets to the AFC Championship Game as a rookie, playing his best football in the biggest games. Sanchez was at his best in the postseason.

That trend would continue in his second year, during which he cut down on his turnovers, throwing seven fewer interceptions and losing two fewer fumbles and generally playing more consistently. Sanchez completed nearly 55 percent of his passes in 2010 and accumulated 3,291 passing yards.

And for the second consecutive year, Sanchez helped lead the Jets to within one game of the Super Bowl.

Sanchez had decided to leave school early, with one more year of eligibility remaining at USC. He had started only 16 games in college, raising questions about how ready he'd be for the NFL. His college coach, Pete Carroll, in fact, went public in saying that he thought Sanchez was making a mistake by coming out early and that he needed another year of college ball to develop.

That rubbed Sanchez the wrong way, though he never said anything negative about Carroll. Sanchez said he believed he was prepared for the scrutiny of playing in New York and for a franchise that hadn't played in a Super Bowl since Joe Namath led the Jets to the title in 1969.

"The kind of pressure, you expect that," he said. "As a quarterback, that's what you signed up for. I learned how to compete and deal with pressure at 'SC and in a large media market in Los Angeles, and things are only going to be bigger and better."

It didn't take long for Sanchez to get the rookie treatment from his teammates once the players convened for minicamp. It didn't help when *GQ* magazine hit the street with a photo spread Sanchez had posed for with model Hilary Rhoda before the draft.

Sanchez's teammates were merciless once they got a hold of it. When he came to work, photocopies of the pictures, some featuring him bare-chested and dressed up in a lifeguard suit, were plastered all over the walls of the building, including the locker room. The pictures also ended up as computer screensavers in offices throughout the building.

More than just a pretty face, Mark Sanchez quickly established himself as a winning quarterback in the NFL, leading the Jets to the conference finals in each of his first two seasons. *John Iacono/Sports Illustrated/Getty Images*

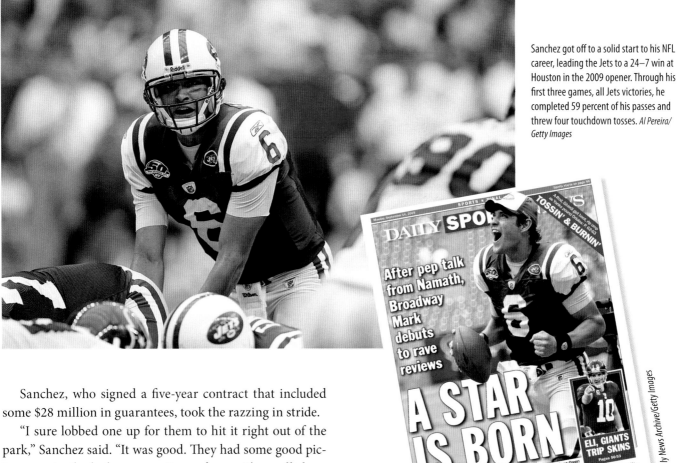

Sanchez got off to a solid start to his NFL career, leading the Jets to a 24–7 win at Houston in the 2009 opener. Through his first three games, all Jets victories, he completed 59 percent of his passes and threw four touchdown tosses. *Al Pereira/ Getty Images*

NY Daily News Archive/Getty Images

Sanchez, who signed a five-year contract that included some $28 million in guarantees, took the razzing in stride.

"I sure lobbed one up for them to hit it right out of the park," Sanchez said. "It was good. They had some good pictures up in the locker room. It was funny. They called me David Hasselhoff and all that."

"He's got thick skin," linebacker Calvin Pace said. "And that's good for a quarterback."

As Sanchez would soon find out, he'd need that thick skin playing under the bright lights of New York.

Not that there was much drama to it, but it didn't take long before Sanchez was named the Jets' starting quarterback. Showing his flair for the dramatic, his first pass of his first NFL preseason game was a majestic 48-yard toss to receiver David Clowney.

"For a rookie to step in on the first play and unleash one, it was pretty impressive," Ryan said. "He showed us everything we needed to see."

GAME TIME

After training camp, it was down to business for Sanchez and the Jets. At the regular-season opener, the Jets whipped the Texans 27–7 in Houston, and Sanchez was terrific, completing 18 of 31 passes for 272 yards and a touchdown.

After the game, his teammates awarded him the game ball.

"That was pretty special," Sanchez said. "I'll hold onto it tight and hope for plenty more."

Amidst the attention given to Sanchez, Ryan's defense suffocated the Texans' high-powered offense and showed a glimpse of things to come.

It got better the following Sunday, when the Jets played their hated AFC East rival, New England, in their home opener at Giants Stadium. Before the season, Ryan had delivered this bold statement: "I didn't come here to kiss Bill Belichick's rings."

Ryan, of course, was referring to the three Super Bowl rings Belichick had won with the Patriots. Those words didn't sit well with the New England locals, who couldn't wait to feast on the Jets and their rookie head coach and quarterback.

The crowd was fired up for the Week 2 meeting with the Patriots at the Meadowlands on September 20, 2009. The fans—along with the Jets defense—helped rattle New England quarterback Tom Brady (12), holding him to 23-of-47 passing in a 16–9 Jets triumph.
Robert Sabo/NY Daily News Archive/Getty Images

The Jets, however, shut down Tom Brady and the Patriots 16–9 and made a rather rousing statement about their arrival.

"We believe that we are the better team today," Ryan said afterward. "We went out and showed it. I think our fans are huge in this victory."

The Jets crowd, indeed, was as loud and raucous as it had been since the Jets last hosted a playoff game in 1998. After the game, Ryan said he was giving the fans a game ball that would be placed in the team's trophy case.

"I thought they were the difference," he said.

Sanchez wasn't bad either, finishing 14-of-22 for 163 yards and a touchdown to tight end Dustin Keller. Brady, who was hit more than 20 times by the Jets defense, was 23-of-47 for 216 yards and an interception.

"The big deal is, we're a football team that should be respected," Ryan said. "Sometimes we talk a little bit, but only because we have confidence in our football team."

As good as 2–0 felt, getting to 3–0 by defeating the Tennessee Titans the following week had Jets fans dreaming of the possibilities. Ryan's talk of a White House visit was being revisited.

The 24–17 win over Tennessee set up a Jets-Saints showdown in New Orleans for a clash of two undefeated teams. Confidence was high, in part because the Jets defense was terrorizing opponents and in part because Sanchez was playing more like a 10-year veteran than a rookie.

That, however, changed inside the Superdome on October 4, 2009.

Sanchez became the inexperienced rookie many expected him to be, turning the ball over four times—three interceptions (one returned for a touchdown) and one fumble in the end zone that was recovered by the Saints for a touchdown. Sanchez handed the Saints 14 points in a 24–10 loss.

"The kid, Sanchez, at times he looked like a rookie today," Ryan said.

"The truth is this team played well enough to win and I let them down," Sanchez said. "My mistakes absolutely killed us. It's tough when the rest of the team plays well enough to win and the quarterback doesn't play very well. . . . There's no excuse."

Sanchez was 14-of-27 for 138 yards, three interceptions, one lost fumble, and a 27.0 passer rating.

"The guys aren't worried," Sanchez said after the game. "It's no cause to start searching somewhere else for another quarterback. I know what happened. I got to the truth of it right away and the truth is I played poorly. Everybody else played well. I didn't. I'll wear this one, take ownership of it and move on."

The problem for the Jets was that Sanchez didn't move on so well. The 3–0 start gave way to a three-game losing streak. The Jets defense let the team down a week later in Miami, allowing a game-winning touchdown in the final seconds.

It got ugly in Week 6 with a 16–13 overtime loss at home to the Buffalo Bills. Sanchez threw five interceptions, including one in overtime, which led directly to 13 of Buffalo's 16 points. The Jets essentially handed the game to the weaker Bills team.

"Just an embarrassing day," Sanchez said afterward. "I've never played like this. Ever. Not even close. This is bad. To be perfectly honest, I don't know if I can play any worse."

Sanchez was 10-of-29 for 119 yards, five interceptions, and a staggering 8.3 rating. He completed half as many passes (five) to Bills players as he did to his own receivers (10).

Rex Ryan conceded that he had considered pulling Sanchez in favor of backup Clemens during the game, but added, "I still believe in him. He gives us the best chance to win, and he will remain our quarterback."

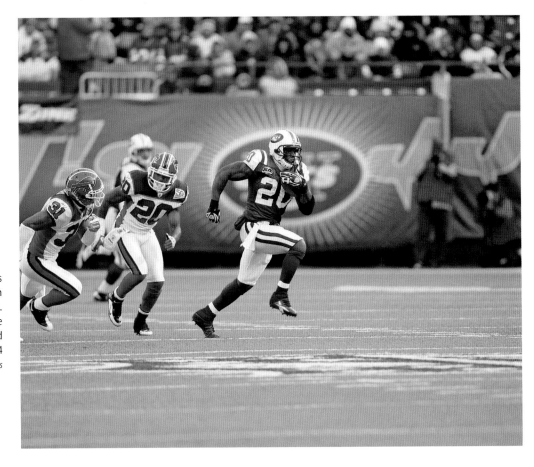

Running back Thomas Jones ran circles around the Buffalo defense on October 18, gaining 210 yards on 22 carries. Unfortunately, the Jets couldn't pull out the victory, losing in overtime. Jones finished the season with 1,402 rushing yards and 14 touchdowns. *Al Pereira/Getty Images*

Making the loss even more disturbing was the fact that the Jets ran for 318 rushing yards—the second-highest total in franchise history—led by a team-record 210-yard performance by Thomas Jones, who scored their only touchdown on a 71-yard run that gave the Jets a 13–3 halftime lead.

"We did a heck of a job on offense in the running game and our defense played lights out and I just gave [Buffalo] the win," Sanchez said. "Credit [the Bills] for catching all those passes, because it was just a poor game accuracy-wise with some misreads. I really let this team down."

The rookie quarterback acknowledged that he needed to "work harder, work smarter, and play a heck of a lot better."

The loss was a big punch in the gut for the Jets, who were now in crisis after thinking Super Bowl just weeks before as the toast of the NFL at 3–0 with their rookie quarterback.

"When we were 3–0, we thought we'd be 6–0 after six games," Keller said.

Veteran defensive end Shaun Ellis called the fall from 3–0 to 3–3 "shocking."

"We deserve every negative thing that's said about us," Scott said. "We are a 3–3 team at the crossroads."

NEW LIFE? NOT SO FAST

The Jets teased themselves the following week with a 38–0 shellacking of the Raiders in Oakland, where they played well in all phases. The win stopped the three-game slide and seemed to soothe everyone's anxiety—at least for the moment.

The one big negative on that day was losing running back Leon Washington to a compound leg fracture. Washington, the Jets' most explosive and versatile player, was out for the season. The leg break was so severe that he stayed behind in Oakland to have surgery while the team flew home.

The loss of Washington would sting the Jets. He was one of the best kickoff returners in the NFL, and he was Sanchez's best pass catcher out of the backfield as an outlet, check-down receiver.

The loss of Washington, however, could not be blamed for what was to come after the win in Oakland—another three-game losing streak.

This one began with a 30–25 home loss to the Dolphins. Miami's Ted Ginn Jr. returned two kickoffs for touchdowns against the Jets' special teams, and New York's rookie

After losing their three previous games, the Jets badly needed a win when they headed to Oakland on October 25. They easily took care of the Raiders, trouncing them 38–0. Calvin Pace (97), who led the team with eight sacks for the season, tallied three in the game. Here he bears down on Oakland's Bruce Gradkowski. *Greg Trott/AP Images*

running back Shonn Greene lost a fumble that was returned 48 yards for another Dolphins touchdown.

Just like in the New Orleans loss, the Jets gave away points like grownups handing out candy on Halloween. They managed to lose a game in which they outgained the Dolphins 378 to 104 yards on offense, had 23 first downs to the Dolphins' 10, and controlled the ball for 35:06 to the Dolphins' 25:54.

Sanchez wasn't the problem in this game. He threw for 265 yards and two touchdowns, ran for another score, and didn't turn the ball over. Thomas Jones rushed for more than 100 yards for the third consecutive week (102) while the Dolphins' "wildcat" offense, which had shredded New York's defense three weeks before, produced just six yards on seven plays. The Jets defense allowed only nine of Miami's 30 points.

"Sometimes things just don't make sense," Ryan fumed after the game. "It stinks. We totally outplayed them but got beat. It's a huge loss for us."

The next game, they found another crazy way to lose in a 24–22 decision to the Jacksonville Jaguars.

This defeat featured another defensive meltdown after the Jets had taken a 22–21 lead with 5:04 remaining. The Jaguars offense, which had no first downs and only 12 yards in the second half to that point, marched 80 yards to set up a game-winning, last-second field goal.

That left the Jets, once 3–0, with a 4–5 record.

"We're on life support right now," right tackle Damien Woody said. "Did we find another way to lose? Yup. This is real, real frustrating, real frustrating. Everybody needs to wake up and realize that the more this stuff happens we're

The New York defense led the NFL in fewest points allowed (236) in 2009, thanks in part to the efforts of veteran defensive end Shaun Ellis. Seen here celebrating his sack of Buffalo's Ryan Fitzpatrick, Ellis was in his 10th season with the club and hot on the trail of Mark Gastineau to become the Jets' all-time sacks leader. His 6.5 sacks in 2009 gave him 68 for his career, six behind Gastineau. *Darren Calabrese/The Canadian Press/AP Images*

Playing with Clemens, the backup quarterback, the Jets easily beat the Bucs 26–3 in Tampa. Suddenly, the three-game winning streak breathed life into their slim playoff hopes. They were 7–6 with three games to play.

That life seemed short-lived when the Jets lost to the Atlanta Falcons 10–7 at home to fall to 7–7. A distraught Ryan said, "This is tough, because we're obviously out of the playoffs. We thought we had a great chance to make it to the playoffs. This is hugely disappointing."

WAIT—NEW LIFE

Twenty-four hours after Ryan had declared the Jets dead and gone from the playoff race, he was informed that his team was not, in fact, mathematically eliminated quite yet.

"First off, I was dead wrong in the playoff scenario," Ryan said. "You would think that the head coach of the team would know the situations. I thought we had to win out. We had a single focus that we were going to have to win six straight games.

"We don't [just] have a possibility; we have a huge possibility—if we'll win out—that we can be in the playoffs. We're actually in a better situation right now, this week, than we were last week at this time. That's unbelievable. We're there. We've got a chance to make the playoffs and, hey, we're going for it."

The scenario, which was complicated and a long shot, was presented by Ryan in a Powerpoint presentation to the players on the Monday after the Atlanta loss. Ryan showed the players how they could control their own destiny entering the final week of the season.

- The Jets had to beat the 14–0 Colts in Indianapolis that Sunday.
- The Jaguars had to lose to the Patriots.
- The Dolphins had to lose to the Texans.

going to be sitting at home watching other teams in the postseason and saying, 'Man, we're better than them.'

"This is the time of year when really good football teams play their best football. This time of year separates pretenders from contenders."

When Ryan was asked after the Jacksonville game about his team's playoff chances, he said bluntly, "Not very good."

"We just spent all of our room for error," he said. "It's ridiculous. Right now, something's missing and we've got to find it."

The Jets wouldn't find it the following week either, losing 31–14 to the Patriots in New England, where Sanchez threw four interceptions in another rookie meltdown. The result left the Jets at 4–6 and with seemingly little chance of making the playoffs.

Fortunately for the Jets, though, after New England they had a succession of cupcakes on their schedule—the Carolina Panthers, Buffalo Bills, and Tampa Bay Buccaneers. The Jets scraped by the Panthers at home 17–6 and then squeaked past the Bills 19–13 in a game played in Toronto. Sanchez suffered a knee injury that would keep him out of the Tampa Bay game.

Although it came against backup quarterback Curtis Painter, not Peyton Manning, Dwight Lowery's second-half interception helped secure the Jets' 29–15 victory over the then-undefeated Colts on December 27, 2009, and helped keep New York's playoff hopes alive. *Al Pereira/Getty Images*

- And either the Ravens had to lose to the Steelers in Pittsburgh or the Broncos had to lose to the Eagles in Philadelphia.

If all those things happened, then the Jets would be facing the Cincinnati Bengals at home in their regular-season finale with a chance to win and get in.

Remarkably, every one of those things happened the way the Jets needed them to.

Making it all the more bizarre, the Jets were able to hold on and beat the Colts 29–15 largely because the Colts pulled their star players, beginning with quarterback Peyton Manning, to rest them for the playoffs rather than go for the magical undefeated season. It was a controversial decision by Colts management and an unpopular one in Indianapolis, but the Jets weren't complaining.

Once the Jets got to that regular-season finale against the Bengals, Cincinnati had already clinched its division title

and a win wouldn't change its postseason seeding. The Jets annihilated the Bengals 37–0 and made the playoffs.

Their next game? At Cincinnati in a wild-card contest the following week.

On a frigid January night in Cincinnati, the Jets beat the Bengals again, this time by a 24–14 score. They were going to San Diego to play the favored Chargers in the divisional round.

"This was just the first step in what we think is going to be a great journey," Ryan said.

As he stood at the podium, Ryan's eyes were red from a moving moment he'd just been a part of inside the Jets locker room when he presented team owner Woody Johnson with the game ball. Johnson's daughter, Casey, had died earlier in the week. Players said Johnson was overcome with emotion when Ryan gave him the game ball. Ryan, too, had tears in his eyes.

"This one was for Woody," Ryan said.

Tight end Dustin Keller breaks away down the sideline on a 45-yard touchdown play during the second quarter of the wild-card game at Cincinnati on January 9, 2010, putting New York ahead 14–7. The Jets defeated the Bengals 24–14 to notch their sixth victory in their last seven games. *Al Pereira/Getty Images*

After compiling only 504 rushing yards in 14 regular-season games in 2009, Shonn Greene ran wild in the playoffs. First he gained 135 yards against the Bengals, and then he scorched San Diego with 128 yards in round two, including this 53-yard touchdown run. The fourth-quarter score gave the Jets a 17–7 edge and helped them on their way to the AFC Championship Game. *Stephen Dunn/Getty Images*

"He was very emotional; you could tell how much this meant to him," Jim Leonhard said of Johnson. "After a win like that, you're on Cloud Nine and you come in here and you look at Woody Johnson's eyes and you realize that it's a game. This goes from football to real life real quick.

"It means a lot for us to get a win for him. We feel like we're helping him cope."

In the game, the Bengals couldn't cope with Sanchez, who played his best game as a pro, completing 12 of 15 passes for 182 yards, including a 45-yard scoring pass to Dustin Keller.

"He had the eye of the tiger today," Ryan said of his rookie quarterback, who had thrown 20 interceptions in the regular season but was playing his best in the biggest games. "He was on fire. He wanted this game in the worst way. I think he's tired of hearing he's the weak link on this football team. One of these days, he's going to be the biggest thing we have on this football team. Maybe that day's coming sooner rather than later."

Now the Jets were going back to San Diego having won six of their last seven games. Many expected the Jets' train to be halted by the Chargers and their high-octane offense. Many, that is, except the Jets.

That's why they went to San Diego and upset the Chargers 17–14 to advance to the AFC Championship Game for the first time since 1998.

Their opponent would be the Colts in Indianapolis, where the controversy had swirled just weeks before. The Jets had become irritated with all the talk that they won solely because the Colts had pulled their starters.

Now the Jets had their chance to shut everyone up and get to the place Ryan had said they were going since the day he was hired—to the Super Bowl.

"I don't think anybody could have drawn it up any better than this," said linebacker Calvin Pace.

"They're not going to respect us," defensive end Marques Douglas said of the Colts. "I'm pretty sure those guys are already making plans to go to the Super Bowl. But we're not going to rest until we're down in Miami for the Super Bowl."

"We definitely feel like this is our year," added guard Brandon Moore. "This is our shot. We're one game away from the big party,"

Receiver Braylon Edwards was fed up with all the talk about how the Jets had gotten lucky and "backed into" the playoffs, saying, "I hope this validates that we belong here."

Rookie quarterback Mark Sanchez (right) seemed poised in leading his team in the AFC Championship Game, but in the end Sanchez and the Jets were no match for the Colts' masterful quarterback, Peyton Manning. *Scott Boehm/Getty Images*

Kicker Jay Feely said, "This win validates everything Rex did. He took a lot of undue criticism. People look at him and sometimes they question the way he acts. But there's a purpose behind everything he does. He came in and had to try to convince this team that we are good enough to go to the Super Bowl—right now, this year."

STALLED OUT IN INDY

It was only fitting to the season that the AFC title game would tease the tortured Jets fan the way this one did.

In 1998, the last time the Jets had gotten this close, they led the Denver Broncos 10–0 before losing 23–10 with a barrage of second-half turnovers. This time, the Jets let a 17–13 halftime lead turn into a 30–17 victory for the Colts in Indianapolis.

Jumping ahead 17–6 late in the first half, the Jets seemingly had the Colts exactly where they wanted them. But

then Manning and the Colts scored 24 unanswered points to crush the Jets' dream and earn their second Super Bowl berth in four years. Indianapolis scored 17 second-half points against a Jets defense that hadn't allowed more than 15 points in a game in their last four games, all wins.

"We expected to go to the Super Bowl," Damien Woody said. "And to come so far—it was right there sitting in front of us and yet so far away. We were 30 minutes way."

The Jets were making big plays on offense, with Sanchez (17-of-30, 257 yards, two touchdowns, one interception) making a bid to become the first rookie quarterback in NFL history to lead his team to a Super Bowl. He connected with Edwards on an electric 80-yard scoring pass in the first quarter and threw another touchdown toss to tight end Keller.

The key turning point came at the end of the first half. After the Jets took a 17–6 lead with 2:11 remaining on a Jay Feely 48-yard field goal, they allowed Manning—a two-minute-drill magician—to march the Colts 80 yards in 58

Braylon Edwards (17) and Wallace Wright (15) celebrate after Edwards' 80-yard touchdown reception gave the Jets a 7–3 lead in the AFC Championship Game at Indianapolis on January 24, 2010. New York built a 17–6 lead before yielding 24 unanswered points. *Joe Robbins/Getty Images*

seconds and cut the lead to four. Manning's 16-yard scoring pass to Austin Collie completed the critical drive.

Several players, including Leonhard and Edwards, hinted that the Jets were rattled by the Colts' scoring drive at the end of the first half, and that they didn't react well to it after halftime.

"We didn't come out in the second half with that same attitude and that same fire," Edwards said. "We got a little complacent, and the Indianapolis Colts, they exposed that, especially Peyton Manning."

Rex Ryan said that late score in the first half "took a lot of wind out of our sails."

"To give up an easy score like that after we'd played so well was disheartening," said Leonhard, who noted that he sensed frustration among the players in the locker room at halftime.

"But we needed to understand we were 30 minutes away from the Super Bowl," Leonhard added. "We had the lead at halftime."

Manning gave the Colts a 20–17 lead when he connected with Pierre Garcon on a four-yard scoring pass with 8:03 remaining in the third quarter, and that was it for the Jets. The Colts put the game away with a 15-yard Manning scoring pass to tight end Dallas Clark for a 27–17 lead with just under nine minutes remaining in the game and capped it off with a 21-yard field goal with 2:29 remaining.

"This will eat us up all offseason," Leonhard said. "When you come up short, there are a lot of thoughts that go through your head. You could see all across this locker room, guys are like, 'Where do we go from here? What do we do now?'

"We feel like we're ready to take that next step. We felt like we were ready this year. Maybe we weren't. But we'll prepare next season to take that next step."

A NEW BEGINNING

The sting of the AFC Championship Game loss to the Colts began to wear off as soon as general manager Mike Tannenbaum began pushing the buttons for his offseason plan, gearing up for an all-or-nothing run at the Super Bowl.

The Jets were saddled with a major obstacle as one of the teams that fell within the NFL's "final four" rule, which stipulated that none of the four teams that reached the conference finals could sign an unrestricted free agent unless they lost one from their own roster. The Jets' problem was that, other than kicker Jay Feely, they didn't have a lot of desirable unrestricted free agents that other teams would come chasing.

So Tannenbaum got to work reloading the roster without signing unrestricted free agents. His first significant move was to trade for underachieving Chargers cornerback Antonio Cromartie, who had been a Pro Bowl performer in

Among the Jets' biggest offseason acquisitions in 2010 was former All-Pro running back LaDainian Tomlinson. Although his production had dipped with San Diego in 2009, in his first year as a Jet, Tomlinson ran for 914 yards and caught 52 passes for 368 yards, making him the team leader with 1,282 total yards from scrimmage. *Al Pereira/Getty Images*

2007 but whose production had slipped the following two years. He was acquired for a 2011 conditional draft pick.

Tannenbaum then allowed Feely to sign with the Arizona Cardinals, replacing him with former Dallas kicker Nick Folk.

Finally Tannenbaum made what turned out to be the blockbuster move of the offseason, trading for receiver Santonio Holmes, who had worn out his welcome in Pittsburgh after a series of off-field incidents. For Holmes, who was in violation of the NFL's substance abuse policy and already headed for a four-game suspension to start the 2010 season, the Jets gave up only a fifth-round draft pick to the Steelers.

The clever element to this plan was the fact that Holmes, Cromartie, and Braylon Edwards, who had been acquired in 2009 from Cleveland for almost nothing, were all considered risks, but they were all playing in contract years in 2010, meaning they had to be on their best behavior if they wanted to be re-signed or become attractive free agents after the season.

Also highlighting the busy offseason was the unpopular release of dependable running back Thomas Jones and perennial Pro Bowl guard Alan Faneca, both crucial locker room leaders.

The Jets signed veteran running back LaDainian Tomlinson, a better pass receiver out of the backfield than Jones and considered a better fit in a two-back rotation with Shonn Greene. Former Dolphins sack machine Jason Taylor was also signed as a free agent.

But the departures of Jones and Faneca were met with skepticism among the players, leading many to wonder if the Jets were messing with a good thing, tinkering with the chemistry that helped them come within a game of the Super Bowl just months earlier.

That skepticism was heightened when training camp arrived and a contract dispute with cornerback Darrelle Revis, arguably the team's best player, dragged deep into the summer and got ugly with sniping from both sides.

All of this drama, of course, was perfect fodder for the cameras that filmed Jets training camp for HBO's *Hard Knocks* series.

The team's decision to appear on the series let viewers in on a very inside look at the Jets and all their characters, beginning with Ryan, whose incessant cursing drew criticism. Among the most offended was former Colts head coach and current analyst for NBC TV Tony Dungy, who chastised Ryan for the salty language.

THE DARRELLE REVIS CONTRACT SAGA

At training camp in 2009, the rookie Sanchez trying to establish himself as the starting quarterback had provided the main storyline to the Jets' first camp at SUNY-Cortland, a college campus in upstate New York. In 2010, it was the Revis holdout that dominated camp.

The holdout officially began on August 1, when Revis failed to report to the training camp site by 5:30 p.m. Rex Ryan, filmed by the *Hard Knocks* cameras, checked Revis' assigned dorm room that night and called out, "Come home, Revis. Come home." Ten days later the coach offered to call off practice and have the entire organization present to meet with Revis and his agents, Neil Schwartz and Jonathan Feinsod.

DARRELLE REVIS

CORNERBACK
2007–

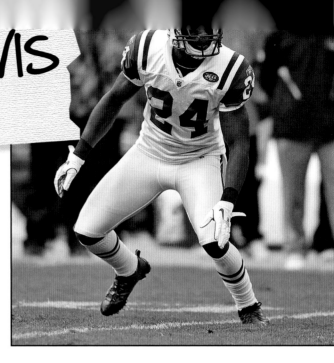

MANY PEOPLE KNEW that Darrelle Revis would be good in the NFL, but few realized he would be this good. In the 2009 and 2010 seasons, Revis forged a reputation as the best shut-down cornerback in the NFL. To illustrate how lost he made opposing receivers feel, he earned the nickname "Revis Island."

Perhaps best defining "Revis Island" was his performance against Indianapolis in the 2011 wild-card playoff game, when he held Colts receiver Reggie Wayne to one catch for one yard. Wayne, who had led the NFL with 111 receptions in 2010, angrily said that he had been a mere bystander in the game and that he shouldn't even have suited up.

Revis was drafted 14th overall out of the University of Pittsburgh in the 2007 NFL draft. The Jets had traded their first-round selection, the first of their second-round selections, and their fifth-round selection to the Carolina Panthers for the chance to move from the 25th to the 14th spot, one ahead of Revis' hometown Pittsburgh Steelers.

Revis started right away for the Jets, the first rookie to do so since Ray Mickens in 1996. Starting all 16 games, Revis ended his debut season with 87 tackles, one sack, one forced fumble, and three interceptions.

His best season was 2009, when he truly forged his "Revis Island" nickname, shutting down some of the NFL's best wide receivers—Houston Texans Pro Bowler Andre Johnson (4 receptions for 35 yards) and New England Pro Bowler Randy Moss (4 re-

Although his contract holdout in 2010 earned him some notoriety, Darrelle Revis' skills as one of the top defensive backs in the game makes him a leader on the Jets defense. *Joe Robbins/Getty Images*

ceptions and 24 yards), to name two. Revis finished second in the Defensive Player of the Year voting to Charles Woodson. Rex Ryan called his season "the best year a corner has ever had, the most impact a corner has ever had in the National Football League."

Although Revis became more widely known because of his 36-day holdout for a new contract in the summer of 2010, his prowess on the field superseded that notoriety. Although he didn't record any interceptions during the 2010 season, his game-changing impact was validated by the fact that he was named to the Pro Bowl for the third consecutive year and earned his second-straight first-team All-Pro selection.

The negotiations between the Jets and Revis' agents during the month of August were very acrimonious at times, and there was some early sniping through the media. On August 12 the two sides issued a joint statement to put an end to the war of words. "From this point forward," the statement read, "all discussions regarding these negotiations will remain confidential." In other words, a media blackout.

On September 4, Ryan had made the unprecedented move of flying down to Florida with team owner Woody Johnson to visit with Revis, his mother, Diana, and uncle, former NFL defensive lineman Sean Gilbert, to make the final push for the contract dispute to end.

The following day, frustrated that a deal was not reached, Ryan stormed out during a conference call with the agents, yelling expletives at them as he left. Nevertheless, GM Mike Tannenbaum was able to work out a deal later that day.

Revis, who was scheduled to make $1 million in 2010, the fourth year of his original six-year deal, ended up missing

The Jets played the role of home team in their preseason matchup with the New York Giants at the newly completed New Meadowlands Stadium on August 16, 2010. The $1.6 billion facility has a seating capacity of 82,566, making it the second-largest stadium in the NFL. *David Bergman/Sports Illustrated/Getty Images*

all of camp and all four preseason games during the 36-day holdout. After accruing nearly $600,000 in fines for the holdout, he agreed to a new four-year, $46 million deal with $32 million guaranteed.

When Revis finally joined the team, on September 6, he was met with a special greeting by his teammates at practice.

As he walked slowly to the practice field, players bowed to their knees and chanted "Revis Christ" and then broke into a slow and steady "Rudy" clap.

Ryan, addressing the players after the practice, told them, "It's up to us now; we have everything we need."

Revis began his press conference by apologizing to the fans and said the process "humbled" him. "I'm happy this is over with so I can play football again," he added.

THE JOURNEY BEGINS

After all the bravado, all the talk of it being a Super Bowl-or-bust year, the 2010 season began with a much-anticipated home opener against Ryan's former team, the Ravens. It was the Jets' first regular-season game at the new Meadowlands Stadium and the first game of the NFL season on *Monday Night Football*.

New York's ballyhooed offense could not have looked worse in the maddening 10–9 loss. Sanchez threw for a mere 74 yards, and the offense controlled the ball for only 21:28, managed just six first downs, and produced only three field goals. All this, after the offseason acquisitions of Tomlinson and Holmes, had fans in a panic.

In the days before the game, Ravens linebacker Ray Lewis had talked about how, with all their bold talk, Ryan and the

Braylon Edwards leaps over New England defensive back Darius Butler to give the Jets their first first touchdown in the New Meadowlands Stadium and tie the game 7–7 in the second quarter on September 19, 2010. The Jets went on to win 28–14. *Al Pereira/Getty Images*

Jets might have written a check they can't cash. After the game, the Ravens rubbed the Jets' face in the loss.

"Rex put a bull's eye on them," Ravens running back Ray Rice said after the game. "Like Ray Lewis said, he put more pressure on them than he did on us. You've got to write a check you can cash, and starting 0–1 isn't going to get you a Super Bowl."

The Jets surely didn't look like the Super Bowl favorites they made themselves out to be.

"That's not who we are; that's not how we play," an exasperated Ryan said. "That was a joke."

That joke would turn into euphoria a week later when the Jets played rival New England and beat them 28–14, outscoring them 18–0 in the second half. And just like that, the swagger was back.

"We're back to being who we think we are," Ryan said after the Patriots game.

"To hear everyone say we were pretenders not contenders, that pissed us off," said Edwards. "Today showed who we really are."

Sanchez, who outplayed Tom Brady and threw three touchdown passes, said, "This is just the beginning for us. It's tough when you lose that first game; it feels like you're 0–10. This game couldn't come soon enough for us."

Damien Woody conceded that, after the loss to Baltimore, "it seemed like the whole world came crashing down."

The only thing that came crashing down in this game, other than the Patriots, was Revis, who suffered a hamstring injury while being beaten by Randy Moss on a 34-yard touchdown pass late in the first half.

For Revis, who during an offseason interview called Moss a "slouch," it was an embarrassing moment. He was not only beaten on the play by the man he ridiculed, but now he was headed for rehab after tearing his hamstring—less than two weeks after ending his contract holdout.

Keeping things interesting off the field, on September 21, just two days after defeating the Patriots, Edwards was arrested for DWI while driving with a couple of teammates in the early morning hours in Manhattan. Ryan responded with a rant to his players about conduct away from the team and benched Edwards for the beginning of the next game.

The Jets, without Revis for two weeks, reeled off four consecutive wins after the New England game, including a 29–20 win against Brett Favre and the Vikings in a Monday night home game.

Consecutive win number five came in Denver, and a game they had no right winning. After Denver took a 20–17 lead in the fourth quarter, Holmes drew an pass interference penalty on a desperation play in the final seconds to set up the winning touchdown. Tomlinson ran it in from two yards to secure the 24–20 victory for New York.

Jerricho Cotchery's dropped pass in the end zone was just one of numerous misplays by the Jets in their 9–0 loss to the Packers on October 31. *Joe Robbins/Getty Images*

CARDIAC JETS

The win over the Broncos sent the Jets into their bye week feeling great with a 5–1 record and with a home game against the Green Bay Packers looming. This is where the season hit its worst skid.

The Jets, looking passive on offense, lost to the Packers, the eventual Super Bowl champs, 9–0 on Halloween. It was the first time they'd been shut out in four years, and it foiled their bid to win a sixth straight game for the first time since 1998.

"It felt embarrassing to be shut out at home," Woody said after the game. "Our personnel and our coaching staff is too good for us to be shut out at home."

"A shutout is ridiculous when you're at home," center Nick Mangold said. "It's disappointing for us, disappointing for our fans."

The most disappointing plays came from the highly touted receiving corps, which dropped at least six catchable passes. The worst of them came in the third quarter, when Holmes dropped a pass on a slant route on which he was so wide open he would have scored had he made the catch. Even Jerricho Cotchery, the team's most dependable receiver, uncharacteristically had a couple of bad drops.

But the misplays weren't limited to the receivers. Punter Steve Weatherford made an ill-advised decision when he faked a punt and ran for it on fourth-and-18 from the Jets' 20-yard line. He came up a yard short, and the Packers converted a 20-yard field goal for a 3–0 first-quarter lead. Then, in the third quarter and the Jets still trailing by just three, Folk was wide right on a 37-yard attempt; he entered the game having made 13 of 15 field goals.

The loss to Green Bay was followed by a series of games that in many ways defined the Jets' season—three wins in a row that came in the closing seconds.

The first was an overtime win in Detroit. The Jets offense was effectively stifled by the Lions through more than three quarters before Sanchez came alive and led New York back from a 10-point fourth-quarter deficit. The young quarterback stunned the sellout Ford Field crowd by completing 10-of-13 for 144 yards on the Jets' last three offensive possessions, leading them to 13 points and a 23–20 triumph. The winning field goal in overtime was set up by a 52-yard catch-and-run by Holmes.

"Mark was at his best when we needed it most," Ryan said.

After going his entire rookie year without a fourth-quarter comeback victory on his resume, Detroit was the second such comeback in three games Sanchez helped engineer.

"You always judge quarterbacks the same way, and that's in wins," Ryan said. "After wins it would be fourth-quarter

Santonio Holmes and Mark Sanchez celebrate in the locker room after their 37-yard pass play in the closing seconds of overtime defeated the Browns and gave the Jets their second consecutive overtime victory on the road. *Al Pereira/Getty Images*

[comebacks]. Can he lead his team back from being down in the fourth quarter? He's had two big ones already this year for us."

And a week later, Sanchez and the Jets would do it again. After being outplayed by the Browns for most of the game in Cleveland, the Jets ripped yet another victory from the jaws of defeat, winning 26–20 in overtime. This time, it was a 37-yard Holmes catch-and-run that provided the game-clinching points with 16 seconds remaining in overtime.

With the victory, the Jets became the first team in NFL history to win back-to-back overtime games on the road.

"We're far from perfect; there's no question about it," Ryan said after the game. "But we're 7–2, and we'll take it. That's what good teams do. At the end of the day, the only thing that matters is the number of wins you've got and the number of losses you've got."

Among the intriguing subplots to the game were Browns head coach Eric Mangini facing the team that fired him two seasons earlier, and Rex Ryan facing his twin brother, Rob, the Browns defensive coordinator.

"Clearly, [the game] wasn't just personal for me, it was personal for a lot of guys," Rex said afterward. "But like I told the guys, at one o'clock, [the Browns] are nameless, faceless objects and that's what you have to treat it as. Whether it's your twin brother, your friend, or whomever, you've got a

job to do. Our goal is to be a champion, and we have to find ways to get it done. That's what we did."

For Rex, the game marked the third time he and Rob were pitted against each other in the NFL but the first since Rex became a head coach. Rex left the building 3–0 against Rob, with his teams outscoring Rob's teams 83–36.

Another stirring, last-second New York win followed a week later. This time the Jets allowed a 23–7 fourth-quarter lead against the Houston Texans at the Meadowlands to disappear into a 27–23 deficit. Then, starting a drive from their own 28-yard line with 49 seconds remaining and no timeouts, Sanchez did it again, channeling his inner John Elway and Joe Montana and engineering an improbable game-winning drive.

Sanchez completed four passes to get the needed 72 yards, the last six yards coming on the game-winning pass to (who else?) Holmes with 10 seconds remaining in the game.

"I was thinking that we've done it over and over this year so I was like, 'All right, let's see how we get out of this this time,'" Jim Leonhard said.

"Obviously, we had our doubts," said tackle Wayne Hunter. "But the way we've been playing these last three games, anything can happen with us."

It was the third consecutive game in which Holmes made the decisive play, and the fourth in five games.

Displaying the poise of an experienced veteran, Mark Sanchez led the Jets on a dramatic game-winning drive to defeat the Texans 30–27 on November 21, 2010. It was the third week in a row that New York eked out a victory on the game's final drive. *Jim McIsaac/Getty Images*

"Santonio's been the home run hitter we thought he was going to be," said Calvin Pace said.

"The guy is a gamer," added Sanchez about Holmes. "The last drive, we're down, no timeouts left, less than a minute and he says, 'All right, let's get it.' That's it. That's all he says."

One play before the game-winner, Sanchez connected with Braylon Edwards on a 42-yard strike down the right sideline to give the Jets a first-and-goal from the six with 16 seconds remaining.

"Can you explain it? Because I can't explain it," right tackle Woody said. "I've never seen anything like this in one season. It seems like it's just one of those seasons, man."

As Ryan explained it, "We keep finding ways to win, and that's what championship teams do. If I have to apologize for every week I will—all the way to the Super Bowl."

Rex Ryan could only look on helplessly from the sideline as the Patriots handed his Jets a good, old-fashioned butt kicking on December 6, 2010. The 45–3 defeat was the worst in Ryan's first two season as head coach. *Rob Tringali/SportsChrome/Getty Images*

THE FINAL STRETCH

A home victory over the Bengals on Thanksgiving, just four days after the win against the Texans, set the stage for the 9–2 Jets to play the 9–2 Patriots at Gillette Stadium in a battle of teams with the best record in the league and the most anticipated regular-season game in years.

The Jets went to New England dreaming of taking control of the AFC East, which the Patriots had dominated for more than a decade. They left devastated, suffering a 45–3 thrashing on national TV. It was the most embarrassing moment of the Ryan era, by far the worst defeat the Jets suffered in the two years he'd coached to that point.

"The biggest butt whipping I've ever taken as a coach," Ryan said. "We were outplayed and outcoached."

These words came after he had told reporters during the week that he was going to New England with the intention of kicking Patriots coach Bill Belichick's butt.

"I came in to kick his butt and he kicked mine," Ryan said. "We knew this was a big division game and we thought we would put a stranglehold on it. We could have been up one game on them and the tiebreaker. Now they've won one and we've won one."

The Jets defense let Tom Brady (21-of-29, 326 yards) have his way, playing pitch-and-catch with his receivers and throwing four touchdown passes. The Jets offense, meanwhile, was simply awful. Sanchez went 17-of-33 and threw three interceptions, all of which came in the second half and led to New England touchdowns.

It was a humbling night for the Jets.

"This humble pie tastes like a car tire and it goes down like peanut butter," said defensive tackle Sione Pouha.

"If you can draw up getting your [butt] kicked, we did it," Pace said. "This was embarrassing."

The night began badly and got worse. By the time the first quarter was over, the stunned Jets were down 17–0. They trailed 24–3 at the half.

"I looked at the scoreboard and said, 'Am I seeing things?'" said Woody. "It all just happened so fast. We were shell-shocked. We got hit with a haymaker. This was definitely embarrassing, but we can't let this snowball. At the end of the day, it was just one loss."

The loss dropped the Jets to 9–3 and into second place behind the 10–2 Patriots. It also effectively ended the Jets' hopes of winning their first AFC East title since 2002.

"We're going to take this like men," linebacker Bart Scott said after the game. "I know there will be a lot of bad things written about us and we'll deserve it. Hopefully we'll see these guys again and get another opportunity."

That opportunity would indeed come six weeks later when the teams met in the AFC divisional playoff round.

Before that could happen, though, the Jets needed to rebound from the 45–3 trouncing. They tried to put the memory behind them when, three days later, Ryan gathered the team together at one end of the practice fields, dug a hole in the ground, and buried the game ball from the Patriots loss.

The symbolic gesture didn't help cure the hangover, however. The following week the Jets lost 10–6 to the Dolphins, another game in which their offense was so poor it spurred New York fans to call for offensive coordinator Brian Schottenheimer's job.

But the biggest storyline from that December 12 game came when Sal Alosi, the Jets' strength and conditioning coach, organized a "human wall" of inactive players along the sideline to prevent opposing players from running out of bounds on punt plays to avoid blocks. Alosi stuck his knee out to intentionally trip Miami defensive back Nolan Carroll.

The day after the incident, which was caught clearly on camera, Alosi issued a public apology. On December 15, the Jets suspended him indefinitely. The NFL conducted an investigation and sent out a memo to all teams making clear that the practice was illegal. The league also fined the Jets $100,000. After the season, Alosi was fired.

The team, meanwhile, was in the throes of going two games without scoring a touchdown and were headed to Pittsburgh to take on the Steelers and the NFL's top-ranked defense. Against those tough odds, the Jets won a gritty 22–17 decision to notch their 10th win of the season and put them in commanding position to claim a wild-card playoff berth.

New York secured the game by stopping the Steelers at their 10-yard line with a tough defensive stand. Reserve

Offensive coordinator Brian Schottenheimer and quarterback Mark Sanchez teamed up to get the Jets offense back on track for a much-needed win against the Steelers in Week 15 of the 2010 season. *George Gojkovich/Getty Images*

cornerback Marquice Cole broke up a pass by quarterback Ben Roethlisberger intended for tight end Matt Spaeth in the end zone on the final play of the game, clinch the Jets' most significant victory of the season.

"We said we were going to come in here and weren't going to leave without a win," Cotchery said.

It was the Jets' first win in Pittsburgh in seven tries. They'd lost their previous two games there by a combined score of 55–9 and hadn't scored an offensive touchdown in nine quarters entering the game.

The victory gave the Jets a two-game lead for the wild-card berth with two to play, and perhaps as importantly it galvanized the team for the playoff run on which it was about to embark.

"We were sinking," said Scott. "We went from fighting for the best record in the league to if we lose this game fighting to get into the playoffs."

"A loss would have been devastating," Brandon Moore said. "You could feel the intensity from the coaches and the speeches they gave. Guys stepped up to the challenge."

Ryan was at the head of the line in stepping up. In the Saturday night team meeting at the hotel, the head coach delivered an impassioned speech to his players and got so worked up that he was in tears.

"He welled up, he got emotional, and we took it as a personal challenge," said Hunter. "Rex is a very emotional guy, and just seeing that passion in his heart and seeing the passion in his eyes fired us up. The game could not come any sooner. It was a long night and long day, waiting for this game to start."

Earlier in the week, the day after the loss to the Dolphins, Sanchez had implored his teammates to "lean on" him and to trust him as their quarterback.

"Mark's speech set the tone for the week," Hunter said. "His speech was intense. . . . It was needed coming from our quarterback.

About Sanchez's speech, Tomlinson said, "When he stood up in that huddle this week and he said, 'I'm going to play better, I'm not going to continue to turn the ball over,' he had that look in his eyes, a look that you had to believe in the guy.

"When your quarterback stands up in front of you and delivers a message like that, you can feel it. . . . He was going to get back into his groove."

Schottenheimer, too, was in a groove in Pittsburgh. One week after Jets fans chanted for him to be fired, Schottenheimer called a marvelous game against the Steelers, playing away from trends and keeping the Pittsburgh defense off balance.

"It was pretty much the Six [Sanchez's number] and Schotty show," Cotchery said. "They were in a zone."

Ryan called Sanchez' game "as gutsy a performance as you'll find. He was absolutely outstanding. I knew he would respond."

Through all the distractions of the season, the Jets managed to win their 11th game of 2010 with a 38–7 triumph over Buffalo at New Meadowlands Stadium. Defensive back Marquice Cole (34) picked off two Bills passes, one of which he returned 35 yards for a touchdown to give the Jets a 10–0 lead. *Jim Luzzi/Getty Images*

But just as the Jets looked to be back on track and in good shape for the playoffs, their world was rocked. Just days after winning in Pittsburgh, an Internet site published videos featuring a woman who appeared to be Ryan's wife, Michelle, in suggestive foot fetish poses.

Ryan, whose voice seemed to be on one of the videos as the person doing the filming, never denied it was his wife. Instead he chose to say repeatedly that it was a "personal matter."

The day the videos came out, Ryan told his players that there was "something coming out" that was embarrassing to him and his family, and he implored them to not let it distract them from their upcoming game in Chicago.

Ryan later addressed reporters and looked as nervous and uncomfortable as he ever had. He invoked the phrase "personal matter" six times while trying to deflect the questions.

To a man, Ryan's players defended their coach.

"That's my man right there," said Scott. "I love him to death, and I'll be right behind him supporting him all the time. That's all I know how to do. It's not Coach Rex, it's Uncle Rex. That's my uncle."

Said Sanchez, "It's a personal matter with Rex, but we're behind him one hundred percent, and it won't affect our team. I totally support him. He's our coach. We'll rally behind him."

Revis described the scene in the team meeting room as a bit surreal, as not everyone knew what was going on. But the All-Pro cornerback echoed his teammates' views that it wasn't a big deal to them but rather was a matter between him and his family.

"At the end of the day," said Revis, "that's his wife, and he can do whatever he wants with his wife. It's not like he's out committing adultery or anything negative."

Still, Revis admitted, "It's always something with this team, and it always will be."

PLAYOFF BOUND

After the win in Pittsburgh, the Jets split their last two regular-season games against Chicago and Buffalo to finish with a record of 11–5, their best since 1998. For the wild-card playoff game, they headed to Indianapolis, where, of course, they had ended their 2009 season with a loss to the Colts in the AFC Championship Game.

Beyond that game, Colts quarterback Peyton Manning had long been a nemesis for Ryan, having solved Ryan's defenses and beaten him in five of six games against him. The only win for Ryan was the 2009 regular-season game in which the Colts pulled their starters in the second half to rest them for the playoffs. In the five Manning-led wins, two

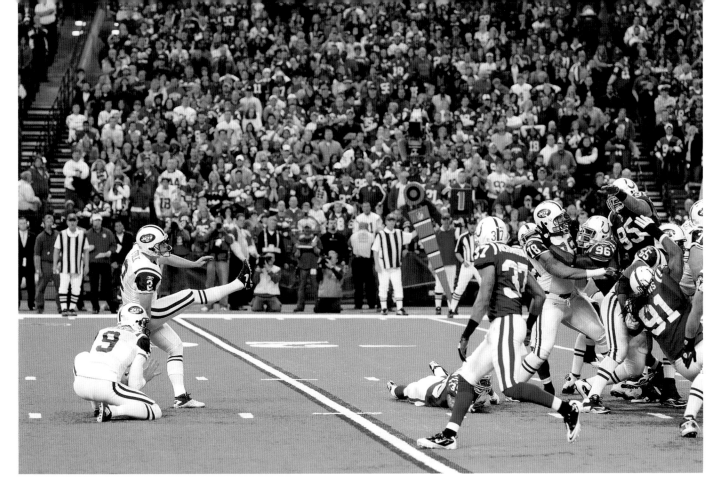

Nick Folk delivers the game-winning 32-yard field goal against the Colts in the wild-card playoff game on January 8, 2011. The 17–16 victory provided some vindication following the loss to Indianapolis in the previous year's playoffs and also sent the Jets on their way to another meeting with the Patriots. *Joe Robbins/Getty Images*

of which came in the postseason, the Colts outscored the Ryan-coached teams 144–53 with Manning going 94-of-150 for 1,321 yards, 12 touchdowns, and two interceptions.

In the days leading up to the wild-card game in January 2011, Ryan called out Manning, saying this time it was "personal." He said he wanted to "put the shoe on the other foot."

"Is it personal? Yes, it's personal," Ryan said. "It's personal against him, Reggie Wayne, all those guys, yeah. . . . Absolutely. Peyton Manning has beaten me twice in the playoffs. That's well-documented. You've got all the stats. But this is about this year, and I've waited a whole year for this."

The wait was worth it. The Jets finally solved Manning and beat the Colts 17–16 on a 32-yard, game-winning field goal by Folk as time expired.

Folk's game winner came after Colts kicker Adam Vinatieri had booted a 50-yarder to give Indy a 16–14 lead with 53 seconds remaining. Manning, whom the Jets defense has bottled up almost all game, had led the Colts to apparent victory by driving them 48 yards to set up the Vinatieri field goal.

After it was over, a euphoric Ryan said, "I'll tell you what, it feels awesome because this is the playoffs and we're moving on."

And where else in this season of endless drama would the Jets move on to?

Foxborough, Massachusetts, of course, for yet another epic game against the Patriots.

JETS–PATRIOTS III

Only one week removed from saying the game against the Colts was "personal" for him against Manning, Ryan ratcheted up the stakes for the New England game.

"This week is about Bill Belichick against Rex Ryan," Ryan said to kick off the week. "It's personal. It's about him against me, and that's what it's going to come down to. When you look at it, both teams are very even. When you look at the players, our teams are solid across the board. If you look at the assistant coaches, we're on level ground.

"This is going to be about me raising my level against Bill Belichick," Ryan went on. "I recognize he's the best, but I'm

Defensive end Calvin Pace inflicts one of New York's five sacks against Tom Brady in the AFC divisional playoff game at Gillette Stadium. New York harassed Brady all night long in the 28–14 Jets win. *David Bergman/Sports Illustrated/Getty Images*

just trying to be the best on Sunday. . . . I recognize that my level has to come up and he's going to get my best shot. He's going to get everything I have on Sunday. If he slips at all, we're going to beat him."

Ryan acknowledged that he had been out-coached in the 45–3 Jets loss on December 6 and did not have his team properly prepared. He also made a point of crediting Belichick as a "Hall of Fame coach" and someone who will go "down in history as maybe the best football coach in the history of this game or close to it."

Ryan was irked that when analysts talked about the Jets–Patriots rivalry all they talked about was the 45–3 game, and not the Jets' 28–14 win at the Meadowlands in Week 2. He became defiant in the face of so much sentiment against his team, which was a nine-point underdog heading into the divisional playoff game.

Asked why he chose to place all the pressure on himself, Ryan said, "I'm the guy that said we'd be in this position again. By the way, we're here. I'm the guy that said we'd play them again. I'm the guy who believes we'll beat them. It comes down on me, nobody else."

Asked if the game would be a "defining" game for him as a head coach, Ryan didn't flinch, saying, "No question. I think that's true."

Ryan said he told Belichick during the post-game handshake after the 45–3 loss, "We'll see you in round three."

The chatter in the week leading up to the game wasn't limited to Ryan. Cornerback Antonio Cromartie called Tom Brady an "asshole" and proclaimed that he hated him. Then Patriots receiver Wes Welker used 11 veiled references to feet in a press conference, a clear shot at Ryan and the foot-fetish flap. Belichick was so incensed by Welker's comments that he benched him for the start of the game.

Culminating the emotionally charged week, former Jets defensive end Dennis Byrd gave a powerful motivational speech at the Saturday night team meeting before the game. A surprise speaker at the meeting, Byrd stood before the players with the actual jersey that had been cut away from his paralyzed body after the collision that ended his career in 1992.

Still, the deck appeared to be stacked against the Jets. The Patriots were 8–0 at Foxborough that season, and Brady was working on an NFL-record 28 consecutive wins at home. The New England offense entered the game having scored 30 or more points in each of their last eight games.

But the Jets were unfazed and pulled off a convincing 28–21 upset for their eighth win in 10 road games. Ryan's defense suffocated the Patriots offense, sacking Brady five

After a week of highly charged words, the two rival head coaches—Rex Ryan and Bill Belichick—hug at midfield following the divisional playoff game between their teams on January 16, 2011. *Jim Rogash/Getty Images*

times—the most he'd been taken down all season—and picking him off once.

The look of fear, confusion, and bewilderment in Brady's eyes was priceless for the New York defenders.

"He was terrified," defensive tackle Trevor Pryce said. "In the first half he was absolutely frazzled. It's shocking because you don't see it very often. The game plan was out of sight. We did some stuff I've never seen a pro football coach do. It was the craziest thing I ever saw. We turned simple things and found a way to make it as complicated as possible, and Tom Brady literally had no answer for it.

"Tom Brady is going to look at the film tomorrow and say, 'Oh, that's what they were doing.' Well, too late mother-f---er. We confused a Hall of Fame quarterback, but we think we have a Hall of Fame coach."

"He was scared straight," added safety James Ihedigbo. "He had no idea where the pressures were coming from."

Welker, who had been a Jets killer in previous meetings, did play after being benched for the first offensive series, but he was a non-factor, stifled by the Jets' secondary, led by Revis.

The Jets had defeated Manning and the Colts in Indianapolis and then vanquished Brady and the Patriots in Foxborough. Now it was on to Pittsburgh for the AFC Championship Game, where they would take on Ben Roethisberger and the Steelers.

"On to Round Three—mission impossible," Ryan said after the New England game. "We came here for a reason. Maybe everyone else didn't believe us, but we believed."

60 MINUTES FROM HISTORY

The AFC Championship Game against the Steelers at Heinz Field on January 23, 2011, marked the Jets' fourth appearance in the conference title game since their lone Super Bowl in January 1969.

Forty-two years had passed since that day when Joe Namath made good on his famous guarantee and changed the course of pro football history.

Fourteen thousand nine hundred and seventy-six days had passed.

Six hundred thirty-one regular season games had been played.

Twenty-three playoff games had been played.

Fourteen different head coaches had coached.

Eight U.S. presidents had held office.

And still the New York Jets were without another Super Bowl appearance.

Sadly for fans who had waited all those years for more glory, the Jets came up short once again in Pittsburgh.

After the Jets had defeated the Patriots in the emotionally charged divisional playoff game, New England receiver Deion Branch predicted a Jets letdown in the AFC Championship Game, saying that the win over the Patriots "was their Super Bowl."

Watching the AFC title game, it was hard to argue with Branch's assessment. The Jets looked like they were sleepwalking through the first two quarters, falling behind 24–0. They did rally in the second half, however, scoring 16 unanswered points before losing 24–19 and falling short of the Super Bowl yet again.

In a particularly cruel irony, despite the horrible start, the Jets had a chance to win at the end of the game, but their trusted defense let it slip away, allowing the Steelers to keep a final drive alive and run out the clock with a couple of key pass plays on third down. The clincher was a 14-yard throw from Roethlisberger to Antonio Brown on third-and-six from the Jets' 40-yard line. With New York out of timeouts, the play iced the game.

It was the final dagger on a night when the Jets curiously didn't look prepared as the Steelers built a 24–3 lead at halftime.

Santonio Holmes celebrates after scoring on a 45-yard pass play in the third quarter of the AFC Championship Game in Pittsburgh. The touchdown cut the Steelers' lead to 24–10 and helped turn the momentum back in the Jets' direction. *Nick Laham/Getty Images*

"We chose a bad time in the season to play our worst half of football," Ihedigbo said. "Defense, special teams, offense—it was just terrible. This hurts a lot more than last year."

The Steelers went up 7–0 on a one-yard scoring run by Rashard Mendenhall that climaxed their more than nine-minute-long opening drive. A 20-yard Shaun Suisham field goal gave Pittsburgh a 10–0 lead before Roethlisberger's 2-yard run at the two-minute warning made it 17–0. Forty-seven seconds later, blitzing Steelers cornerback Ike Taylor sacked Sanchez and forced a fumble that was recovered by William Gay and returned 19 yards for a touchdown—24–0 Pittsburgh.

Sanchez (20-for-33, 233 yards, 2 touchdowns) appeared to injure his right shoulder on the play. He lay motionless on the ground for several moments before laboring off the field, but he returned on the next series and drove the Jets downfield to set up a 42-yard Nick Folk field goal that cut the lead to 24–3 with nine seconds remaining in the half.

Sanchez and the Jets finally got themselves together for the second half. A 45-yard touchdown pass to Holmes cut the lead to 24–10 less than eight minutes into the third quarter.

New York had an opportunity to reduce the deficit to a lone touchdown after setting up a first-and-goal from the Pittsburgh 2-yard line. But the No. 1–ranked Steelers defense stuffed them on four downs. The goal-line stand ended on a LaDainian Tomlinson run into the line for no gain on fourth down with 7:44 remaining in the game.

That wasted a 17-play, 80-yard drive that took 8:07 off the clock. But the Jets managed to cut the lead to 24–12 on the very next play when Roethlisberger fumbled the snap and was touched down by linebacker Mike DeVito in the end zone for a safety.

The Jets then made it 24–19 on a 4-yard Sanchez scoring pass to Cotchery with 3:06 left to play. That, however, was as close as they would get. The Jets never got the ball back, failing to stop the Steelers on the ensuing possession and leaving them again haunted by what might have been.

"We played a good half; we never played a good game, and that was the difference," Ryan said. "You get to this point, you've got to play a great game against a great opponent, and we played a good half and that was it."

"This was our year," Cotchery said in the hushed visitors' locker room afterward. "Last year hurt, but this hurts even more because this was our year and the Steelers took it from us."

Ryan's eyes were red from crying when he stepped to the podium for his post-game press conference. He called it the most crushing loss of his career.

"Of course it's emotional," Ryan said. "We came up short. One game short again. It cuts your heart out. . . . Our goal for next year won't change and it'll never change. We're going to chase that Super Bowl and chase it until we get it. And then we'll chase it again after that."

Veteran linebacker Jason Taylor, playing his 14th NFL season, called it "the toughest loss I've ever been a part of."

"We were so close you could see it, you could smell it, feel it," he said.

"There's no tomorrow now," said Sione Pouha. "We go home now."

It was a familiar, sad refrain from the Jets, who always seem to be headed home too early, destined to watch the Super Bowl on television instead of playing in it.

Asked if he would change anything about the season, Ryan said, "I would change the outcome of this game and that's the only thing I would change. We don't need to apologize to anybody. We'll be back, you'll see."

The Jets had a big hole to dig themselves out of at Heinz Field, falling behind the Steelers 24–3 by halftime. New York gradually chipped away in the second half, cutting the lead to 24–12 after tagging Ben Roethlisberger in the end zone for a safety. *Al Bello/Getty Images*

Although the team's history may be peppered with more moments of frustration and disappointment than joy and celebration, the enthusiasm of Jets fans remains high. Dreams of a long-awaited return to the Super Bowl continue to provide inspiration. *Per-Anders Pettersson/Getty Images*

AFTERWORD
by Woody Johnson

Robert W. "Woody" Johnson, 2010. *Leon Halip/Getty Images*

IT WAS NEVER a dream of mine to become principal owner of the New York Jets, because honestly I never thought it was possible.

Like so many of my generation, I was drawn to the Jets while I was in college and Joe Namath was playing for the Green and White. He was such an engaging character with the white shoes, the fur coat, the Fu Manchu mustache, and that western Pennsylvania drawl.

He was also a heck of a player and a great leader, but there was so much more to that title team, including the likes of head coach Weeb Ewbank, the only coach ever to win a championship in both the AFL and the NFL, and an underrated defense that held mighty Baltimore at bay in Super Bowl III.

The Jets were an 18½-point underdog when they faced the Colts on January 12, 1969, but they were dominant in a 16–7 win. Here was this league—the AFL—that really didn't have a chance, and here comes this guy—Joe Namath—who had the ability to excite everyone in the country.

Then he makes the guarantee, leads his teammates to an upset for the ages, and the football world is turned upside-down. Moments like that are why we all are drawn to sports, because it reminds us that belief has no boundaries.

When we purchased the Jets from the Hess estate, I stated, "We want to emphasize that we are totally dedicated to bringing a winning and a championship team to this area." That objective hasn't changed, and I feel better about where we are as a team today than at any point since January 2000.

In addition to pursuing another Super Bowl, we had to get a new home. We've actually built two new homes. The team and the fans share a new state-of-the art stadium at the Meadowlands, which made its debut in 2010, and we also made an important addition with a new practice facility in Florham Park, New Jersey, that houses the team and all our employees.

Woody Johnson with the inaugural members of the Jets' Ring of Honor at New Meadowlands Stadium, August 2010 (left to right): Johnson, Winston Hill, Joe Klecko, Curtis Martin, Don Maynard, Joe Namath, Weeb Ewbank's son, and General Manager Mike Tannenbaum. *Al Pereira/Getty Images*

I am committed to winning, and I view that as a state of mind. If you want to be an elite franchise, you have to put your resources behind the players, coaches, employees and fans, and I really believe we're doing just that.

Average doesn't cut it. You need people, on both the football side and the business side, who strive every day to be the best at what they do. Talent only gets you so far; you need hunger and heart, too.

Our head coach, Rex Ryan, always talks about playing like a Jet, and I'll never forget a play that wide receiver Jerricho Cotchery made in Cleveland during the 2010 season. After injuring his groin on his route, he hopped around for awhile and then proceeded to get open for Mark

Sanchez and make an amazing diving catch. Sure, the athleticism he displayed was incredible, but it was the selfless effort by a player who wouldn't give up on his teammates that made me most proud.

Our next step is to cash the check. While back-to-back trips to the AFC Championship Games were nice, nobody's goal in the organization is to come close to the top. We won't be able to say "We did it" until we hold the Lombardi Trophy in our hands.

I still get excited to walk through the parking lots at our home games and talk with the Green and White faithful. I always tell them, "We're working for you," and there is plenty of work left to be done. This dream is more than possible.

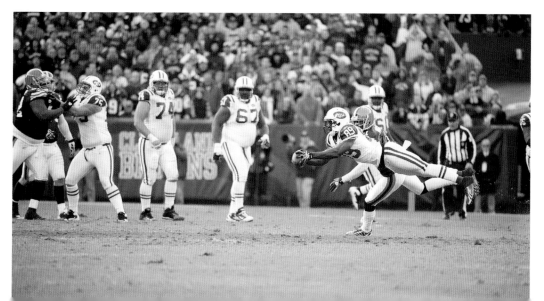

Jerricho Cotchery's diving catch against the Browns in November 2010 exemplifies for Woody Johnson what it means to "play like a Jet." *David E. Klutho/Sports Illustrated/Getty Images*

APPENDIX

New York Jets All-Time Record Book

(through the 2010 season)

NEW YORK JETS YEAR-BY-YEAR

Year	W–L–T	Postseason	Points Scored	Points Allowed	Head Coach
1960	7–7		382	399	Sammy Baugh
1961	7–7		301	390	Sammy Baugh
1962	5–9		278	423	Bulldog Turner
1963	5–8–1		249	399	Weeb Ewbank
1964	5–8–1		278	315	Weeb Ewbank
1965	5–8–1		285	303	Weeb Ewbank
1966	6–6–2		322	312	Weeb Ewbank
1967	8–5–1		371	329	Weeb Ewbank
1968	11–3	2–0; Super Bowl champions	419	280	Weeb Ewbank
1969	10–4	1–1; lost divisional round	353	269	Weeb Ewbank
1970	4–10		255	286	Weeb Ewbank
1971	6–8		212	299	Weeb Ewbank
1972	7–7		367	324	Weeb Ewbank
1973	4–10		240	306	Weeb Ewbank
1974	7–7		279	300	Charley Winner
1975	3–11		258	433	Charley Winner, Ken Shipp
1976	3–11		169	383	Lou Holtz, Mike Holovak
1977	3–11		191	300	Walt Michaels
1978	8–8		359	364	Walt Michaels
1979	8–8		337	383	Walt Michaels
1980	4–12		302	395	Walt Michaels
1981	10–5–1		355	287	Walt Michaels
1982	6–3	2–1; lost AFC championship	245	166	Walt Michaels
1983	7–9		313	331	Joe Walton
1984	7–9		332	364	Joe Walton
1985	11–5	0–1; lost wild card round	393	264	Joe Walton
1986	10–6	1–1; lost divisional round	364	386	Joe Walton
1987	6–9		334	360	Joe Walton
1988	8–7–1		372	354	Joe Walton
1989	4–12		253	411	Joe Walton
1990	6–10		295	345	Bruce Coslet
1991	8–8	0–1; lost wild card round	314	293	Bruce Coslet
1992	4–12		220	315	Bruce Coslet

1993	8–8		270	247	Bruce Coslet
1994	6–10		264	320	Pete Carroll
1995	3–13		233	384	Rich Kotite
1996	1–15		279	454	Rich Kotite
1997	9–7		348	287	Bill Parcells
1998	12–4	1–1; lost AFC championship	416	266	Bill Parcells
1999	8–8		308	309	Bill Parcells
2000	9–7		321	321	Al Groh
2001	10–6	0–1; lost wild card round	308	295	Herm Edwards
2002	9–7	1–1; lost divisional round	359	336	Herm Edwards
2003	6–10		283	299	Herm Edwards
2004	10–6	1–1; lost divisional round	333	261	Herm Edwards
2005	4–12		240	355	Herm Edwards
2006	10–6	0–1; lost wild card round	316	295	Eric Mangini
2007	4–12		268	355	Eric Mangini
2008	9–7		405	356	Eric Mangini
2009	9–7	2–1; lost AFC championship	348	236	Rex Ryan
2010	11–5	2–1; lost AFC championship	367	304	Rex Ryan

INDIVIDUAL HONORS

New York Jets Ring of Honor

(2010 inductees)

Name	Position	Years with Jets
Weeb Ewbank	coach	1963–1973*
Winston Hill	tackle	1963–1976
Joe Klecko	defensive lineman	1977–1987
Curtis Martin	running back	1998–2005
Don Maynard	wide receiver	1960–1972*
Joe Namath	quarterback	1965–1976*

* Member of the Pro Football Hall of Fame

First-Team All-Pros

Name	Position		Years with Jets
Larry Grantham	LB	5	1960–1964
Marvin Powell	T	3	1979, 1981, 1982
Mark Gastineau	DE	3	1982–1984
Bob Mischak	G/TE	2	1960, 1961
George Sauer	WR	2	1967, 1968
Gerry Philbin	DE	2	1968, 1969
Joe Klecko	DL	2	1981, 1985
Kevin Mawae	C/G	2	1999, 2001
Nick Mangold	C	2	2009, 2010
Darrelle Revis	DB	2	2009, 2010
Art Powell	WR/DB	1	1960
Bill Mathis	RB	1	1961
Joe Namath	QB	1	1968
Don Maynard	WR	1	1969
John Elliott	DL	1	1969
Matt Snell	RB	1	1969
Wesley Walker	WR	1	1978
Pat Leahy	K	1	1978
Freeman McNeil	RB	1	1982
Joe Fields	C/G	1	1982
Al Toon	WR	1	1986
Mo Lewis	LB	1	1998
Tom Tupa	QB/P	1	1999
John Abraham	DE	1	2001
Curtis Martin	RB	1	2004
Leon Washington	RB	1	2008

Pro Bowlers

Players with three or more Pro Bowl selections.

Name	Position		Years with Jets
Winston Hill	T	8	1964, 1967–1973
Kevin Mawae	C/G	6	1999–2004
Larry Grantham	LB	5	1962–1964, 1966, 1969
Joe Namath	QB	5	1965, 1967–1969, 1972
Marvin Powell	T	5	1979–1983
Mark Gastineau	DE	5	1981–1985
Don Maynard	WR	4	1965, 1967–1969
George Sauer	WR	4	1966–1969
Joe Klecko	DL	4	1981, 1983–1985
Matt Snell	RB	3	1964, 1966, 1969
Verlon Biggs	DE	3	1966–1968
John Elliott	DL	3	1968–1970
Rich Caster	TE/WR	3	1972, 1974, 1975
Freeman McNeil	RB	3	1982, 1984, 1985
Al Toon	WR	3	1986–1988
Mo Lewis	LB	3	1998–2000
Curtis Martin	RB	3	1998, 2001, 2004
John Abraham	DE	3	2001, 2002, 2004
Nick Mangold	C	3	2008–2010
Darrelle Revis	DB	3	2008–2010

PLAYER RECORDS

CAREER OFFENSIVE RECORDS

Most Games 250 — Pat Leahy, K, 1974–1991
Most Points Scored 1,470 — Pat Leahy, K, 1974–1991
Touchdowns Scored 88 — Don Maynard, WR, 1960–972

Passing Records

Quarterback Wins 60 — Joe Namath, 1965–1976
Pass Attempts 3,655 — Joe Namath, 1965–1976
Pass Completions 2,039 — Ken O'Brien, 1984–1992
Completion Percentage (min. 500 att.) 65.7% — Brett Favre, 2008 (343/522)
Passing Yards 27,057 — Joe Namath, 1965–1976
Most Passing Yards/Game (min. 30 g) 199.1 — Chad Pennington, 2000–2007 (13,738/69)
Most Passing Yards/Attempt 7.40 — Joe Namath, 1965–1976 (27,057/3,655)
Touchdown Passes 170 — Joe Namath, 1965–1976
Most Interceptions Thrown 215 — Joe Namath, 1965–1976
Fewest Interceptions/Attempt (min. 250 att.) 2.18% — Brooks Bollinger, 2004–2005 (6/275)
Quarterback Rating (min. 250 att.) 88.9 — Chad Pennington, 2000–2007

Rushing and Receiving Records

Rushing Attempts 2,560 — Curtis Martin, 1998–2005

Rushing Yards 10,302 — Curtis Martin, 1998–2005

Rushing Yards/Carry (min. 200 carries) 4.89 — Bruce Harper, 1977–1984 (1,829/374)

Rushing Touchdowns 58 — Curtis Martin, 1998–2005

Receptions 627 — Don Maynard, 1960–1972

Receiving Yards 11,732 — Don Maynard, 1960–1972

Yards per Reception (min. 150 rec.) 18.96 — Wesley Walker, 1977–1989 (8,306/438)

Touchdown Receptions 88 — Don Maynard, 1960–1972

Total Yards from Scrimmage (rush. + rec.) 12,741 — Curtis Martin, 1998–2005 (10,302 + 2,439)

Longest Run from Scrimmage 90 yards — Johnny Johnson, 9/25/1994, vs. Bears

CAREER SPECIAL TEAMS RECORDS

Kicking Records

PAT Attempts 584 — Pat Leahy, 1974–1991

PAT Made 558 — Pat Leahy, 1974–1991

PAT Percentage (min. 50 att.) 100% — Jay Feely, 2008–2009 (71/71)

Field Goal Attempts 426 — Pat Leahy, 1974–1991

Field Goals Made 304 — Pat Leahy, 1974–1991

Field Goal Percentage (min. 50 att.) 84.4% — Jay Feely, 2008–2009 (54/64)

Longest Field Goal Made 56 yards — Nick Folk, 10/17/2010, @ Broncos

Most Punts 553 — Chuck Ramsey, 1977–1984

Total Punt Yardage 22,718 — Curley Johnson, 1961–1968

Yards per Punt (min. 200 punts) 43.7 — Ben Graham, 2005–2008 (9,876/226)

Longest Punt 98 yards — Steve O'Neal

Return Records

Most Kickoff Returns 243 — Bruce Harper, 1977–1983

Most Kickoff Return Yards 5,407 — Bruce Harper, 1977–1983

Yards per Kickoff Return (min. 30 ret.) 28.73 — Leon Burton, 1960 (862/30)

Kickoffs Returned for Touchdown 4 — Leon Washington, 2006–2009

Longest Kickoff Return 106 yards — Brad Smith, 12/27/2009, @ Colts

Most Punt Returns 183 — Bruce Harper, 1977–1983

Most Punt Return Yards 1,784 — Bruce Harper, 1977–1983

Yards per Punt Return (min. 30 ret.) 16.17 — Dick Christy, 1961–1963 (679/42)

Punts Returned for Touchdown 4 — Dick Christy, 1961–1963

Longest Punt Return 98 yards — Terance Mathis, 11/4/1990, vs. Cowboys

CAREER DEFENSIVE RECORDS

Most Interceptions 34 — Bill Baird, 1963–1969

Interception Return Yardage 608 — Erik McMillan, 1988–1992

Most Interceptions Returned for Touchdown 5 — Erik McMillan, 1988–1992

Longest Interception Return 100 yards — Aaron Glenn, 9/15/1996, @ Dolphins

Most Sacks 74 — Mark Gastineau, 1981–1988

Most Fumbles Forced 26 — Mo Lewis, 1991–2003

Most Fumbles Recovered 18 — James Hasty, 1988–1994

Most Fumbles Returned for Touchdown 2 — Greg Buttle, 1976–1984; Mark Gastineau, 1981–1988; Erik McMillan, 1988–1992

SINGLE-SEASON OFFENSIVE RECORDS

Most Points Scored 145 — Jim Turner, K, 1968

Most Touchdowns Scored 15 — Thomas Jones, 2008

Passing Records

Quarterback Wins 12 — Vinny Testaverde, 1998

Pass Attempts 590 — Vinny Testaverde, 1998

Pass Completions 343 — Brett Favre, 2008

Completion Percentage (min. 100 att.) 68.9% — Chad Pennington, 2000 (275/399)

Passing Yards 4,007 — Joe Namath, 1967

Most Passing Yards/Game (min. 10 g) 286.2 — Joe Namath, 1967 (4,007/14)

Most Passing Yards/Attempt (min. 100 att.) 8.69 — Joe Namath, 1972 (2,816/324)

Touchdown Passes 29 — Vinny Testaverde, 1998

Most Interceptions Thrown 30 — Al Dorow, 1961; Richard Todd, 1980

Fewest Interceptions/Attempt (min. 100 att.) 1.01% — Vinny Testaverde, 2003 (2/198)

Quarterback Rating (min. 100 att.) 104.2 — Chad Pennington, 2002

Rushing and Receiving Records

Rushing Attempts 371 — Curtis Martin, 2004

Rushing Yards 1,697 — Curtis Martin, 2004

Rushing Yards/Carry (min. 50 carries) 6.94 — Bruce Harper, 1983 (354/51)

Rushing Touchdowns 14 — Thomas Jones, 2009

Receptions 93 — Al Toon, 1988

Receiving Yards 1,434 — Don Maynard, 1967

Yards per Reception (min. 25 rec.) 24.35 — Wesley Walker, 1978 (1,169/48)

Touchdown Receptions 14 — Art Powell, 1960; Don Maynard, 1965

Total Yards from Scrimmage (rush. + rec.) 1,942 — Curtis Martin, 2004 (1,697 + 245)

SINGLE-SEASON SPECIAL TEAMS RECORDS

Kicking Records

PAT Attempts 50 — Bill Shockley, 1960

PAT Made 47 — Bill Shockley, 1960

PAT Percentage (most att. without a miss) 100% — Pat Leahy, 1986 (44/44)

Field Goal Attempts 47 — Jim Turner, 1969

Field Goals Made 34 — Jim Turner, 1968

Field Goal Percentage (min. 15 att.) 88.89% — Mike Nugent, 2006 (24/27)

Most Punts 99 — Brian Hansen, 1995

Total Punt Yardage 4,090 — Brian Hansen, 1995

Yards per Punt min. 50 punts) 45.28 — Charley Johnson, 1965 (3,260/72)

Return Records

Most Kickoff Returns 60 — Justin Miller, 2005

Most Kickoff Return Yards 1,577 — Justin Miller, 2005

Yards per Kickoff Return (min. 15 ret.) 30.68 — Bobby Humphery, 1984 (675/22)

Kickoffs Returned for Touchdown 3 — Leon Washington, 2007

Most Punt Returns 51 — Leon Johnson, 1997

Most Punt Return Yards 619 — Leon Johnson, 1997

Yards per Punt Return (min. 15 ret.) 21.28 — Dick Christy, 1961 (383/18)

Punts Returned for Touchdown 2 — Dick Christy, 1961 and 1962; Santana Moss, 2002

SINGLE-SEASON DEFENSIVE RECORDS

Most Interceptions 12 — Dainard Paulson, 1964

Interception Return Yardage 227 — Darrol Ray, 1981

Most Interceptions Returned for Touchdown 3 — Otis Smith, 1997

Most Sacks 22 — Mark Gastineau, 1984

Most Fumbles Forced 6 — John Abraham, 2001 and 2005

Most Opponent's Fumbles Recovered 4 — accomplished 7 times

Most Fumbles Returned for Touchdown 1 — accomplished 32 times

INDEX